D1563520

A Thinking Man's Guide to Pro Hockey

Books by Gerald Eskenazi

Hockey

A Year on Ice

Hockey Is My Life

The Story of Hockey

A Thinking Man's Guide to Pro Hockey

A Thinking Man's Guide to Pro Hockey

Gerald Eskenazi

E. P. Dutton & Co., Inc. | **New York** | **1972**

796.9
E

Published simultaneously in Canada
by Clarke, Irwin & Company Limited, Toronto and Vancouver

SBN: 0-525-21731-2
Library of Congress Catalog Card Number: 72-82710

FOR MY MOTHER

Contents

1. The Canadian Thing   9
2. The Players   17
   The Goalies   17
   The Goal-Getters—The Forwards   35
   The Forgotten Men—The Defense   61
3. The Thinkers   72
   The Coach   72
   The General Manager   90
   The Scouts   98
4. The Officials   103
   The Referee   103
   The Linesmen   111
   The Minor Officials   114
5. What You Don't See   128
   Training Camp   128
   The Routine   137
   The Media   146
6. Exploring the New World—Expansion   184
7. Strictly Personal   205
   The French Connection   205
   The Clutch   208
Index   219

1 | The Canadian Thing

If you're an American the first thing about hockey to realize is that it's not like any other sport you've known. Hockey players are not like you and me. They take the ice without teeth, with arms in casts, jaws wired, knees braced. "Baseball players?" Reggie Fleming, a hockey ruffian, once said with a sneer. "Why, they don't play if they've got a hangnail."

Now that hockey has burst upon the American consciousness, with teams from coast to coast, north and south, it is becoming a sport that doesn't have to be confined to the wheat fields of Saskatchewan, or the rolling countryside of Kitchener, or the natural ice in the lakes of Quebec. Yet, emotionally we're still not prepared for it. Canadians are, and that tells us something about Canada, as well as the game it loves.

Virtually all of the National Hockey League's performers are Canadian. Their attitude to the game has been honed with their background. When they're eight years old and learning that the team comes first, that winning is everything, that you play with broken teeth—well, that will carry over into their big-league careers. Imagine even Little League mothers in the United States putting up with this attitude. It wouldn't happen.

For many Canadian youngsters, hockey is life. Small cities

everywhere have rinks, and the highest rated telecasts in that country are the Saturday night games showing either the Vancouver Canucks, Toronto Maple Leafs, or Montreal Canadiens. With only 20,000,000 people, the options are not as great as they are in the United States, where tens of thousands of its 200,000,000 population get college scholarships in football, basketball, baseball, tennis, golf, and even rodeo. How many of these sports are big-league in Canada? How many offer a road to riches up north? None, really. In football and basketball, college is the only training ground for pros, but in Canada, it is looked at as a detour en route to the N.H.L. It slows you down, you don't get the competition, you're not getting the ice time, you're not improving. So now you have a boy 19, or 20, or 21, and he's been playing hockey since he was a pre-teen. He hasn't been to college. He's lucky, in fact, if he was graduated from high school. What is he fitted for? Hockey.

In 1967 the National Hockey League passed a rule that a player may not turn pro until he's 20. Before then, 75 percent of the players hadn't graduated from high school. Take a kid whose father was eking out a living on a dirt farm, or who worked in a copper mine for $100 a week, and you had a 17-year-old who would gladly leave high school to turn pro.

The system perpetuated dropouts. Youngsters of 14 were signed to "C" cards or letters of intent, that, in effect, signed them to a team for life. Take Bobby Hull, for example. When he was 14 his parents signed the card, making him Chicago Black Hawks' property. He was way ahead of the other boys his age at Point Anne, Ontario. In order to help him improve, the Hawks sent him to a better club. However, that was 150 miles from his home. So he packed up—at the age of 14, mind you—and went off to play hockey. He lived in a boarding school and his rent and tuition were paid. He also played more than 60 hockey games a year, getting up at 5 in the morning to practice, getting home late after a game.

"I used to cry myself to sleep, at first," he recalled. "I missed my mother and father. After a while it wasn't so bad. They'd come to visit me on weekends."

That story was repeated with other boys all over Canada with slight variations. Some clubs gave the boy the tuition money if the youngster decided not to attend school. The incentive to quit school was obvious. Far from home and guidance, teen-agers were hardly in a position to make intelligent judgments about how they'd spend their futures and didn't worry about diplomas. They were making more money than their fathers. Even if they stayed in school, they still received spending money.

"Sure I got paid when I was in the juniors," said John Ferguson of the Montreal Canadiens. "I was married. I had to raise a family. We all took the money."

Amateur hockey taught them at an early age that winning was essential. Most clubs, from bantam to peewee to juniors, were sponsored by big-league clubs who wanted to develop players and poured money into towns that might not have a first-class hospital, but had a rink that measured big-league dimensions of 200 by 85 feet. The coaching varied in quality, but generally was superior to the coaching on the same levels in the United States sports of basketball, football, and baseball. After all, the New York Yankees didn't "own" 10-year-olds in New Jersey and weren't really concerned with how well they developed.

The boys in Canada played under N.H.L. rules, in which checking was permitted in all the zones of the ice, and the only concession to their age was that they wore helmets. The coaches knew that not only were the players being scouted at all times, but also that they were constantly being eyed. So you played to win, and you taught the different tactics that go with winning in hockey. If your coach was like Ferguson's, you were told, "Never become friendly with a player who isn't your teammate. Avoid talking to them, don't socialize with them. Learn to hate them."

And at times there were the tough jocks, like the fellow who's now in the Ranger organization. During a game one of his 10-year-olds failed to hit properly. The coach was furious with him and chewed him out between periods. In anger and frustration, the coach picked up the boy and hung him by the suspenders on a clothes hook.

The boy dangled there, while the other youngsters watched and said nothing. Just then, the team's general manager walked in, saw the boy, and asked, "What the hell are you doing there?" The boy replied, "The coach put me here." Taken aback, the general manager replied, "Well, you just stay there."

Years later, reflecting on the incident, the general manager said, "It was a hell of a thing to do to a kid. But when he told me the coach hung him up there, I didn't want to undermine the coach's authority. So I let the kid dangle."

Presumably, the boy learned how to hit, learned not to back off. Before they reached a sense of manhood, of values that could enable them to make intelligent decisions that might not be "manly," according to society, they lived in a subculture that demanded you retaliate. Their manhood was tested when they were 10 years old. They learned also their first hockey cliché: "If you can walk to the bench, you can play."

Cesare Maniago, a goalie, apparently never learned that well enough. Early in the 1966–67 season, when it appeared he had taken the No. 1 Ranger job away from Ed Giacomin, he got rapped in the mouth with a puck. He skated back to the bench. Between periods, Coach Emile Francis asked him, "Are you ready?" Maniago replied, "I don't think I can go on." The next day Giacomin was told he had the job. Maniago was finished as a Ranger.

"Look closely enough at a tough hockey player and I'm sure that in the background you'll find a father who pushed him, who demanded manliness." The comment is a New York psychiatrist's, who sees the game a little more clearly since his own son joined a league. "I can't believe this violence doesn't carry over into other areas," he says. "It's impossible to channel hostility as though you were pointing a flashlight, directing the beam in one direction only."

Yet, hockey players are not bombastic and it is an exceptional few—a Rocket Richard, a Derek Sanderson, a Boom Boom Geoffrion—who will boast or put down another player. Does that mean that hockey makes a player self-effacing? No. It might simply mean that that's the way Canadians are: low-keyed. They shun the braggart and the bigness, much like the American Middle West does.

They dress for a game without fanfare. First they take out their false teeth and drop them into paper cups. Then they put on the gear that protects their kidneys, shoulders, groin, kneecaps, and toes. They know they will be hurt, that sometime during the evening they will be bruised.

"Their tolerance to pain is remarkable," says Dr. James A. Nicholas, an orthopedic surgeon prominent as the man who operates on Joe Namath's knees. "Hockey players are the most uncomplaining athletes I've met."

Part of it, of course, is due to their conditioning. Leg ailments that would sideline players in other sports heal quickly. And if there's an injury above the knees, it virtually goes unnoticed. A major reason is that these players have been on skates from the time they were three or four. The skating motion is natural, and they have developed tremendous thrusting power in their legs. They are constantly stopping and turning, falling, leaping, churning. And they have another advantage over, say, football players. When you slip on the ice you have give. Your ankle doesn't remain planted. It moves—or slides—with the force exerted on it. Most football injuries occur from what has been called the "locked-knee syndrome." The foot, encased in a shoe with cleats that dig into the turf, is wrenched one way and the rest of it goes the other way. Result: all sorts of leg problems.

But injuries aren't allowed to stand in the way of the play. At a Ranger practice some years ago, Dave Balon missed his man and sailed into a metal support post. He was knocked unconscious. Only a few players skated over. The rest remained either on their bench or on the far side of the ice, taking practice shots. When Balon finally was revived, Rod Seiling said, "You just didn't feel like practicing today, did you?"

Hockey players have a need to play down injuries, as if by denying that someone else is hurt they won't recognize their own vulnerability. This is something else they get when they're youngsters. You look away when a nasty accident has occurred. And, if they were like Derek Sanderson, whose father refused to listen to complaints about injuries, you just went back and continued playing.

Jim Krulicki, a youngster who had some success in the Rangers' organization, was traded to the Detroit Red Wings during the 1970–71 season. When the season was over, the promising wing quit the game. "They don't care about you," he said. "I didn't realize it until I was traded. But now that I think about it, I remember the times I played when I was younger and my knee hurt. They told me it was nothing, that there was really nothing wrong. So I continued to play with a bad knee. Then later the doctors told me I could have been seriously crippled playing with the bad leg. I was too young to know any better."

And yet . . . hockey can be the most joyous of events. It has the ingredients of spectacle—players and fans drawn together under one roof, close to one another. The brilliance of the uniforms, the light flashing off the blades, the speed and skill of plays executed at 30 miles an hour, the roaring of the fans, the shouting of the goalies, the instant gratification of a goal. The game is so heated that in no other sport can one score so quickly turn a game around, or can the fans be so quixotic in their loyalties, shifting their affection in the middle of a busted play. The fans, because of their proximity to the action, are an integral part of the game and the players feed off the crowd reaction. If the fans demand blood, you're certain that eventually some will be spilled.

When they're booed, the players deny the home fans make a difference. It is more than coincidence, though, when during the 1970–71 campaign the home teams won 307 games, lost 153, and tied 85. That is double the number of victories as losses. And how do you account for the fact that the Pittsburgh Penguins, who won only three games on the road while dropping 25, sported 18 victories and 12 defeats at home?

That same season the Rangers were superb at home, winning 30 and losing only twice. The two losses tied a league record for fewest home defeats. But on the road, the New Yorkers won 19 and lost 16. Several conclusions are possible: the visiting team is tired from traveling; the home team knows its ice so well it turns it into an extraordinary advantage; there is a psychological factor at work that cannot be measured.

As far as travel goes, it is obvious that a club flying from Minnesota to Boston will not get much rest. Their plane might arrive at 3 A.M. for a game that night. But by the same token, Boston might very well have been on the road, too. More often than not the visiting team has at least a day in the city before a game, and the home team has not been settled at home for any significant length of time.

The home ice surface is important. Each rink has its nuances. The Red Wings used to have a favorite play in which the center would rap the puck off the boards, and his winger would scoot down the alley, time the rebound, and blast a shot at goal. Familiarity with the rink's sideboards was essential to this play. Boards in different rinks have different "give." The Wings are fortunate in that they practice on their own rink. For every game they play there they stage twice as many practices. But when the Rangers lost only two games in New York, they went through only one scrimmage on their home ice. Not all clubs can practice on their ice because of the many uses expensive arenas must have.

Tired players often get a lift on familiar territory. The fans goad them on to performances beyond the players' normal abilities. The clubs with the three poorest records in 1971—Vancouver, Detroit, and California—had respectable combined home records of 51 victories and 54 losses. On the road, they were 15-90.

Even the top clubs are content with a draw on the road. A .500 mark away from home virtually guarantees a club a winning record and a playoff berth. A favorite cry of the Bruins after a road loss is "Just wait till we get them in Boston." Not only does a club's play improve, but also the competitors become bolder. Johnny McKenzie, a smallish Bruin right wing, has said, "They wouldn't dare do that to us back home." The comments usually come after another team takes liberties with Boston. At Boston Garden, McKenzie is cheered lustily for his checking. He relishes it and becomes a super-pest. But away from home, he is not half the belter. He knows he will not get the encouragement from Toronto fans, say, that he does from the bellowing Boston rooters.

Some players, of course, are equally brutish at home or away. Gordie Howe of the Wings never backed away. His techniques, honed after years and years of learning just what was detectable, worked everywhere. "You're working a game," Referee Vern Buffey once said, "and you see a player is down. You know that Howe did it. But how can you prove it?" Howe probably was the league's unofficial greeter. The first time he faced the Rangers' Brad Park, he flicked out his stick after Park checked him. Park went down with a sliced cheek, the cut missing his eye by a fraction of an inch.

"I'm young," said Park later. "I'll have time to get even." Welcome to the National Hockey League, Brad.

2 | The Players

The Goalies

"A goaltender's mother always worries," said a Long Island mother whose son was stopping shots in a kids' league.

Goalies themselves worry. If there is one man connected with the sport who should be on the fine edge of madness it is the goalie. That is why his teammates pamper him, why they run so quickly to his defense if another player shoots the puck after the whistle has blown, or dares touch the goalie's uniform. The goalie is the last line of defense. The players know it—and the goalie feels it.

They may very well have the most demanding job in sports, stopping (or trying to) 30 and 40 shots a game that zero in at speeds up to 110 miles an hour. There isn't always time to stop and set. The muzzle velocity of a Bobby Hull drive from 10 feet out is frightening. Yet the goalie must stand there and take it. He can't skate out of the way, nor can he just wander trying to shake off the pressure. He is fixed to his cage and he must wait.

They react differently to the pressure. Before he put on his pads and chest protector and knee guards and mask, Glenn Hall usually threw up. He would talk freely of how he detested playing goal.

Even during a game, he sometimes called time out to go to the locker room. Yet Hall was one of the very best. His goals-against average never went over three a game in each of his N.H.L. seasons. But his average went above that figure seven times during Stanley Cup play. Even the great ones feel pressure.

Classically, the goaltender started because he was the poorest skater. Not good enough to become a forward or defenseman, he would plant himself in goal, where he could hold on to the posts for support or rest his back against the crossbar. Major-league goalies don't like to admit this fact. They usually say it is what they always wanted to do. However, anyone going to see a pick-up game or a young league in action will usually spot the poorest skater immediately—it's the goalie. But he'd better learn pretty quickly. Today's hockey demands mobile netminders. In the sport's early days, though, goaltenders by rule had to be fixed to one spot. They weren't even permitted to go to their knees to stop shots. They had to stand and try to split without falling if they were to kick out a low shot to the side. The rule was changed when Lester and Joseph Patrick, two of hockey's greatest innovators, started their league in western Canada in 1912. Soon, the National Hockey Association, the N.H.L.'s predecessor, adopted the ruling. In the early pro days, a goaltender didn't have to be much of a skater. He only had to keep his footing. There weren't many radical goaltending changes in technique for the next 40 years. Then Jacques Plante came along with the Canadiens. The wiry Plante, a true character but a virtual hockey philosopher, changed most of the ideas of goaltending. First, he wandered. He actually moved around the ice going for the puck. Goalies had been content to let long shots roller-coaster off the boards, where it would travel behind the cage and come out along the other side. The puck could wind up on an enemy's stick before a defenseman could stop it. Plante, however, went behind the cage to stop the disk, leaving it there for one of his own men. If an opponent was bearing down on him, Plante merely shot the puck away.

Plante had no fear about coming out to the sides of the ice, either. Often, he would pick up a loose puck and shovel it to a teammate, starting an offensive burst. Although he played goal recklessly, Plante was as much a worrier in his way as Hall was. He also was an egocentric of mammoth proportion. After a shut-out, he'd blow kisses to the crowd, and skate around the rink in a victory lap. But if a goal were scored against him, he'd usually blame a teammate's error. His bombast and his hypochondria often made Coach Toe Blake livid. Blake put up with Plante be-cause Plante delivered—especially in the playoffs. For five straight years he posted the fewest goals-against in Cup play. Blake, who never had any formal training in psychology, burned whenever Plante's individualism showed through. Judged by to-day's standards, Plante's idiosyncrasies might not appear so grave. But hockey players, mostly unsophisticated, were hardly equipped to deal with emotions. Nor were their coaches, or general manag-ers. So when Plante one day told Blake he was going to wear a mask, Blake growled, "Awright, if you really want to." The mask was another Plante revolution. He had kept one in the locker room. But he hadn't worn it during a game. Then he played a game against the Rangers in New York, shortly after Halloween. He stopped a puck with his face—and it knocked him out. In those days—and it wasn't so long ago—teams didn't keep two goalies around. You waited until your goaltender was revived, or stitched up, and then you continued play. Blake went back to the trainer's room after Plante was taking time coming around. He asked his goalie if he could continue. "Only if I wear the mask," Plante replied. Plante put on the mask. When the Madison Square Garden crowd saw him, they tittered. One fan yelled, "Hey, Plante, Halloween's over!" Plante never took off the mask again.

Was it goaltending that made Plante a hypochondriac? Nobody knows. But he did have asthma as a child, and a host of allergies. Goaltending didn't help. There was a time when Plante couldn't play in Toronto. He claimed he was allergic to the city. He had a bright idea: He'd sleep in a motel on the outskirts of Toronto and go into town just to play. That worked fine for a time. But one night, Plante dreamed he was in Toronto—he woke up wheezing. Over the years, from Montreal, to the Rangers, to the St. Louis

Blues, Plante's strange reaction continued. It didn't matter what club he played for. In 1970, when he was 41 years old, it appeared he had reached the end of his distinguished career. He was traded from the Blues to Toronto. Instead of suffering from asthma, Plante turned in his best season in 15 years. His 1.88 average was the best in the league. And where was Plante's favorite place to play during the 1970–71 season? Toronto. Indeed, he had a reputation for being a homer, of not liking to play anyplace else but Toronto.

It is not so difficult to see why goalies worry. From high in the stands, the net doesn't look so big. To a goalie, it looks like a cavern. The net is 6 feet wide and 4 feet high. If the average person held both arms stretched to the side, it wouldn't reach from one side of the cage to the other. In other words, there's a lot of net to shoot at. There are 24 square feet of open space. Standing erect, and allowing for a body width of 2 feet, a goalie would cover only 8 square feet of space. How well you protect the other 16 square feet is what goaltending is all about.

When you start to talk about "playing the angles," and "covering up" you run into a problem. You take away from the spontaneity of goaltending. Analyze it to death and it becomes a mere technical feat. Goaltending, ultimately, is intuitive. Still, it is based on sound principles. The fastest pair of hands in the world cannot move quicker than a slap shot. Until the expansion of 1967 made the two-goalie system mandatory, not many young goalies were seen. The six clubs carried one netminder, and he usually was no kid. Goaltenders always were among the oldest of players. There was no substitute for experience—not even quick reflexes. Terry Sawchuk was the classic example.

He may have been the greatest goaltender. Certainly, he was the finest at playing the angles. There were no mathematics involved, at least not consciously. When a goalie plays the angles, he is making the shooter aim for the open portion of the net that is hardest to hit. If a skater, for example, is moving down ice to the goalie's left, the goalie moves to the left. He thus protects the "near side," that portion of space closest to the shooter. In order to score, the shooter must angle his shot farther to the goalie's right, or to the shooter's left. It's easier to shoot for the near side. But if this were all there was to Sawchuk's magic, he never would have achieved stardom. It was the subtle differences of inches, moving left or right, that made him such an outstanding angle man. If an opposing shooter, for example, is slightly to the left of center, the goalie doesn't move all the way to his left. That would give the shooter a virtually straight-on shot at the rest of the net.

A goalie must have the instincts for just the right lateral movement. Watching Sawchuk, you had the feeling you were watching a punching bag. More shots hit him straight on—without his having to move once the shot was taken—than any other goalie. He had judged the probable place the puck would wind up. Probably one-third of all the shots in the game are hit directly at the goalie. Some have gone there because the shooter wasn't able to get off a better shot. But the others have landed on the goalie's body because the goalie was in the right place.

Playing the angle also means cutting down the angle. Place your hand in front of your face. You see a lot of hand. Place it six inches farther back, and you can see more of whatever is behind the hand. The same is true for goaltending. When a goalie comes out to meet an onrushing player, that player sees less net than if the goalie were back in the cage. It is almost a cardinal rule that on a clean breakaway, or a penalty shot, the goalie comes out— far out—from the "crease." The crease is a rectangular box, 8 feet across and 4 feet deep, directly in front of the net. That is the goalie's territory. While he is in that rectangle, he may not be checked. And no goal is allowed if an opposing player is standing in the crease—even if he hasn't shot the puck. The exceptions are when the player has been pushed into the crease. During a penalty shot, it isn't unusual to see a goalie come 20 feet out. He is not only cutting down the angle, but also hoping to goad the puck-carrier into making the first move. On a penalty shot, though, the goalie cannot make his move out of the cage until the shooter has touched the puck. Then the fun starts.

A lone oncoming shooter against a goaltender is the true one-to-one relationship. The shooter against the goalie. It is a pure confrontation. Each player has been programed for such an occasion. The shooter is a deadly, skilled professional, able to put the puck in with a forehand or backhand shot. He has practiced thousands of shots. He can hit the upper corner or the lower corner. He can slap the puck or he can take a more delicate wrist shot. The goalie knows his own weaknesses. He knows how quickly he can bring his stick up to bat a puck away, or how deftly his throwing hand can spear a puck in midair. He knows how much he can rely on his feet to kick out the disk. And he must also know the shooter, what he prefers, how his backhand is, how quickly the shot travels.

Once the goalie comes out to meet the shooter, the goalie goes through his tricks, some meaningless, others used perhaps to psyche the skater. Some goalies start to move laterally, swaying side to side, keeping the shooter off balance, attempting to make him guess where the goalie will be a second from now. At all costs, the goalie must not commit himself, must not lose his balance. He must be able to adjust to a sudden shift. If the goalie can pressure the shooter enough, the shooter must find another way to get off a shot. He might be forced to take the shot on his backhand, which is just what the goalie wants. The backhander is not nearly so accurate.

Sawchuk had a stripper's flare for enticement. He would come out of the net to meet the attacker. He would purposely let the shooter see net space over one of his shoulders. Sawchuk knew the skater would try to put the puck there. Sure enough, the inviting cage beckoned, and the opponent would let fly. But Sawchuk had already prepared himself for the shot. Whoosh! His stick would go up, or his hand would come out like a cobra's tongue—and the puck was knocked away. Sawchuk had good reflexes. But there were those who had better. His anticipation and his knowledge of the angles were unsurpassed.

Goalies today will let a player see the net intentionally, too. But just a little piece of it. Even if they can't stop the shot, they figure that the puck would have to be driven so accurately that the odds against it going in favor the netminder. When does a shooter have the edge? Hardly ever. Except for the rare chances at an unguarded net, a player's best chance will come during a penalty shot. During the 1967–68 season, eight such shots were taken. Only two went in. In the 1969–70 campaign, three were tried—all unsuccessfully.

There are few instances during a game, though, when a goalie has all the time he needs to set himself. His most relaxed times, of course, are when the puck is on the other side of the ice. There is a danger, though, of relaxing too much. Ed Giacomin of the Rangers, after seeing easy shutouts against expansion clubs elude him, keeps himself prepared all the time.

"I'd be watching the guys really put it to the other goalie," says Giacomin. "I wasn't in the game, really didn't feel a part of the action. Then the other team would come down, take an easy shot —and there went my shutout. But when you're being pressed, that's when you're sharpest."

So true. Anyone who has seen a goalie peppered with four, five, six shots in a row has the feeling he's watching a headless chicken gyrating. The goalie at these times is so fired up he's not really aware of what he's doing. If he stopped to think about the ridiculous situation he was in, he'd probably fold.

Some clubs whose goalies are not so expert like to discount goals-against average. They claim that more shots were taken against them. Certainly, the shots-on-goal statistics can be misleading. It is, first of all, extremely difficult to score a goal in the National Hockey League. In fact, it's tough enough just to get a shot on net. One of the most clever stick-handlers and shooters, Stan Mikita of the Black Hawks, had 39 goals during the 1969–70 season. He averaged fewer than five shots a game. That was for approximately 25 minutes' work. Most clubs will take between 20 and 30 shots during a contest, about one for every two minutes' of actual play. During Mikita's big year, more than 30,-000 shots were taken. Fewer than 2,700 goals were scored. The league averages under 10 percent in shooting efficiency. Goalies say that 60 percent of the shots are hit straight at them.

The goalie is under pressure even during a face-off. There are two face-off spots in each defending zone, 25 feet out from the goal. Each spot is angled out from the goal. Perhaps once or twice a season a player will score out of the thousands of face-off opportunities. But the goalie has to be prepared for that one rarity that will go in. He does it by keeping his knees together, stick on the ice in front of him, and hunched. Because of the tangle of players in a face-off, the goalie is screened. He needs a view of the action. He also should be standing a little bit out from the net, closest to the face-off spot. This gives the player who takes the face-off only a difficult far corner to shoot at.

All goalies want to score. None have, at least not in the National Hockey League. It seems strange, given the number of chances they have had over the years. Probably one-sixth of the hockey games played are decided by only one goal. That means that at least once in six games, a team will have to pull its goalie out of the net in the closing seconds in a last-ditch effort to tie the game. More often than not, a player from the team with the lead will put the puck into the empty net to foil the strategy. Why shouldn't at least one goalie have been able to hit the empty net on the other side of the ice? The problem is quite simple, really. During those final seconds, the goalie on the winning team is contending with six, and not five, attackers. He has all he can do just to stop the opposition from scoring. Because there are so many players on his side of the ice, he doesn't have the room to maneuver, or the time to set up. And if he did have the chance and shot the puck, it could go wide. If it did, he would suffer an offside, which means a face-off right near him.

Under a 1970 ruling, it will be just about impossible for a goalie to score. That year, Gary Smith of the Oakland Seals was intent on becoming the first goalie to score. He grabbed the puck and took off. But he was halted before he could get off a good shot. The league, fearing for the life of its goalies (who are fair game out of the crease), made it illegal for a netminder to skate past center ice.

The goalies had been hockey's iron men, playing virtually the full schedule. In some ways, it was easier than being a forward or defenseman. You didn't have to worry about body contact. You didn't have to skate all-out. The game was simpler. Life, indeed, was simpler. It began to get a bit more complicated when Boom Boom Geoffrion came along with the Canadiens. He got the nickname because of the sound his slap shot made when it boomed off the boards. The slap shot had been shunned. It was too showy, too inaccurate. You got your goals, said the traditionalists, by hard work. Geoffrion's slapper introduced a new element. But things really changed when Bobby Hull put a curve on his stick. Life was never the same again for the goaltender.

Actually, Mikita, Hull's teammate on the Black Hawks, was the first to use the curve. During a practice session Mikita accidentally broke the blade of his stick. Just for fun, he decided to continue playing with it. He whipped a shot at goal—and discovered that the puck did tricks. He tried a few more shots, and the disk dropped or hooked, or even rose.

To Mikita, a pugnacious little player who has learned to use every edge, it was as if he had discovered fire. He quickly told Hull about the phenomenon. They went to the locker room and grabbed some sticks. Then they carefully bent them under a door. A new era, a torturous one for the goalies, had begun.

In Hull's hand the curved stick, looking like a scythe, became the ultimate weapon. Before the curve his shot had been clocked at nearly 110 miles an hour. That alone made the netminders nervous. Consider the possibilities with the curve: the puck comes in at 330 feet a second. Suddenly it dips. Or drops. Or starts to wiggle. It drove goaltenders mad. Hull's goal production, meanwhile, soared. Soon, the curved stick became a standard production item. Some players' curves were more, some less. Goalies weren't the only ones to complain. The management of teams that didn't have a fearsome shooter didn't like it. They got a rule passed that prohibited the curve from exceeding 1½ inches. Now it may be only half an inch.

Still the slap shot continued. Youngsters stopped imitating the league's fancy stick-handlers and began practicing the slap shot.

Goalies, who had more teeth than any other players, suddenly started to lose theirs. They began stopping shots with their faces. At first, Plante was the only one to wear the mask. He was alone for more than 10 years. Then, one by one, the others put them on, too. While the curved stick mania was at its height, hockey further taunted the goalies—it expanded.

In 1966 there were six teams. In 1967 there were 12. The players were going west of the Mississippi for the first time, to Oakland, Los Angeles, Minnesota. They were getting tired. They were losing their effectiveness, they were bowing to the pressure.

"You finish a game in Minnesota," relates Cesare Maniago of the North Stars. "You need time to unwind from all those slap shots. But no. You've got to rush to catch a plane to New York. On the plane you're not relaxing. You're thinking of the goals you let in. You try to sleep, but you just can't. So after a while, you don't even try. Then you land in New York. Because of the time difference, it's an hour closer to morning. You get in the airport at two in the morning. By the time you get into bed it's three o'clock. You're still tense. You try to sleep. You've got a game that night. Sometimes, I don't roll over till four or five."

Enter the two-goalie system. It had to happen. For many goaltenders the pressure was just too much. Al Smith of the Pittsburgh Penguins said, "We're brought up in Canada that it's a do-or-die game, that with every goal that goes in behind you, you can be gone." Multiply those goals over more than 70 games, divide them by cities north, south, east, and west—and you've got a desperate situation.

Now there isn't a club in the big leagues that doesn't use two goalies. Most of the clubs split the schedule down the middle between netminders. Some even use three. The two-goalie system had a curious effect. Sure, it made the physical aspects of goaltending easier. But goalies, as we know, are worriers. The two-goalie system increased this mental aspect of the game.

"You're always hoping you're going to play," says Maniago. "When I used to back up Eddie Giacomin, it was a big disappointment to find the coach chose him. I prepared myself mentally to play for a day and a half. It's like telling a quarterback or a pitcher that they won't start. You work like heck in practice and find out you're not going to be in the game."

During the 1970–71 season, Jack Norris was the back-up to Denis DeJordy at Los Angeles. "I worry as the back-up man," Norris admitted. "I only play every third or fourth game, and wonder what'll happen if I do badly. You can't play as well when you come in infrequently, and then you have the added burden of producing. You wonder if you'll get another chance if you have a bad game."

The deployment of the goaltenders is a problem for coaches. Some alternate the players every other game. The pure two-goalie system probably reached its height with Doug Favell and Bernie Parent, the Philadelphia Flyer rookies, during the 1967–68 season. Parent played 37½ games while Favell played 36½. Each was sharp. They knew when they were going to play, and they were ready. But in the second season, Parent forged ahead as Favell slumped. Favell was relegated to a secondary position. He discovered: "I got lazy. I found I didn't care as much as when I saw action. The longer you don't play, the tougher it becomes to get up for a game. There was no incentive to practice."

When Harry Sinden coached the Bruins, his goalies were Gerry Cheevers and Ed Johnston. Sinden had a different strategy. He'd play one goalie until the club lost. Then he'd switch. If that goalie was in the nets for a loss, the switch would again be made. Scotty Bowman at St. Louis had another technique. He had two aging, great goalies in Glenn Hall and Jacques Plante. When one played, Bowman didn't even dress the other goalie. He would call up someone from the minors to sit on the bench. Bowman figured that Plante and Hall, at their advanced ages, needed a complete rest. He would tell the one who wasn't playing to wear street clothes and sit in the stands. The maneuver backfired one game in New York. Hall got injured. Bowman wasn't about to put in the minor-leaguer, but he had no choice. The back-up goalie went in. He took a few listless swats at practice shots, and suddenly collapsed. He complained that a slap shot had injured him and he was unable to continue. However, even while the goalie was warming up, Bowman had sent a messenger to find Plante. Bowman knew there was no way he was going to let the untried goalie play against the Rangers. With Bowman claiming that his two "dressed" goalies couldn't function, the referee allowed him to use Plante. The rule was changed shortly: Only players in uniform, and on the bench, can get into a game.

There are those coaches who don't even tell the goaltenders which one will start until game-time. The coaches think it keeps the players sharp. The goalies claim it makes them nervous. "You have to be ready," says Norris. "Physically and mentally. That's why I'd like to know my schedule a month in advance. You might get 10 shots against you in the first 10 minutes when you've been out for a while. You have to be ready for the bombardment. And yet, you're just making the adjustment to merely being on the ice."

Giacomin was the most famous iron man. While most other clubs were employing two goalies, the Ranger netminder played and played. For four straight seasons he played at least 65 games a year. In each of those seasons, he was bad in the playoffs. Giacomin insisted the long hours had nothing to do with it. His coach, Emile Francis, said Giacomin thrived on work. But Francis wanted to have a back-up goalie. The trouble was he could never find anyone he trusted. All the other goalies in the league attributed Giacomin's postseason problems to overwork. Sanderson, the Bruins' center, added, "It's just not possible for him to be sharp after playing the whole schedule. You need to be fresh for the playoffs. Everyone knows that."

So Giacomin toiled and toiled, earning all-star honors, amassing more shutouts over the four-year span than any other goalie—and losing in the playoffs. Then Gilles Villemure came along in the 1970–71 campaign. At last, Giacomin had a competent replacement. For the first month, Giacomin still played most of the games. Then, suddenly, he was rotated. His goals-against average went down. His playing was sharp, and he turned in shutouts at an even better average than before. He should have been happy. But he wasn't.

"I read the papers, and I see where Gilles is doing so well," said Giacomin. "I go into a game and it's in my head what Villemure has been doing. So I try a little harder. Maybe I shouldn't have to worry about competing with him—but I do. It only makes more pressure." Even while he was turning in the best goals-against average of his career, and adding eight shutouts in only 45 games, Giacomin insisted he was sharper when he played all the games.

He finally admitted after the playoffs, though, that perhaps it was all for the best. He was outstanding in the Stanley Cup games. But there was a nagging doubt. "I wonder how many shutouts I would have had if I had played the whole season," he said.

Until Gerry Desjardins, the Kings' goalie, was traded to Chicago during the 1969–70 season, he played in almost all Los Angeles games. At one point he moaned, "I don't know why they keep playing me. I can't get up for all the games." His coach, Larry Regan, had no choice. "I had to get up," said Desjardins. "They averaged 37 shots a game against me. What could I do?"

Gary Smith was the Seals' goalie during 1970–71. His coach, Fred Glover, told him, "I just can't afford to give you a rest." So Smith went on the firing line, game in and game out. He admitted there was a tendency to let down with a bad club. "I give up seven goals one night, five the next," he said. "I let in 120 goals in 40 games. What's one more goal? I let down. When you're losing, what does another goal matter? I don't feel the need to stop them —but I should."

Having two goalies around requires a defense that can adjust. The greatest display of individualism in the sport is demonstrated by the goaltender. Some like to leave their nets. They're known as wanderers, a throwback to the days when they played for bad teams in the minors and had to do a lot of work themselves, or didn't trust their defense to get the puck.

Some goalies don't like to catch the puck. They bat it to the sides. Others haven't mastered that technique. They stop everything with their body. By choice, Tony Esposito is a body-blocker. He leaves more loose pucks in front of him, after they've banged off his body, than any other goalie. His defense must have quick sticks to knock the pucks away. A goalie such as Sawchuk not only knew where he should be when the puck was coming but also what he was going to do with it once he saved it. Goalies should be aware of who is near them, both teammates and opposition. It doesn't do much good to deflect the puck to the left if an enemy player is scooting down that side. The goalie must plan whether he wants to glove the shot, or bat it straight out, or smother it with his body, or angle it. It's easy enough for a defense to adjust to a goaltender. But when two goalies are playing, often the defensemen must play differently for each. Some goalies like to handle the puck, drop it behind the cage for a defenseman or pass it out to him. The back-up may not. It is essential that goalies talk to their rearguards, on the ice and off. Some goalies find that shouting is good for them. It relieves their tension.

There also are some goaltenders for whom a club will play better, just as there are some quarterbacks who will receive sharper blocking from the offensive line. A rookie goalie invariably will receive all sorts of help. It's simply because the players don't trust him, and check furiously to make sure he's not tested often. Other goalies, because of their personality, will invite less than 100 percent effort by their teammates. Still others are so good that their teammates believe liberties can be taken, and the club becomes more offensive-minded when he's playing. They think that even if they make a mistake by pressing too deeply into the other end, their goalie can halt a breakaway.

Emotionalism plays a key role in how well a goalie is protected by teammates. The classic example came in the 1928 Stanley Cup final. It was the Rangers against the Montreal Maroons, in a best-of-five series for the Cup. The Maroons won the first game. The Rangers' goalie was Lorne Chabot, who performed well but got no scoring support. Midway through Game 2, a shot by the Maroons' Nels Stewart rammed into Chabot, above his left eye. An intermission was called as Chabot, followed by his teammates and Coach Lester Patrick, went to the dressing room for repairs. There they got the bad news from a doctor: Chabot couldn't continue.

Patrick then asked the Maroons for help. Strange as it sounds, all rinks kept spare goalies around, sitting in the stands, for an emergency. Thus, someone from the home team's farm club often filled in for the opposition. It sounds incredible now. But that's the way things went then. Goalies simply played every game. Why carry an extra man—at a salary, of course—for only one or two appearances? You might as well use a player from the opposition, hockey's brain trust reasoned. This particular night it backfired. The Maroons didn't have anyone sitting around. There were two goalies from other clubs as spectators, though—Alex Connell of Ottawa, and a minor-leaguer named Hughie McCormick. Patrick asked if the Maroons would permit the Rangers to use either of them. The Maroons refused. Patrick, starting to feel panic, went back to his dressing room. Did any of his players feel competent to play goal? No one did.

Patrick, 44 years old, with a handsome head of gray hair that earned him the nickname of The Silver Fox, announced solemnly: "I'm going to play goal, fellows. Check as you've never checked before and help protect an old man."

Psyched out of their minds, the Rangers turned into brutes. They body-blasted everyone in a Maroon uniform. Incredibly, the Rangers won in overtime, with the old man permitting only one goal. It was a lasting display of just what a team can do for its goaltender. They protected Patrick as if he were an old man about to be attacked by muggers.

An unwritten rule exists in hockey that you don't hit a goalie, even if he's out of his crease. It has been traditional, probably starting because a team would be out of luck if its goalie got hit so hard he couldn't continue. There was no back-up. An even more valid reason for not hitting a goalie is that the other team can do the same to yours. Possibly an element of fair play is at work here. Goalies, by the nature of their business, are not accustomed to hitting or being hit. They don't expect to be rapped and aren't prepared for it. This doesn't mean they're angels. Gerry Cheevers of Boston thinks nothing of swinging at an opponent as the player glides along in front, as if to say, "You've got some nerve trying to score against me!" He was lucky to get away with it. He has played for the roughest, toughest team around. If the opponent retaliated, the consequences wouldn't be pleasant. The Bruins are one team that leaps in if anyone bothers their goalie.

Another cardinal sin is the firing of the puck after the whistle has stopped action. You just don't shoot when the goalie isn't prepared if it doesn't count. His teammates will probably retaliate at the proper time. That doesn't bother Derek Sanderson. "Some goalies get rattled when I shoot after a whistle," he says. "So I'll take the shot. If it bothers them, that's fine. I'll do anything to win." That includes taking a poke at goaltenders at times, especially when they meet behind the cage. During the 1969–70 playoff series against the Rangers, a six-game affair that set a Cup record for penalties, Sanderson had been particularly hated by the New Yorkers and their fans. Before one face-off, Giacomin, exasperated, skated out to Sanderson and said, "We're getting a bonus if we take care of you tonight." Sanderson replied, "That's cool." Later, the devilish Sanderson said to newsmen, "I don't think Eddie knew what 'cool' meant."

Goalies, however, must remain cooler than their teammates. Until 1971 other players didn't get fined if they tried to break up a fight, or attempted to hold an enemy at bay. But if a goalie leaves his crease during a brawl, he receives an automatic two-minute penalty, and is subject to a $100 fine. One of the stranger sights in sports is to see an all-out fight while the goaltenders watch from opposite ends of the ice. Of course, they sometimes forget. During a playoff series with Toronto in 1971, Giacomin raced 200 feet to fight with the Leafs' goalie, Plante. Plante had gone to a teammate's help, and it was two against one. "I just wanted to even things up," Giacomin explained after he charged Plante. When goalies receive penalties, they don't sit them out. But a player from his team who was on the ice during the infraction must spend the time in the penalty box.

The only standard the public is aware of for judging goalies is the goals-against average. That is the one most publicized, and it is the only one that leads to an award—the Vezina Trophy. The Vezina is given to the goalie, or goalies, for the team permitting the fewest scores. To be eligible, a goalie must have played in at least 25 of his team's games. From the time it was first presented in 1927, until 1964—a span of 38 awards—the trophy was presented to only one goalie a year. But the advent of the two-goalie system changed that. Over the next seven years it was shared by two goalies on six occasions. The exception was Tony Esposito, who turned in a remarkable rookie campaign in 1969–70 with Chicago, where he set a modern record of 15 shutouts and appeared in 62⅔ games.

The award is worth at least $1,500 to the overall winner. But the leader (or leaders) for the first half of the season and the second half of the season each receive $250. In addition, the overall runner-up gets $750. During his big season, Esposito earned $2,000—he also led each half. Three St. Louis Blues goalies— Plante, Hall, and Ernie Wakely—shared runner-up money.

Georges Vezina is the man for whom the goaltending award is named. Yet, a cursory look at *his* averages would be misleading. It indicates the unreliability of statistics taken out of context. In his first 12 seasons with the Canadiens, his goals-against average was never better than 3.2 for any season. He had a five-year stretch when it was 4.0 or worse. His career average was 3.49. That is about a goal a game higher than today's top netminders.

But Vezina's era, 1911–26, was one in which players scored five, six, or seven goals in a game. It was a time, for the most part, when goalies couldn't leap or dive to make saves. They had to rely on the speed of their hands or feet, and had to play the angles.

Just how do you judge a goalie's effectiveness? It's not always easy. The most perfect indication would be to judge two goalies from the same team, assuming they play the same type of opposition at home and away. Then you could logically consider that any differences in the won-lost records, and the goals-against average, were significant. Take the Canadiens' goalies during the 1970–71 season, Rogatien Vachon and Phil Myre. Each played against similar opposition. Vachon played in 47 games, Myre in 30. But Vachon's average was 2.64 and Myre's was 3.11. With Vachon in the nets, the Canadiens won 23 and lost 12. With Myre, they were 13-11. It is clear that Vachon had the superior season. That same campaign, Roger Crozier and Joe Daley shared the nets for the first-year Buffalo Sabres. With Daley, the club won 12 games and dropped 16, quite respectable for an expansion club. But with Crozier, they won only 9 and lost 20. Yet Crozier had a 3.68 average to Daley's 3.70. Who was the better goalie? Strictly on won-lost averages, it was Daley by a wide margin. However, Daley generally wasn't selected to play the toughest opposition. Crozier was. Crozier would yield three or four goals to Montreal or Boston or New York and the club would lose. But if Daley yielded three or four to the weaker clubs like the Seals, or Pittsburgh or Vancouver, the Sabres could still score enough to overcome those goals.

Cheevers and Johnston, the Bruins' goalies in 1971, used to get miffed when they read that goaltending was Boston's only weak spot. The criticism came because of the seemingly endless number of 8-5, 7-4, 9-6 games that Boston won.

"Sure, there are games we let in a lot of goals," Johnston acknowledged. "But those only came in after we got a big lead and we let up. You should judge by what we do in the close games."

Big leads never prevented Plante from trying his best when he was with the Canadiens. Always in the back of his mind was the Vezina Trophy. But the other great goalies of his era, Hall and Sawchuk, had a different mental approach. They wouldn't consider it a tragedy to yield a goal when they had a big lead. Hall and Sawchuk had high-scoring teams, too, but their defenses were not nearly so expert as the Canadiens'.

Coach Scotty Bowman, who had Plante and Hall with him at St. Louis, believed that the philosophies of the clubs the pair played with in their primes were different. "Montreal remained a solid team even with a big lead," said Bowman. "They didn't like to get sloppy. But Glenn's teams just didn't defend as well."

Hall was the perennial runner-up in the Vezina race. He played for a powerhouse in Chicago, and a few of the big scorers were concerned with their goal-scoring averages at the expense of yielding goals.

"I was once fighting for the Vezina in the final week of the season and the players didn't even know it," Hall said. "They were just intent on getting their own goals."

Compassion for the goaltender has increased in recent years. The maximum curve allowed has been lowered to half an inch. The slap shot still bugs them and even a half-inch curve is a magic wand in the hands of Hull. That may explain why goalies have become so pugnacious in recent years, using their sticks to trip or jab opposing players.

Johnny Gottselig, a Black Hawk player of the 1930's, recalled the untimely death of the team's goalie, the great Charlie Gardiner, just a few months after the team won the Stanley Cup.

"I think his whole life was shortened by goaltending," said Gottselig. "He was always alone. Goalies are probably the loneliest guys in the world."

The Goal-Getters—The Forwards

"When you see a guy in another uniform," said Boom Boom Geoffrion, "you're seeing a guy who's your enemy. He's trying to take bread out of your mouth. And I'm not going to let him."

"Bread" to most forwards means goals. Watch even a practice session, and you'll see the forwards moan when a goalie stops them. You'll see them take 15-foot slap shots at open nets when no one else is on the ice. There is something so completely gratifying—and necessary—about putting the puck in the net that the average hockey player's life is built around that one thing: scoring. When Geoffrion was at a training camp, a rookie defenseman stood between the Boomer and the goal. Up went Geoffrion's stick. Down went the defenseman, off for five stitches.

"I give him five," explained Geoffrion, in the patois of hockey. "He was in my way."

Only half the players on the ice, though, should be primarily concerned with scoring. These are the three forwards. And their alignment is incredibly simple. The center usually stays in the middle, the left wing stays on the left, and the right wing on the right.

When you hear hockey people talk of someone "playing his wing" they mean that he remains on his side of the ice as much as possible, and doesn't wander. It is also known as positional hockey. That is what the textbooks teach. If a right wing, for example, always played on his side of the ice he not only would be in position for offensive thrusts, but also would be properly positioned for defensive play. That's right, defensive play. Two defensemen alone can't stop the opposing team. Thus, forwards are continually shifting their own roles. When they've got the puck they're on offense. When the opposition has it, they're on defense.

You rarely hear of goal-scorers being dubbed "two-way players." That is an almost polite way of saying a player is pretty good, but not much of a shooter. But in order for the average competitor to make it in the N.H.L., he'd better be a two-way player. Only a few can become the really big goal-scorers. To the layman effectiveness is measured by how many points a player picks up. But to most general managers, the really significant figures are the "plus-or-minus" statistics.

The goals are the most glamorous numbers in the sport. Next come the total points—the sum total of goals and assists. It's a funny system. If two players on the same team touch the puck directly leading to a goal, those two players pick up assists. The goal-scorer gets a goal. But three players have picked up 1 point apiece. Certainly, the instances where the player who receives the "second" assist—and really deserves 1 point—are rare. Yet, that's the way it's figured.

They used to joke in Montreal about Rocket Richard getting an assist while he was sitting on the bench. When an official scorer has enough leeway so that he can grant points to three-fifths of the skaters for a team on one play, there is easy opportunity to add on assists for players who the scorer might favor. But you don't hear much of that these days. Still, it does seem strange that a player who might have fought off a check, controlled the puck, and shoveled it between a mass of players to a teammate who scores receives the same point as a player who might have got the puck behind his own net, passed it to another skater, who in turn passed it to a goal-scorer. Some people believe the second assist shouldn't be worth anything, or at best only half a point. They also say that if an assist is worth a point, then a goal should be worth 2 points in the scoring parade.

The league, however, reasons (quite well) that all these points make for a team effort. The league's policy is that it often is as difficult to get off a good pass that leads to a goal as it is to score that goal. Why shouldn't the man who makes the assist be rewarded? The league also believes that it should not have a specific honor for the leading goal-scorer. Although hockey is the most trophy filled sport, the only scoring trophy the league gives—the Art Ross Trophy—is for the overall point leader.

Richard was paid to score goals. He is perhaps the only super goal-scorer never to lead the league in total points. He is, in fact, one of the few among the top career point leaders who had more goals than assists—544 goals, 421 assists. Richard, the first player to score 50 goals in a season and 500 for a career, came close to leading in total points only once.

The fact that he was denied set off the most bizarre chain of events the sport has witnessed. It was March, 1955, and Richard was on top of the league standing—in total points as well as goals. He already had led the league four times in goals scored. But now he was approaching his 34th birthday and the fans realized this might be his last shot at the elusive total-point crown. It had never seemed terribly important before. Richard, however, had heard for years the criticism that he was a selfish player. If he could gain the overall scoring title he would show his critics. Only three games remained in the regular season after a Sunday night contest at Boston. The game at Boston was the last one the Rocket appeared in that season.

He got into a fight with the Bruins' Hal Laycoe, then swung at a linesman who tried to break it up. For his actions Richard was suspended for the remainder of the regular season—and the playoffs. He was a few points ahead of Geoffrion when Clarence Campbell, the league president, announced the suspension. Immediately, Geoffrion was questioned by newsmen and fans: Would he try to win the scoring title while Richard was unable to compete? Geoffrion replied, "Are you putting bread on my table?"

As soon as the suspension was made known, Richard received calls from fanatic fans who said they would get Campbell. At the Canadiens' next game, a few fans threw eggs and tomatoes at Campbell and one fan rushed and tried to hit him. Campbell, surrounded by police, refused pleas to leave. But soon the entire Forum emptied—a stink bomb exploded filling the arena with noxious fumes. The game was forfeited, and fans went on a rampage outside, breaking windows, looting stores, overturning cars. After a night of rioting, order was restored in Montreal.

Geoffrion, however, continued to receive threats. There were bomb scares and several callers said they would kidnap his children if he picked up any more points and passed the Rocket. Geoffrion, his home cordoned off by police, nevertheless played the remaining games. He beat out Richard as the point leader.

No hue and cry would have arisen if Geoffrion had been the leader in "pluses." That is one aspect of the game that doesn't capture the fancy of the fans. A player receives a "plus" if he's on the ice for a goal by his team with both squads at equal strength. Conversely, he gets a "minus" if he's skating when the opposition scores. Short-handed goals and power-play goals don't count in this ranking.

Some of the game's top players have been minus throughout a season. During the 1969–70 campaign, Red Berenson was a big gun in the West Division with 33 goals and 39 assists for 72 points. Yet he was minus 3. His teammate on St. Louis, Tim Ecclestone, had only 16 goals and 21 assists for 37 points—but was plus 7. That same season Dave Keon paced Toronto with 32 goals, 30 assists for 62 points. He was minus 15. Paul Henderson, a teammate, had 20 goals and 22 assists for 42 points, yet was plus 14. Which players were the more effective?

Judging by the statistics, the easy answer would be: the plus player. But there are a number of variable factors at work. Keon was used with inexperienced, younger players. Henderson was on a line with the great Norm Ullman and the outstanding Ron Ellis.

Those are three players who can produce, and also play defensively.

Another factor to consider when judging a player's effectiveness, is who the opposition has thrown against him. Some coaches like to use a "checking" line against another club's top scorers. The checking line is concerned with defense, rather than scoring. Other coaches, though, often will toss their top scorers against the other squad's top scorers. Both lines will be scored against in these situations.

Other variables include the players plus or minus average in relation to the team average, and the amount of ice time he sees. Gil Perreault of Buffalo, the rookie of the year in 1971, had one of the worst minus figures in the league. Does that mean that Buffalo was better off without him? Definitely not. Perreault was told by his coach, Punch Imlach, not to worry about the defensive aspects of play in his first year, but to learn how to score in the big leagues. And Perreault also was on the ice more than other players. When you play for a bad team and see a lot of ice time, you're going to play when you're tired. You're going to see action in the waning minutes of a game when the coach wants to keep the score respectable and you're losing.

Were Keon and Berenson poor defensive players? Ask their coaches. Both players were their respective teams' top penalty killers. They had to be excellent defensively.

Jean Ratelle of the Rangers was plus 8 for the 1969–70 season. His left wing, Vic Hadfield, was minus 3. That is a swing of 11 goals. During long and sometimes bitter negotiations the following season, Hadfield's general manager and coach, Emile Francis, pointed to the minus figures when he offered Hadfield a contract. It appeared he had enough ammunition.

Hadfield countered with some facts of his own. He was injured for part of the season, and missed games when the club was scoring a lot of goals during extended winning streaks. Also, he often stayed on the ice a bit longer than his teammates, who might have been quicker getting off on line shifts. Hadfield played on some other lines occasionally.

Bobby Hull was probably the most celebrated minus player. Until the Hawks changed their style a few years ago, he consistently wound up with negative figures. When he set a goal-scoring record of 58 in 1968–69 and set a right-wing record of 107 total points, Hull was minus. The Hawks' style then revolved around Hull. He was always at center ice, looking for the breakaway pass. He would wander from his wing when he had the puck, leaving his side of the ice unprotected. As a result, the opposition had many breakaway chances. Hull also played with different linemates, and each of them was looking to set him up rather than concentrate on the basics of the game. When the Hawks changed their style, they became winners—and Hull became a plus player.

Just what are the basics of the game for forwards? Ideally, it means playing your position. The center is the focal point of the attack. Most centers, like most players in the N.H.L., shoot left-handed. Centers must be able to control the puck equally well from the forehand or backhand because of the constant passing to their wings. A left-handed center, for example, will be making a backhand pass to his left wing and a forehand pass to his right wing. Since the center usually is the man who will bring the puck up ice, he must be able to control the disk, keeping it from the opposition, and be able to put a pass on his wings' sticks while the three are moving at nearly 30 miles an hour and harassed by the opposition.

Most right wings are right-handed shots and most left wings shoot left-handed. Richard was the notable exception. He was a left-handed shot playing right wing. Whenever the puck came to him, it usually arrived on his backhand. He had to switch the position of his stick to curl the puck on the inside of his blade. Richard was unusual, though. He had a remarkable ability to shoot the puck off his backhand. Since most goalies are accustomed to seeing forehand shots leveled at them, Richard's backhander, hard and accurate, presented a problem to the other netminders—even though his backhand wasn't as good as his forehand.

A center's stick-handling ability is necessary on the very first play of the game—the opening face-off. In virtually every case, the centers meet in the face-off circle. Because they have carried the puck so often and for so many miles, centers are usually the most experienced stickmen, and their talents are necessary to win a face-off. Boston's Derek Sanderson has made a science of the face-off. It may not be crucial when the puck is dropped at center ice, but when there's a face-off near a goalie, it can lead directly to a goal. Sanderson thinks he's the best, and claims he can win 90 percent of the face-offs. In one game, he says, he won 38 face-offs and lost once. Sanderson advises that if you want to pass the puck to your teammate on the left, you fade to the right. Then, when the puck is dropped, you move in the direction of your pass. If Sanderson is up against a player who's extremely fast on the draw, Sanderson stays a bit outside, lets the opponent win the face-off, and then charges him just as the puck hits the other player's stick. The player is off balance and theoretically could lose the puck.

"One of the key elements to winning a face-off is cheating," says Sanderson. "You've got to cheat because it's too difficult to win most of them fair and square." He also tries a bit of psychology. Sometimes he talks to the linesman, saying "Don't drop the puck until I'm ready." The other center, says Sanderson, begins to wonder when Sanderson will be ready.

It is important to know the official's style of puck-dropping. The referee drops the puck only to start a game or after a goal. At all other times, a linesman drops it. Some officials drop the puck to the side, letting it hit the ice before the players' sticks do. Others might hold the disk a certain way, giving a clue to when they're ready to let it go.

Before the face-off, the center should have an exact idea of what he wants to do with the puck. He tells his teammates his plans and they know what to expect. During a normal face-off— when a team isn't short-handed—it is difficult for the center to interfere with his opposite number on the dropping of a puck. The referee is watching the face-off pretty closely. During certain situations, to be described later, a center can get away with a fair amount of bodily contact.

Okay, the game's ready to begin. The center moves toward the face-off spot at center ice. He faces the goal he will be attacking. Behind him his defensemen are ready, protecting their own goal. To his right is his right wing. To his left is his left wing. The easiest move for a center to make is to propel the puck behind him. But he has to know his opponents. If they're a club such as the Montreal Canadiens, they'll be streaking goalward. A center wouldn't want to pass toward his own defensemen in such a situation. If they miss the puck, the Canadiens are home free.

The center in this instance has told his right wing he'll try to get the puck to him. He does. Once the club has the puck, it is on offense. Each role is highly specific. The ultimate aim is a goal. To get one, all the club has to do is bring the puck in, avoid getting checked or losing it, and get a shot past the goalie. The execution is the hard part. The three forwards should be moving as a unit, lateral with one another. The center carries it as long as he can. His first obstacle is to get the puck in the other team's zone, beyond the blue line. If he can't carry it all the way himself, he looks for a free wing. If they're being bothered by the other team, then he'll have to shoot the puck in and hope his club can control it. It's not always such a hit-and-miss affair as it seems. The Detroit Red Wings got many goals during their great years by using the boards at the Olympia. The center would send in a long blast that rebounded back. The wing on whose side the shot came out to would time the rebound and get to a certain spot just as the puck did. Boom—a shot on goal. If a skater can't bring the puck in, he might take a long shot at the goalie. He knows the puck won't go in, but he knows that he and one of his wings might be able to play the rebound. Some goalies hit the puck straight back. Others knock it to the sides. Still others like to catch it and hold it. If they hold it for more than three seconds there's a face-off. So the center should be aware of the goalie's habits.

If a center has been able to pass to one of his wings at the blue line, the center then drives down the middle, hoping for a return pass. This is, perhaps, the most fundamental attacking play in hockey. However, since the opposing center is usually right in front of him, it is not quite as easy to perform as it seems.

Some centers are masters of the change of pace, or the head fake. Take the Black Hawks' Mikita. He can get off a shot on goal that will be low and hard while he's looking to his right, apparently trying to spot his man. Mikita also has a variety of head and shoulder fakes that alarms opposing centers and defensemen. Just at the moment it seems he has committed himself to cutting left, Mikita has the ability to shift to the right and get behind his man. He does it with quickness rather than brawn. At 5–9 and 165 pounds, Mikita may well be the smallest N.H.L. player to lead the league in scoring. Coaches usually like their centers to be big, in height and weight. A taller center means he has a "longer" stick, can sweep the puck away from the opposition, or can keep it at arm's length. And brawn is important for a center for most clubs ask their centers to be able to dig the puck out of the corners, or go behind the net where the action gets close.

This is another offensive area for the center. If he has been unable to bring the puck in, or pass off, then he might shoot the puck off the boards. If the shot has wound up on the right side of the ice, the right wing and the center chase it. If it goes to the left side, the center and left wing go in deep for it. Clubs will almost always send in two forwards for the puck, unless they feel they're outmanned and want to avoid risking being caught short. But when the two men go for the puck you won't see them charging it willy-nilly. The job of the first man is to take the opposing player —who will be going for the puck, too—out of the play. The first man in "plays the body." He's not concerned with getting the puck. The second man in, though, tries to control it. While the center and the right wing, say, have been battling for the puck in the corner, the remaining wing should be stationed in the "slot" —an imaginary point midway between the blue line and the goal. It is the ideal place to shoot from, since the shooter can see the entire net in front of him. Now that the center has the puck, he will attempt to pass it to his teammate in the slot. Once the man in the slot has the disk, he is a pretty good bet to score. But if the puck can't be moved out to him, what does he do? Nothing. He waits. And if the puck is shoveled to the left side, then the left wing leaves the slot and chases it, along with the center. The right wing then moves into the slot, and the process begins again.

It is at times like this that players have to keep their heads. Often the intoxication of attack makes a player forget himself. That's when they wander from their positions, chasing pucks all over the ice. And it is just at these times that breakaways by the opposition take place. Some players are so conscious of playing their position and not getting caught deep, that they don't present much of a scoring threat. Ron Stewart, who played 20 years and scored more than 270 goals, was such a performer. As soon as he saw the possibility that he might have a battle for the puck, he backed up, ready to defend. It wasn't that he was afraid of the contact. His style was geared to always thinking about what might happen if he lost the puck while deep in the opponent's end. It was a styled honed during his years on the Maple Leafs, a tough club in the early 1960's that worked hard, but played for a few breaks. They never took chances.

No matter what style of attack a team has, it must change as soon as the other team has possession. The club that doesn't have the puck is now playing defense. Once the attack has failed, the center backs up toward the middle, the right and left wings are ready to halt the opposing team's wings—the right wing will be taking the opponent's left wing, and vice versa. Now the center is trying to halt a play rather than start one. He is the key defensive player of the forwards. He should be attempting to harass the other club's puck-carrier, but still be able to get back in position to take the other center. If a center's stick is crucial to the attack, it is equally valuable when he's playing defense. He uses his stick almost like a billiard cue, trying to hit the puck away. The wings, meanwhile, are backing up, keeping their respective opposing wings in front of them. The wings should also have their sticks on the ice. It's easier to block a pass if the stick is already at ice level, rather than swinging at it from hip level. While the wings back up, they stay away from the boards, cutting down the attacking wings' angle. If the attacking wing tries to cut between the defending wing and the boards, the defender can ram the player into the boards. By keeping an opponent close to the boards, you are also keeping him from getting off a straightaway shot.

Some players are followed more closely. The good ones have their "shadows," an opponent whose job is, simply, to halt the star from scoring. The shadow will not concern himself with the other players, only with the man he is to stop. In the case of Bobby Hull, a left wing, several squads have assigned right wings who oppose him whenever Hull gets on the ice.

Being a shadow is a thankless job. It requires a player to be unselfish. While Hull is out there, the shadow must forget his instincts to go in deep for the puck when his club is attacking. Hull made the shadow famous and the shadow made Hull angry. The shadow came to stay during the 1965 Stanley Cup finals, when the Hawks faced the Canadiens. The Montrealers assigned Claude Provost to guard Hull, and the move set up an intriguing series of confrontations between the pair.

Provost, a square-jawed forward who could double for the wrestler, the Swedish Angel, was, according to Hull, the best shadow. He was clean but clinging, and he respected Hull. Not every club could afford to put a shadow on Hull. If a team took one of its top players to bother Bobby, it meant that its overall punch was weakened. The Canadiens, though, were a power-packed squad, filled with talent. They could take one of their top men, put him on Hull, and still have enough firepower left.

Before the 1965 playoffs, everyone had been aware that certain players had been assigned to guard Hull. But Provost brought the torment to an art form. During the 1964–65 season Hull had a brilliant year. He had 39 goals in only 61 games. He was to win the most-valuable-player award and he was to win the Lady Byng Trophy for gentlemanly conduct combined with skill. He had amassed only 32 minutes in penalties.

In the first round of Stanley Cup play he was brilliant. The Hawks, who had finished third during the regular season, defeated the first-place Red Wings. With Crozier in the nets, the Wings had posted the second-lowest goals-against average in the league. Crozier, only a rookie, led the league with six shutouts. But in the seven-game series against stingy Detroit, Hull accounted for a record-equaling eight goals. Only two other players had ever scored so many in a Cup series. It seemed that nothing would stop Hull.

His fans had conveniently forgotten about Provost. As soon as the final series against the Canadiens began, it was obvious that Hull was going to have a rough time. Provost became bonded to him. Provost was the super-shadow, the prototype. A right wing, Provost dashed over the boards whenever Hull was on the ice. It didn't matter what Montreal line was playing. If Hull was out there, Provost would be, too. In the first three games, Hull was kept off the scoreboard. In Montreal, the fans cheered wildly for Provost. At Chicago, he was booed when he appeared. Soon, Hull was losing his cool. When he saw Provost approaching he'd shift to the other side of the ice; when he was tied up, he'd swing his elbows wildly. Provost accepted the role as shadow, although one had the feeling he didn't relish it.

"I feel bad for Bobby," he said. "But that's the way I got to play him. I have to stay ahead of him and get the puck. If I don't, and he winds up . . ."

It was perhaps the first time that a shadow received genuine appreciation. Today, shadows have a bit more recognition. But nothing approached the tension that was developing in that playoff. Provost stood 5-9, and weighed 168 pounds. He was an inch shorter and 25 pounds lighter than the burly Hull. Provost knew he was getting on Hull's nerves. "You can tell Bobby's angry," he said. "He's playing the body more. He never used to hit me so much. But when he plays the body he doesn't play the puck. I don't blame him, though. I bet no one ever watched him so closely."

Provost's job made a nervous wreck—of Provost. "I can't sleep," the Canadien said. "I think about the game all the time. I try to get it off my mind, watch some TV. I ask the guys what they're doing this summer. I know they don't like me in Chicago. But I'm not in a popularity or beauty contest. If I was, Bobby would win."

Hull finally broke loose in the fourth game, with two goals in a

6-0 victory. But those turned out to be the only goals Hull got as the Frenchmen won the Cup in seven games. The shadow had come to stay. Hull, who had gotten only 32 minutes in penalties in 61 regular-season games, wound up with 27 penalty-minutes in 14 playoff games.

The shadows went after Hull following the dramatic proof of the 1965 playoffs that he could be stopped. Yet, the following season Hull became the first man to get more than 50 goals in a season. His record 54 was part of a record point total of 97. Who was to stop him in the 1966 playoffs, in which the Hawks would face the Red Wings again? Hull, after all, had scored eight times against Detroit in the playoffs the year before.

This time the Detroiters had a fiery player nicknamed Super Pest—Bryan Watson. Used as a substitute, Watson had played 70 games for Detroit in the 1965–66 season—and had only two goals. He was a spare defenseman or spare forward, not considered much of a player. Coach Sid Abel of Detroit decided to make a dramatic move to halt Hull. He made Watson a regular right wing. Whenever Hull was out, Watson would be, too.

Hull is only human. Early in the first game Watson picked a fight with him. Both went to the penalty box, but not before Hull shouted at Watson, "Well, if that's what you want to do—then it's idiot's delight." Clearly, Hull had been ruffled and served notice that he would hit back.

That is just what Abel wanted. Hull became so angered as the games wore on that he forgot about playing. Once, he even picked a fight with Watson, banging Watson's head against the protective glass and cutting him with a stick. But Watson's tactics were working. He didn't hamper Hull just physically. He taunted Hull by talking to him constantly. Hull was so unnerved he could get only two goals in six games, and the Hawks were eliminated. Ironically, Watson, a two-goal scorer during 70 regular-season games, also got two goals in the six playoff games. Super Pest had not only stifled the Master, but also had scored as many goals as the man who had just shattered the single-season scoring record.

During a lull in one of the games, Hull was standing next to

Gordie Howe. The two old pros were watching a fight in which Watson was tangling with a Black Hawk. "Gordie," said Hull, "wouldn't this game be much nicer without the animals?"

It certainly would be much nicer for the superstars. Phil Esposito of the Bruins, who somehow manages to plant himself in front of the goal and get off seven or eight shots every game, complains, "There's so many clutchers and grabbers in this league, it's unbelievable." Esposito, Hull, and Bobby Orr maintain that the referees allow them, in particular, to be abused. The mediocre players scoff at such talk. The marginal ones insist that they are singled out whenever they cleanly check a top star.

Many players say their reputation dictates what the referee will call. John Ferguson of the Montreal Canadiens, for example, says that when he played "the refs were always quick with the whistle." Perhaps it's an analogous situation to the policeman who picks up known criminals for every felony.

It's no doubt true that many of Ferguson's penalties were meted out by officials who were overreacting to the sight of the brawny Canadien. But Ferguson was no angel. Before an important game, he'd map out his fighting strategy. "I'd try to plan how the game would go," he explained. "Then I tried to figure out when would be the best time to start something." Ferguson played on the same line as Provost. Although Ferguson was a left wing, and theoretically on the other side of the ice from Hull, he'd be on the ice whenever Hull was. If Hull eluded Provost, Ferguson was there.

Claude Ruel, Ferguson's coach, once said, "Let's start something." So Ferguson punched Hull. Later that season Ferguson and Hull met again. This time, Hull's jaw was wired and he wore a helmet and face guard to protect the broken jaw. Hull threw a punch and Ferguson knocked him down. He kneeled over the fallen Hull. "I had a clean shot at him," Ferguson remembered. "I saw him looking up at me with real hate in his eyes. I didn't hit him. I would have been the biggest rat in North America if I had."

Ron Stewart was one of the better shadows, who usually played Hull cleanly. Because of the respect each player had for the other, a sort of friendship followed, based on the situation each found himself in. Stewart, anticipating Hull to come on the ice for the next shift, hopped over the boards. He was ready before Hull was. When Hull came out, Stewart skated over and said, "What? Are you shadowing me again?"

Rejean Houle of the Canadiens is the latest of Montreal-based tormentors of Hull. After a game during the 1971–72 season, Houle admitted, "When Bobby gets past me, I've got to trip him. It's the only way I can stop him."

Some players make a career of being pests. Reg Fleming was one such type. In his first 10 seasons in the N.H.L. Fleming never scored more than 17 goals in any campaign. His yearly statistics are filled with such figures as seven or four or eight goals. Yet, he saw action in virtually every game he played. Fleming wasn't so much a "shadow" as he was a "policeman." He wasn't a good enough skater to be the shadow. But every club needs a policeman, someone who keeps the opposition honest, someone who barges in when a teammate is being beaten up.

"I'm smart enough to know I couldn't have lasted unless it was for the fighting part," Fleming admitted. "I'm no scorer, and not much of a skater. I learned early in my career that if I was going to make it, I'd have to be the fighter on the club."

The easiest path for a fan to take, when seeing a policeman such as Fleming, is to consider the player stupid. Certainly, players like Fleming are noted for taking "dumb penalties." Or what appear to be dumb penalties. But how many times has a Fleming been sent on the ice by his coach with instructions to "start something." The point is, the Reg Flemings of hockey have specific, and often important, functions. When a club is down, when it's not hitting, when the opposition is running all over it—that's when a belter can be effective. One good shot to the body can unbalance the other team, lift the spirits of a club, raise the noise level of the fans. The Rangers' Brad Park admits that at times he'll "really lay a player into the boards" just to shake up the hometown fans, whose support is essential.

This is not to suggest that penalties are completely thought out.

No doubt, Fleming received so many penalties because his style dictated that he did. After four or five years in the league, when a player doesn't receive recognition for his skills—only his fighting ability—it's natural for him to continue playing a certain role. Thus, Fleming, or Ted Green of Boston, or Keith Magnuson of Chicago reacted in ways that had proven successful. They were rewarded at contract-time for their fighting qualities, and they received fan acceptance for their crowd-pleasing antics.

The image as a fighter was a source of constant irritation to Orland Kurtenbach, a quiet giant who earned the sobriquet as the man "with the fastest fists in hockey." In quiet moments Kurt would reflect on his career and say, "They never talk about the 100 points I got in the juniors. All they want to talk about is 'the other thing.' " The "other thing," of course, was his fighting ability. He generally was recognized as the best one-punch man in the sport. Yet, he never (or hardly ever) started fights. He was the perfect policeman. His role was to break up something before it got out of hand. He came out of the West as a top scorer. Yet he never had a 20-goal season in the N.H.L. until he was 35.

"I'm not in a position to go around and tell people, 'Hey, there's more to me than being able to fight.' People put you in a certain niche, and they like you to stay in it. It's simpler for them to think of you as a one-dimensional person. But I never thought about the fighting thing. It's a shame that the public did. They always thought that part of me was more important than the fact that I could score," said Kurtenbach.

When players speak of penalties, they usually classify them as "dumb" or "smart." Dumb penalties are for tripping and holding. It shows you haven't played your man right—and have to resort to illegal tactics to stop him. When Vic Hadfield came up with the Rangers he took many dumb penalties. Even he admits it. In his first full year with the club he led the league with 151 minutes in the penalty box. "I couldn't stop my opponent, so I wound up fouling him," says Hadfield.

As the years went by, Hadfield became a better player and a consistent 20-goal man. His penalty minutes dropped. That didn't mean that Hadfield wasn't playing as aggressively. "I took penalties—sure," he says. "But they were good penalties. Boarding and charging are good penalties. They show that you're trying. You're not committing them because you've made a stupid mistake and in desperation have to commit a foul."

As a rule, forwards will be penalized most often for physical fouls—boarding or charging. Usually, they don't have to resort to tripping. Those are the kind of penalties—restraining fouls—that defensemen pick up when there's a danger of their man eluding them and making it toward the goal.

Once a club is penalized, its formations change. By the same token, the club with the man advantage also does things differently. Under a normal penalty situation, a club will have a one-man advantage for a maximum of two minutes. If a goal is scored during that time the penalty is over. If there is a delayed penalty—if the team that has been fouled is keeping possession of the puck—and the club scores, no penalty is assessed. That play is rare. Usually a club plays the entire two minutes. A squad with an excellent power play will score about 25 percent of the time it has the advantage. An average team will score once in every five times. On the other hand, a team that kills 85 percent of the penalties against it—about seven out of eight times—is really doing its job. Most clubs kill 80 percent of their penalties—they allow one goal for every five power-play opportunities.

Now the question arises: Who do you use on the power play, or to kill penalties? The Montreal Canadiens' power play of the late 1950's was so formidable that it wasn't unusual for the club to score twice during the two minutes the opposition was shorthanded. Because of the Canadiens' destructiveness the league changed its rule. Once a goal is scored, the penalty is over. The exception is for a major penalty, such as slashing and injuring a player. Anytime a player is sent off for more than two minutes for such an infraction, the team plays a man short for the duration of the penalty, no matter how many goals are scored.

Selecting players for such situations isn't a cut-and-dried affair. Penalty killing is usually done by the regular defensemen. But the forwards who are employed to kill penalties aren't necessarily the same ones who see action throughout the game. This doesn't mean that subs are the rule. Some squads don't like to use regular forwards to kill a penalty. It drains the players. The teams used to be able to keep a player or two around just for penalty killing. Now that the rosters are smaller, even marginal players must be able to do more than be a pest for two minutes while the other club has the advantage.

Ideally, a penalty-killing forward is unselfish. Rarely do you see a penalty killer take risks to score. His job while he's out there is to subvert a natural desire to put the puck in the net. He should be fast. Because the club is short-handed, there's more ice to cover. Some players turn a short-handed situation into scoring opportunities. They know that on a power play there is a good chance for the club with the advantage to get careless about defensive play. During the 1970–71 season Dave Keon of the Maple League got a record eight goals while his squad was a man short. That's half a season's total-goal production for the average player.

Keon, and another expert penalty killer, Sanderson, have a fantastic talent for anticipation. They don't go charging after loose pucks and attempt to bring them up ice. They can sense when they have the odds in their favor—when the opposition won't be able to get to the puck before they do. Ed Westfall, Sanderson's teammate, is another quality penalty killer. Perhaps a short-handed goal's greatest value is its demoralizing effect. It's bad enough when a goal is scored at any time, since a team averages about 3.5 goals for the entire game. But when a club has the advantage and gets scored upon, it can have disastrous effects. In the 1970 playoffs against the Rangers, the Bruins scored twice on one penalty while they were a man short. The Rangers had started to press after allowing the first goal, left themselves open, gave up another breakaway—and that was it.

Centers usually seem to predominate among the penalty killers. For one, their sticks are generally quicker. They are accustomed to covering a huge amount of surface and are good skaters. They also are experienced at face-offs, and when a team is killing a penalty a face-off is most critical. Lose a face-off in your end when you're a man short, and it is virtually certain to wind up as a shot on goal.

In killing penalties, the standard formation is the box defense. You can't use a man-to-man coverage, quite obviously. So you play a zone. Because the puck can be passed so quickly, it would seem that penalty killing is all but impossible. But the league has made a concession in the rules: the team that is a man short can clear the puck the length of the ice and not be faced with an "icing" call.

For practical purposes, we will call the two forwards on the penalty-killing unit the right wing and the left wing. When the opposition has the puck in the short-handed team's zone, the defending right wing should be between the slot and the opponent's left wing. The left wing on the short-handed squad should be in the same position on the other side of the ice. Once the puck is moved around the penalty killers will have to keep their heads. The opposition may try to "sucker" a player into the slot with a pass there. If, say, the defending right wing runs to the slot, a quick pass back to the left point leaves the man there free for a shot. Because there is so much territory to cover, it is essential for the defending forwards to be adept with their backhand. They will not always have the time to position the puck properly on their sticks, and they'll have to get rid of the puck quickly—no matter where it is. The wing on the defending club always maintains his position between his opposing wing and the slot. So the box formation will move, shifting to the left and right, as the opponents move.

Although no icing is called against the short-handed team, it still is subject to offsides penalties—that is, a player for a short-handed team can't handle a teammate's pass that's gone over two lines. That is basic, but it is even more essential to remember this in a short-handed situation. You don't want to make a mistake and touch a two-line pass. If you do, you've got a face-off in your end. When Larry Jeffrey played for the Rangers in 1969 he made the mistake—during a playoff game. It came against the Montreal Canadiens. He was apparently successfully killing a penalty when he reached for a pass. It was offside. The Canadiens got the face-off in the Ranger end, and scored. The Rangers lost the game.

Pressure does funny things to people. Afterward, Jeffrey admitted, "I just forgot what the situation was." Yet, Jeffrey had been exclusively a penalty killer throughout the season, appearing in 75 games. He never made that mistake once during the regular campaign.

If being one man short is unnerving, imagine what sort of stress players are under when they're two men down. The situation doesn't present itself very often. Referees aren't as quick with their whistles against a team that already has one man in the penalty box. But on those rare occasions when it happens, the short-handed team is presented with extraordinary problems.

The dimensions of the playing surface don't change. There is still the same amount of ice to cover. When a team is two men short, it employs one forward and two defensemen. That one forward is responsible for an inordinate amount of space. He must cover the two point men—who are about 70 feet apart—and the man in the slot. It is physically impossible to be in three places at once. In this situation, he is virtually reduced to being a harasser. He can't hope to stay on top of the disk. The team that's two men down employs a triangle defense. The two defensemen stay back, on either side of the goal. The lone forward is the point of the triangle. He shifts in the direction the puck moves.

Sanderson (his name keeps cropping up in sticky situations) is without equal as a pest when his team is two men short. He admits that he does things to embarrass the opposition when he can. Sanderson is so unpredictable, and keeps the other team off balance so well, that his reputation precedes him and a club often makes mistakes simply because Sanderson is out there.

Clubs usually have two sets of forwards to kill penalties, and both see action during a short-handed stint. Which pair is used first depends on several factors. If, for example, there is only a minute or so left in the period, the coach probably will use his top outfit first and go to the end of the period with it. But if the line has just seen action, it is doubtful the coach would use the same players to start off a penalty-killing job. If nothing else, penalty killers must be fresh and alert. Another factor in deciding which penalty-killing teams to use is: who was the player penalized? Say, for example, it was Westfall. The coach might not use Sanderson in the first wave of penalty killing. Sanderson usually skates on the same line as Westfall. He would use Sanderson toward the end of the penalty. Then when Westfall returns to the ice, he just goes into his regular alignment with Sanderson.

It is apparent that forwards do more than try to score. On poorer clubs, in fact, they probably are playing their defensive roles for longer stretches than their offensive roles. But all clubs, good or bad, are in the ultimate attacking position when they have a power play going on.

The top scoring line will see the majority of the action during the power play. The only time it won't is when it has just been on the ice for a protracted stretch. On a power play, clubs often employ four forwards and only one defenseman. It depends on the talent available. The extra forward would take up a position at one of the points. In effect, he is also a defenseman since he stays back, parallel to the other defenseman. It isn't always necessary to use four forwards. If a club is blessed with a defenseman with a whistling, low slap shot, he can be used on the power play. But whoever plays the point should have a good, low, accurate shot.

The shot must be low so it may afford rebound opportunities. It is difficult for goalies to catch low line drives. They usually bat them out, keeping the puck in play. Once the puck is hit out, the team with the man advantage generally can get a shot at the rebound. Although it might appear dangerous for a club to play with only one defenseman, it really isn't. On the power play the team has a man advantage. The short-handed club won't be taking many chances. Thus, the club with the power play can concentrate on attack, with a minimum of worry.

It is on the power play that the fans will see a majority of long shots. Under normal conditions, a slap shot is wasted. But because the slap shot means rebound chances, the point men will fire away at will, knowing that the other club can't clear the rebound as easily because it has one less player on the ice.

There are rare occasions when a club has six skaters to the

other team's five. These happen during a delayed penalty, or in the closing seconds of a game when a team that is trailing tries a last desperate measure to score. During a delayed penalty, of course, the team that committed the penalty cannot score. The play is dead once the offending team touches the puck. So the team that has been sinned against can pull its goalie, and replace him with another skater, without worrying about a goal being scored. It is possible for a team to put the puck accidentally into its own net. If this happens during a delayed penalty, the goal counts. But this sort of mistake hasn't happened in years. When the goalie leaves the ice during a delayed penalty, he is replaced by a forward—usually a center—who immediately rushes to the slot. Play is still in progress. With the extra man in the slot, all areas of the attacking zone are covered—the right wing has the right side and right corner, the left wing has the left side and left corner, the center has the job as rover. He goes to the right or left, depending where the puck is. The defensemen, of course, are at their respective points. The same alignment is used if a club puts out six skaters in an effort to tie the score. The move rarely works. After all, it is easier to prevent a team from scoring than it is to score.

Some players have made a career out of feasting on power plays. In his first few seasons in the big leagues, Yvan Cournoyer saw most of his action on the power play. Small at 5-7 and 165, Cournoyer was considered too fragile to be a regular, especially on the powerful Montreal clubs. During the 1966–67 season, Cournoyer played part-time—yet he got 25 goals. Twenty came on the power play. It is doubtful if any other 20-goal scorer ever achieved the feat of getting 80 percent of his scores on the power play. Another small man, Camille Henry, regularly scored 40 percent of his total goals on the power play. Henry was only 5-8, and weighed 145. His personal high was 18 power-play goals, achieved during the 1962–63 season when he amassed 37 goals for the Rangers.

Both players were fast, and exceptionally quick around the net. Playing during the man advantages, they had less worry about body contact than they would have under normal conditions. They were able to station themselves in front of the net for deflections and rebounds. If it weren't for the power-play opportunities, it is doubtful if Henry could have played 13 major-league seasons. Cournoyer, however, got his chance as a regular and became a top star—simply because he was too fast to catch. He still enjoyed power-play success. When he got 37 goals during the 1970–71 season, 18 came with the man advantage.

The big guns are well aware that the power play can fatten their averages. In the 1970–71 season, the 12 top goal-scorers had 509 goals, an average of about 42 a man. But nearly 30 percent of their goals—148–came on the power play.

"How can I reach the 30-goal mark," Rod Gilbert once asked, "if they don't use me on the point in the power play?" Gilbert had been replaced on the right point by the most famous point man of them all, Boom Boom Geoffrion.

While the Boston Bruins were breaking all sorts of records in the 1970–71 season, Phil Esposito amassed a record 25 power-play goals among his 76-goal total. He got most of them from in front, after shoving players away and making a groove for himself a few feet from the net. Esposito was aware that some observers didn't give him all the credit he thought he deserved.

"It's not fancy, I know," said Esposito. "But they don't pay me to be fancy. They pay me to put the puck in the net."

To put the puck in the net requires a forward line. But a coach doesn't simply take his top center, left wing, and right wing and throw them together. A certain chemistry takes place in a line, and not all players can blend together. The most successful lines have been composed of a stick-handler (usually the center) who can control the puck and make the plays. Then one player must be the gritty sort, able to tangle in the corners and retrieve the puck. Then another player must be the gunner. If you get players with more than one quality, that's fine. But you can't make up a line of three shooters, or three diggers or three stick-handlers—if those are their only attributes. In recent years several top lines have been formed, and each of them displays perfectly the separate ingredients that go into the making of a trio.

When Frank Mahovlich was traded to the Detroit Red Wings

after an outstanding career with Toronto, he was put on a line with Gordie Howe and Alex Delvecchio. It isn't always a good idea to put a club's top goal-scorers on the same line. That weakens other lines. And when you have two potential hall-of-famers in a Mahovlich and Howe, you could run into a situation where each is jealously protective of the puck and wants it for himself.

Yet, the line set a record during the 1968–69 season of 114 goals. Mahovlich registered 48, Howe had 42, and Delvecchio added 24. The chemistry worked. As usual, Mahovlich had more goals than assists. But it didn't affect the line. Howe and Delvecchio were the diggers, and both were expert stick-handlers, allowing the other members of the line to get in position.

The Rangers have had Jean Ratelle at center, Vic Hadfield at left wing, and Rod Gilbert on the right side. In 1971–72, they became the first line in history to score 40 goals per man. Hadfield is a tiger in the corners. He does the dirty work for Ratelle and Gilbert. Getting banged around—and doing some banging—certainly slows a player down. Wouldn't Hadfield be a more effective scorer if his linemates worked as hard?

"Not necessarily," says Hadfield. "Every player has a certain style, one that works for him. If I tried to become a long-range shooter, or hovered around the net all the time, I wouldn't be as effective. I've always been comfortable with my style. If I played on a line where the other guys did the corner work I don't think I'd score as many goals. In fact, I probably wouldn't do as well."

Ratelle and Gilbert are two of hockey's finest, and cleanest, players. Each takes his lumps. But teamed with Hadfield they are a formidable threesome. Ratelle possesses brilliant stick-handling qualities. He allows his wings to get set up with his extraordinary ability to hold the puck while being badgered. Gilbert is the exciting shooter, with a devastating slap shot.

On the ice they appear to be going through a choreographed routine. Automatically Ratelle follows Hadfield to the left side, with Gilbert hovering around the slot. When the puck is in Gilbert's corner, Ratelle is there while Hadfield gets to the slot. Few passes are wasted by this line, which was formed in 1966 and improved each year. Part of the reason for their success, they say, is that they shout to one another.

"The guys let me know where they are," explains Ratelle. "Even with my back turned, if I hear Rod or Vic shouting I can tell where they are and try to hit them with a pass."

The most feared trio in recent years had the Bruins' Esposito at center, Ken Hodge on the right side, and Wayne Cashman at left wing. Among the 35 league records the Boston team shattered during the 1970–71 season were the marks for most goals by a line and most points by a line. The Esposito trio had a total of 140 goals and 336 points. That broke the previous goal mark by 26 and the point total by 73. Amazing.

Here again we have the stick-handler (Esposito), the worker (Cashman), and the long-range shooter (Hodge). Of course, the line was twice-blessed. Esposito also became the greatest single-season scorer in history.

Rebound attempts made this line so formidable. Esposito can't be moved in front of the net. ("He's a damned tree there," says the Rangers' Rod Seiling.) When Hodge would blast away, Esposito was there for the rebounds. When Cashman would fire the puck laterally to Esposito from the corner, Esposito was in position to shoot. If the puck was knocked out, he still was there to shoot.

The three lines—Delvecchio's, Ratelle's, and Esposito's—were scoring lines. There are other types of lines in hockey. If a club is fortunate, it can have three distinct lines—one for checking, one for holding (or maintaining status quo), and one for scoring.

The scoring line is the No. 1 line. It puts the goals on the scoreboard. Although the players on this line aren't necessarily selected for their defensive abilities, at least one of the players should be competent at back-checking—stopping the opposition in the opposition's attacking zone.

The checking line checks—vigorously. Generally it is placed against the other team's top line. This checking line must be composed of unselfish players. Usually it's an experienced line since most youngsters aren't aware completely of the game's defensive aspects. Sanderson, the pest, has centered the most famed checking line of recent years. His right wing has been Westfall, and swing men have been used on the left side. Indeed, in his first five years in the league Sanderson played with eight different left wings. He always claimed that not having a regular left wing hindered his growth and effectiveness, yet he was a consistent 20-goal man. He was only plus 8 during the Bostonians' highly successful 1969–70 season, when it outscored the opposition by 61 goals. Here was a perfect example, though, of the potential tyranny of statistics. He was always out against the other team's best line.

Another successful checking line was dubbed "The Old Smoothies." This was a Ranger trio of Phil Goyette (center), Bob Nevin (right wing), and Don Marshall (left wing). They were together four years. Unlike Sanderson's line, which had more enthusiasm than experience, the Smoothies did their job matter-of-factly, rarely rattled. They made few mistakes. Each of the players was accomplished defensively, and each played his position perfectly. It wasn't an exciting line to watch, but it got the job done.

Some players might never receive recognition if they weren't on the right type of line. The Los Angeles Kings had three players, Juha Widing, Bob Berry, and Mike Byers, who were expendable with other clubs. They skated together during the 1970–71 campaign—and each scored at least 25 goals. Dave Balon had been a professional for 12 years and had never scored 30 goals. With the 1969–70 Rangers, though, he was made the left wing on a line centered by Walt Tkaczuk—and Balon scored 33. He led the club again the following season with 36 goals. In Tkaczuk, he found the perfect center for his style, which is goal-hovering. Balon is most effective around the net, where he puts his quick stick to good use on rebounds and deflections. If he doesn't have a center who can control the puck deep in the other team's territory, Balon is only half as effective.

A Cournoyer, a Balon, or a Henry couldn't have functioned as well if they played on the same line with a similar type of player. They needed bigger men on their line to get the puck to them and to keep the defense busy. Another thing a small man must have going for him is the opposition's respect for his linemates. If a small man gets battered around, and his teammates don't help him by retaliating, then the little guy is done for. The opposition's defense just has to push the small man around.

Ultimately, points are the lifeblood of a line, or player. If they can't get the points they talk about the pluses. Fred Shero, who was named the Philadelphia Flyers' coach in 1971, remembers a minor-leaguer who wasn't much of a goal-scorer. On one shift, someone on his team scored. When the player came off the ice Shero asked who got the goal. "I don't know," replied the player. "But I was in on it."

The Forgotten Men—The Defense

"All you newspaper guys want to talk about after a game are the scorers," said Arnie Brown, a defenseman. "You never come over to us to ask questions. But as soon as a goal is scored—boom, we get the blame."

There probably is more truth than alliteration in what Brown says. Fans are quick to say, "The defense let the goalie down." Often, it is just as true to say, "The forwards let the goalie down," since the forward should have a man covered.

If defensemen aren't necessarily goal-scorers, and their names don't often appear in the statistics, how do they get their kicks? It isn't easy. No instant recognition follows the solid, game-in, game-out defenseman who plays his position, doesn't get trapped too often, and does a solid job. But behind every shoulder shrug that says "I don't care" when a defenseman is asked about recognition, there lurks a secret goal-scorer. How else do defensemen get applause from fans?

Brown once berated a reporter who didn't choose him as one of the game's three stars. Did Brown feel his defensive work had been overlooked? Not at all. Said Brown: "How the hell could you not pick me? I had a goal and an assist!"

Every discussion of defensemen must start with Bobby Orr. Sure, there were great defenders before him. There are great ones now. But none of them ever scored 30 goals or had 100 points. Orr made the public aware of the extraordinary capabilities a defenseman can have. He brought a new dimension to the game—a rushing defenseman who could outscore 99 percent of the forwards in hockey. Since Orr joined the league in 1966 defensemen have been split into two categories: a "defensive defenseman" and an "offensive defenseman."

The split was necessary because no defenseman could possibly be compared to Orr for overall ability. So some coaches and general managers would talk about their own defenders being "better defensively." And old-timers, who winced when Orr started a rink-length rush, would recall the old days when rearguards played classically, not rushing, not taking chances.

Soon, Orr was being labeled as "great, but . . ." The "but," of course, was his supposed lack of defensive play. Is it a valid argument? Probably not. A defenseman is doing his job if he stops the opposition, and protects his goalie. That is virtually a definition of what a defenseman should be. However, when a fellow like Orr has a direct hand in 139 goals—which he had during the 1970–71 season, with 37 goals and 102 assists—that means he's been keeping the puck away from his own goalie. And isn't that what a defenseman is supposed to be doing—keeping the opposition away? If he does it by scoring, isn't that even better?

Orr's effect cannot be overestimated. He has influenced tens of thousands of young players who now believe defense doesn't breed anonymity—it breeds scoring. On the other hand, Orr has also shown the advantages a team can have by possessing defensively-oriented defensemen. Unless a rearguard is a Bobby Orr, or at least has a few of his talents, he will not be so effective as the defenseman who lays back, aware of his own shortcomings, and is content to play a standard game.

Brown is a good example. After a slow start, his career with New York took shape. He developed into a solid defenseman. Then a bad thing happened to him—he started to score goals. One season he had more goals than any other defenseman except for Orr. So Brown became goal-directed. He would lead rushes up ice, neglecting his post. When he went for a substantial number of games without a goal, it bothered him. He began allowing players to get around him for breakaways. Soon, Brown was traded. But his long-time defensive partner and good friend, Rod Seiling, remained. Strangely enough, when they first started out, Seiling was not as popular with New York's fans. He didn't hit. Fans in most hockey cities like to think that their defensemen should be bruisers who crunch opponents into the boards. A Seiling, a J. C. Tremblay of Montreal, a Bill White of Chicago—they are among the best. But they are not Bobby Orr or even, for example, a Louie Fontinato. Fontinato was the sort who banged everyone in an enemy uniform. As opposed to a Seiling or a White, who could protect their goalies by poking the puck away from opponents, or knew how to maneuver them into the boards, the Fontinato types charged and roughed-up and hit.

The brawny belters have their place, too. Some teams keep them around for peace-keeping purposes. Some teams have had a history of being small and nonviolent, and acquire a rugged defenseman to change their image. Watch a young defenseman in his first major-league games. The chances are that he'll hit indiscriminately. They think that's the way they can impress the fans—and their coach. It probably is. When a giant of a defenseman named Rick Foley came up to the Black Hawks in 1971, he smashed a few people. "I want them to know I'm around," he explained.

That same season, the Hawks' Keith Magnuson set a record of 291 penalty minutes. Yet, he was reprimanded by Coach Billy Reay when the playoffs began. "Don't take so many stupid penalties," he was told. Magnuson, an intuitive player, was unnerved. Hitting had been his style, and so was fighting. You don't amass 291 minutes just for charging. Many 10-minute fighting penalties are included in that total. But when Magnuson was told to think first, his style was affected. He became uncertain during the playoffs and his hesitation showed as opposing players went down his lane and were able to consistently elude his once-damaging body checks. Magnuson wasn't dumb. Thinking didn't hurt him. But not playing his game hurt him.

Just as there is a certain chemistry in putting a forward line together, there is a proper mix in defensive alignments, too. A Magnuson could never be teamed with a Fontinato. Or an Orr with another rushing defenseman. Ideally, one defenseman is the type who can bust out, carry the play when he has to. The other is more traditional. His instincts are to back up, to cover the open side when he has to.

The best defensive combinations over the last few years have illustrated this. Orr has been teamed with Dallas Smith. On Chicago, Pat Stapleton (the rusher) goes with Bill White (the traditionalist). At New York, which has been unusually blessed, Brad Park has gone with the conservative Dale Rolfe and the classic Seiling has been teamed with Jim Neilson.

Even the scoring figures for these defensemen indicate the type of game they play. Orr had the marvelous 1970–71 year of 37 goals and 102 assists for 139 points. His partner, Smith, collected only 7 goals and 38 assists for 45 points.

Stapleton had 7 goals and 44 assists for 51 points. White, who usually was on the ice when Stapleton was, had 4 goals and only 21 assists for 25 points.

Park had 7 goals and amassed 37 assists for 44 points. Rolfe, who played most of the season with Detroit before being traded, had a total of 3 goals and 16 assists for 19 points.

Neilson got 32 points on 8 goals and 24 assists while Seiling accounted for 27 points on 5 goals and 22 assists.

Obviously, one partner is shooting more and picking up assists when the forwards bat in rebounds. And just as obvious, one partner is going in deeper on rushes. Yet, it all blends together. As an indication of how well the defensemen fit, all of them received votes in the all-star balloting.

There are, of course, a right defenseman and a left defenseman. But unlike most right wings, the vast majority of right defensemen shoot left-handed. A right-handed shooting defenseman is a prize. Some clubs don't have any. However, the disadvantage of receiving the puck on the "wrong" side of the stick isn't as great for a defenseman as it is for a forward. Most of a defenseman's attempts will come from the point, where he'll have a bit more time to set up for a shot than a forward will in close to the action.

Orr shoots left, plays right. Who cares? When Orr is out there his defensive partner must be especially sensitive to Orr's break-away possibilities. So should the Boston right wing. Often, the Bruins' right wing when Orr is on the ice is playing more defense than Orr is. When Orr drives down the middle with the puck, someone has to take his place on the blue line. It should be the right wing. When a forward fails to cover for Orr, that leaves Orr's defensive partner all by himself. The same is true of any other defensive combination. That is why it is axiomatic—a rushing defenseman must be paired with a stay-back defenseman. A team can get by with having a traditional defensive combination on the ice together—but it takes its chances when it puts out two rushing defensemen.

Rarely will a team suit up fewer than five defensemen for a game. Occasionally, a club might dress six. But five is the average. Two regular defense teams are employed—and they see most of the action. The fifth man is used to spell a tired player, or if one of the defenders is penalized. Because defensemen generally aren't handling the puck on long rushes, they can play longer shifts than the forwards. While a forward line might skate only for 90 seconds, defensemen can easily play for two minutes at a stretch, or longer if the situation warrants.

Perhaps the first consideration in grooming a defenseman for the big leagues is size. Although no one in the N.H.L. is truly massive or gigantic in height, the defensemen are usually among the bigger players. One thing is certain: they aren't the smallest players on the team. In 1971–72, the average National Hockey League player stood 5-11¼ and weighed 183.7 pounds. Not many defensemen were under those figures. There were about 290 players on N.H.L. rosters the beginning of the season. Only a third of them were defensemen. Yet, of the 30 players who stood 6-2 or over, 18 were defensemen. To quote Milt Schmidt of the Bruins, who was asked what he looks for when he signs defensemen: "If they can fit through the door, I don't want 'em."

Size is so crucial for a defenseman because there's no one be-hind him—except for the goalie. A defender must be able to stand his ground and halt an onrushing player who has momen-tum. He must be physically able to stand the bruises that come when you take a player into the boards. And his height is an ex-tremely important factor when he's standing on the other team's blue line, playing the point. How many times have you seen a tall defenseman raise his big mitt and keep a flying puck in play when the other team tries to clear it? It happens often. Size makes up for skating ability with some defensemen. In fact, if a defenseman can't skate, he'd better be big. Or else he should consider a career in the minors. A fellow like Wayne Hillman, who played for four different clubs his first 10 years, was 6-1 and 205. He never got more than five goals in a season, or 17 assists in any one cam-paign. He was slow. But he was honest. He used his weight and when an opposing player was coming down Hillman's alley he was certain to be hit.

If it weren't for size, Hillman would have remained in Buffalo, where he spent his first four seasons as a professional. His brother Larry performed for 12 different clubs. He skated a little better than Wayne, but his value was mostly as a bruiser, too. Andre (Moose) Dupont, an aptly nicknamed defenseman who stands 6-1 and weighs 200, assessed his role when he was given a major-league tryout. "They bring me up to hit," he said. "So that is what I must do to look good." He proved it by drawing a penalty in his first turn on the ice.

The most controversial defenseman of recent years was the Bruins' Ted Green. Nicknamed Terrible Teddy, Green built his reputation as a vicious fighter. During a brawl he thought nothing of using his stick. But he was also a formidable puncher, perhaps the quickest to use his fists in hockey. Give Green a check—legal or not—and he would bounce off the boards flailing away. Green was a symbol of the Bruins, a club dubbed "The Animals." When-ever they skated onto the Madison Square Garden ice, the New York organist, Eddie Layton, would play a bouncy version of "Talk to the Animals." It angered Green and his teammates, but brought chuckles from the Garden fans. As the years went by, Green became one of the best defensemen in the game. He had an accurate shot from the right point, and he played his position well. He even cut down on his belligerency. But for Green, it was always the fights his fans remembered. Like the time he speared Goyette in the spleen, sending the mild-mannered Ranger to the hospital. Green's violation elicited an angry response from the New Yorkers' president, Bill Jennings, who implied that a bounty would be placed on Green's head. Any Ranger who gave it to Green would pick up a bonus.

Green's stick finally led to one of the most bitter fights the league had seen. During an exhibition game with St. Louis in 1969 Green and Wayne Maki waggled their sticks at each other. Green brought his up and then turned away, figuring it was over. But Maki came down with the stick hard and smashed Green in the head. Green suffered a fractured skull. Although there was a cry, temporarily, for helmets and stiffer fines for stick-fighters, there was not that much sympathy for Green. Yet, the former meanie captured the respect of players and fans when he made a comeback the following year, after sitting out a season. He admits, though, that he didn't feel comfortable until another player picked a fight with him. That told Green that the opposition wasn't going to feel sorry for him anymore, that if he bothered them they would bother him. That's the way he wanted it.

In contrast to a Green, there was Red Kelly. When Kelly played for Detroit he was a defenseman (when he was traded to Toronto he was converted to center). Kelly was such an extraordinarily clean player that he won the Lady Byng Trophy as a defenseman three times. He is the only defenseman, except for Earl Reibel, to win the Lady Byng since 1950. It is simply impossible to have low penalty minutes and be a defenseman for the average player.

In one respect defensemen are like goalies. They get the blame. "The thing about being a defenseman," said Larry Popein, "is that the fans always notice your mistakes. You're back there, naked. If a guy goes around you, everyone sees it. But if he goes around a forward, no one notices because there are so many players at close quarters."

It's true. Because the defenseman is usually the last player in front of his goalie, he looks bad when a goal is scored. He generally is the player closest to the action, to stopping the goal-scorer. If the defenseman keeps his head, and does his job right, then he can compensate for lapses made by his own teammates. Take a simple play. A club is bringing the puck out of its end, on an offensive rush. Some clubs like a defenseman to handle the puck behind the net and pass it out to a waiting center, who starts the rush. If the right defenseman has the puck behind his net, the left defenseman doesn't rush out to be in on the play. He guards the goal—to prevent a score in case his fellow defenseman's pass-out is intercepted. Once the play has moved beyond his blue line, then he can safely leave his goalie alone.

As a rule, a team must always have at least one defenseman near its goalie when the puck is in the team's end. Say the play is hovering around the goalie. The right defenseman goes into the left corner if the puck is shot there, while the left defenseman stands his ground near the goaltender. If the puck swings to the other corner, the defenders switch positions.

Some goalies don't like their defensemen in the way if the other team is shooting long-range. They are afraid that if a hard-hit slap shot hits the defenseman it might ricochet off at a crazy angle—and head toward the goal. There are times, though, when a defenseman can't dare leave the goal area. If the other club has a man in the slot, the defenseman must try to hamper him from getting off a shot. During tangles that follow, screened shots go in and the goalie can't do a thing about them. Is the defenseman at fault? No. He's doing his best trying to clear the area.

There are some defensemen who have a talent—or is it insanity?—for blocking shots. These are the rearguards who offer themselves as human sacrifices by going to their knees in front of players who are taking slap shots and stop the shots with their chests (they hope). Stapleton is one of the best at this tricky business. He claims he can tell if the puck is going to be kept low by the way his opponent shoots. Also, if he's close enough to the player the puck hasn't had a chance to be airborne.

But the defensemen's finest moment occurs when their team is short-handed. At times like these they must avoid getting entangled with another player, unless the defenseman is trying to freeze the puck behind the net or in the corner for a face-off. During these trying moments the skills that go into a finished hockey player are most needed by the defenseman, who doesn't usually get the chance to display all the tricks he's learned. A backhander —and control of it—is essential. And not for shooting. It is needed for clearing the puck, for making split-second decisions. A defenseman must be able to turn either way from trouble, and to pass the puck away from trouble. Orr and Seiling are two of the best at this. Watch Orr spin away from trouble by doing an about face without losing a stride.

In these critical seconds, a knowledge of the boards can be helpful. A defenseman just doesn't throw the puck out, attempting to get it down ice. He has to see where the opposition is set, and where his men are. Many goals are scored because a frightened defenseman had the puck behind his net and wanted to get rid of it at all costs. There's nothing wrong with freezing the puck behind your net and forcing a face-off. Teams usually don't score off a face-off.

The boards can speed a puck to the other team's zone if the puck is hit right and the defenseman is familiar with the boards' peculiarities. The board is also used to ricochet a pass to a teammate. But if the right spot isn't hit, the teammate doesn't get it. Since the opposition has an extra man, the chances are good the enemy will come up with the disk. While he's doing his various bits of business, the defenseman must be watching the play. It is essential that a defenseman know exactly where he's passing the puck. He doesn't drop it behind him if he's not sure there's a teammate ready to scoop it up. If he's got the puck in front of the net he should have a wide view of the action. If he's facing the net and can't see behind him, he doesn't simply shoot the puck to his rear. He tries to knock it to the corner. Because of the angle, you can't score from the corner.

A defenseman must "feel" the puck, especially when he's behind his net. He can't look down at it. You get the feel after years of experience. When Ted Green came back after his injury, which had caused some paralysis, he found that he had lost his feel for the puck. You can't be looking down at the disk when you're so close to your goalie. You must be looking out for the opposition. There's nothing a forward likes to see more than a defenseman who's keeping his head down. Zap! The defenseman gets creamed, the puck squirts loose, the other team gains control.

Next to Orr, perhaps the most intriguing defenseman to watch is Tremblay of the Canadiens. He plays defense with a sense of humor. His stick is a baton and he whirls it as though listening to his own beat. Tremblay may be the best stick-handler in all hockey. He has the uncanny ability to embarrass the opposition —and anger it—with little tricks, such as passing the puck between an opponent's legs—and then taking the pass himself. His stick-handling ability is especially valuable in penalty killing since he can eat up so much time all by himself. If the enemy dares force him and attempt to take the puck away, J. C. can switch positions and take off, leaving the other man flatfooted. Or Tremblay can spot an open man and the Canadiens are off on one of their classic short-handed breakaways.

No matter how expert a defenseman is, though, he must play part of the basic box defense when a club is short-handed. That means the right defenseman stands in front of the goalie and to his right, while the left defenseman stands in front of the goalie, to the left.

Coupled with his adherence to basic rules, a defenseman can take advantage of his shooting abilities. But he must be smart enough to know when not to take a chance.

When Vic Stasiuk took over as coach of the California Golden Seals in 1971, he found himself with a young club that yielded more goals than any other team in hockey.

"The trouble is, everyone thinks he's Orr," said Stasiuk.

"The kids read that the big guns—an Orr, a Park—are making the money and now even defensemen want to be goal-scorers." Stasiuk also touched on another problem—expansion. "It used to be that when a young defenseman came up he had been schooled in a team's system. He knew just what style of play a club had and he could adapt. But now we don't have the kids in the juniors anymore. We have to train them under pressure, and there isn't always time."

Even long-time hockey writers tend to gravitate toward the goal-getters after games. After one contest, Gerry Cheevers sat shaking his head. "Hey," he said to a newsman. "See that guy over there? His name's Dallas Smith. He skates with Bobby Orr."

3 | The Thinkers

The Coach

At ice level the game is another world. Just for fun, take a walk behind the players' bench sometime during a game. What you'll feel is a different experience from what you receive in the stands. You'll feel surrounded by crowd, by noise, by smoke. There will not be the perspective that a higher seat affords. Players whiz by in a blur. The overhead lights, refracted through the haze, give the scene a surreal quality. Players leap over the boards in a seemingly erratic pattern, going and coming. On the bench the players crane their necks for a look at the action, or stand and shout. The trainer screams. In this bizarre milieu, the coach must be able to make split-second decisions. He must know how many men he's got on the ice. He must sense which way the momentum is going. He must know who is doing what to whom, what the score is, how much time is left, how much his players have left.

But the game situation, while the most significant aspect, is only a part of a coach's job. If he hasn't drilled his troops correctly, if he doesn't have their respect, if he hasn't prepared them under all conditions, then his coaching could be ineffectual. All his strategy could be wasted if he hasn't laid the proper groundwork.

Time is one of the coach's biggest problems. There just isn't enough of it. The training-camp season begins the first week in September. The regular season begins a month later—and ends early in April. Then playoffs can go until the middle of May. The difficulties of paperwork, travel, scouting, and coaching are extraordinary. For this reason, during the 1971–72 season, only three of the fourteen teams had men who served both as coach and general manager. In 1969, with only 12 clubs, there were six general manager-coaches.

Because hockey has grown so quickly—and on such a broad scale—there are few people around who can cope with the dual roles. When a club played in 1967, there were only five other teams to worry about. A team faced each opposition club 14 times. It was easy enough then to know the personnel on the enemy. After three or four games, a coach had a pretty good idea which of his lines could handle the lines on the opposition. Suddenly, in 1970, there were 13 other teams. A team faced each of them only six times, often months apart. Who were these players on the new clubs? Many of them didn't even know their own teammates, let alone the opposition.

Coaching problems were magnified. The coach of the expansion club had to mold a team out of players who were unfamiliar with one another's styles, who had been schooled in different farm systems. Meanwhile, the coach of an established club found his own depth watered down because of the player drafts that had stocked the new teams. And he had to know the opposition's strengths and weaknesses the first time they met. There weren't many chances to adjust and get the enemy team the next time they faced. There weren't that many "next times" anymore.

Meanwhile, another factor led to added difficulties in coaching. Before 1967 players could make the big leagues at any age. They could be 17 or 18 years old. They belonged to amateur farm teams of the big-league clubs. But it was obvious that the new expansion teams could never compete successfully unless they had a chance to grab promising junior players. So control of all the amateur players in Canada was taken out of the hands of the N.H.L.

and placed under the Canadian Amateur Hockey Association. No boy could be drafted by an N.H.L. team until he was 20 years old.

This rule allowed thousands of youngsters to complete their high school education and enabled many more to go on to college. As each year passed, the academic ability of boys making it to the pros increased. That meant a new breed of player was coming, shaped by forces in college and shaped by an increased awareness of the world around him. Indeed, he was growing up in the turbulent youth movement of the late 1960's and early 1970's, when old values were reexamined and when the so-called generation gap was at its height. These new players had long hair and wore modish clothes. They believed they should be treated as individuals, a cry being heard in sports in the United States, especially on the campuses of big-time athletic colleges. The new type of player was coming up—but in many instances he found himself face to face with the old-breed coach. Something had to give, or at least someone had to adapt.

Still, there were coaches who looked for the old values. They believed that desire was bred by poverty, or at least middle-class values. They said that the new breed was more interested in making it for reasons other than salary, and that this cut down a boy's effectiveness.

A few years ago Jake Milford, a long-time minor-league coach and general manager, was discussing one of his long-haired players. "His family coddled him too much," said Milford. "Why, they even bought him a car." When the player read what Milford had said, he told Milford—a kindly man—to mind his own business. "When I'm on the ice, I'm yours," the player told him. "But my private life is my own."

"It used to be that a player gave out 110 percent," said Fred Shero, who made it to the N.H.L. as a coach in 1971 with Philadelphia. "But there's less desire around today. If a guy can't make it with Montreal, what's he got to worry about? He knows there are so many expansion teams around, he can make it with one of them."

Wren Blair, the general manager of the Minnesota North Stars, served as coach in the club's first few expansion years. He didn't want the two jobs.

"The problem today is finding a coach who can relate to the new breed of younger player," said Blair. "I'm having a hell of a time finding a coach who's young enough to talk to them. The old ways are finished. You can't just tell a kid to play for you because you're the boss. You've got to find ways to motivate the new player. The old threats, the old ways, don't work anymore. This is going to be the biggest problem hockey is going to face over the next years."

Yet, when Shero took over the Flyers he immediately issued an edict that forbade long hair, sideburns, or mustaches.

"It will take them time to conform," Shero acknowledged. "But they will conform. If they don't—well, Jean Beliveau retired and Gordie Howe retired and we still have hockey."

Shero explained the reason for his rule: "It's a form of discipline—and we must have discipline. And we must conform in order to win." Perhaps his most engaging explanation on the subject was the following: "We have to rush to catch planes, and a fellow doesn't have time to dry his long hair after a game. That's a good way to catch cold and miss a game."

But on the subject of mustaches, Shero gave his true feelings on the values he believed a team must have. "No group can be an individual," he said. "It's unity or else."

Meanwhile, the millionaire owner of the Flyers, Ed Snider, walked around with hair worn approximately the same length as Ben Franklin's.

No matter how he achieves it, a coach must have unity. Perhaps Shero achieved it by other measures. There is more to being a good coach than having your players agree with you. They must respect you, and want to play for you. There are rare instances where a club can win without complete respect for the coach. The Montreal Canadiens of the 1968–69 season are the example. They finished first under unpopular Claude Ruel and won the Cup. But the Canadiens, as always, are an exception. They are joined together, first of all, by the French-Canadian bond that encompasses nearly all the players on the team. Their tradition is such a proud one that it often seems irrelevant who is coaching them. The Canadiens had enough of a self-image, with such stars as Jean Beliveau and Henri Richard to lean on, that they overcame their dissatisfaction with Ruel.

"I'm the guy everyone's looking at," says coach-general manager Emile Francis of the Rangers. "I've got to show them I know what I'm doing on the bench during the games and on the ice during the practice sessions. Players have to be led, and they have to be instructed."

The process begins in training camp, with 50 or more players trying to get a spot on a club that might carry 20 during the season. Immediately, the coach attempts to instill the demands of hockey into his players. He might start it with a little pep talk when the players get on the ice. But mostly he does it by example. Players quickly learn what they may not do. Some coaches are lenient about extra pounds. Most aren't. If a player reports to camp considerably overweight he probably will be fined, or at the least be run ragged. The coach has a pretty good idea of his personnel, and what he needs. Unless some potential superstar is in camp, the coach doesn't tamper with his established lines. He leaves the chemistry alone.

But what of the expansionist coach? He must have a feel for putting players together. The chances are that virtually none of his players has skated on the same line with a teammate, or on the same defensive tandem. The coach also has to evaluate what type of team he will send out, based on the personnel. Will it be an attacking squad or a defensively-oriented club? Often, he won't know until he's seen his players together how they react as a unit. There is also a mix in overall personnel. You don't throw out a bunch of rookies on the ice. You need an experienced player to go along with a young skater.

The blend of youth and age was in large measure responsible for the remarkable success Scotty Bowman achieved with the St. Louis Blues. He was the 1967 expansion team's coach and general manager. He coaxed some old stars out of retirement. He had some marginal players who were let go by the established teams. The club was focused on goaltending, especially when he had Plante and Hall. The old and the precocious worked within a framework of strict positional play. The formula succeeded. In the first four years of expansion, the Blues were the only new club to post a winning record. No other expansion club even had one .500 season.

But the average coach goes into camp with a pretty good idea of who will emerge as the regulars. The difficulty comes in deciding who should stay after the stickouts have been selected. In the 1971–72 season, for example, each club could dress 17 skaters and two goalies for each game. That meant 19 starters. The hard part came in figuring which 17 players to choose. A coach needs three lines, and five defensemen. That makes 14 skaters. In choosing the lines, some picks are automatic—for example, a proven trio. There usually is a prechosen second line, too. But only a few clubs are blessed with three established lines. The players on the third line have to be adroit at other aspects of the game besides scoring—penalty killing, for example, or good defensive work. Once a coach comes down to a choice of marginal players for his third line, he wants versatility. This aspect is even more necessary for the three "odd" players the coach selects to round out his 17 skaters.

When a man isn't good enough—or experienced enough—to make one of the three starting lines, he must be valuable in other areas. The coach must decide what specific players he needs for the type of club he's molding. He might want to keep a bullish player around who's not reliable enough as a starter, but who can come in off the bench and perhaps throw his weight around. Reg Fleming has been such a performer throughout his career. Or perhaps the coach is looking for extra men who can play most effectively when the team is short-handed and rarely will get a chance to start. But with such a small roster, a coach can't keep a man around merely for penalty killing. He has to know that the player can also take a turn in case of an injury to a regular.

Some players can come in off the bench cold and be useful.

These are the types a coach must look for, and he must be able to spot the potential. "You can tell if a man's warmed up on the bench," says one coach. "You can tell by the way he's hollering —how much he's in the game. And during the intermission some of them like to exercise to keep ready. When you see players like that, you know they'll be able to jump right in."

Say a coach has two pretty good penalty killers as extra men, and wants to keep only one. He must weigh the other factors: what positions can the penalty killers play? If, for example, the coach has three regular right wings he might be shopping for a fourth as a spare. If he has three regular left wings, and one of his centers can play the left side, too, then he might be looking for a penalty killer who can play the right wing since he has emergency depth on the left.

Many other considerations go into choosing the final team. Can the coach afford to put out a younger player and give him time to develop? Or is the coach under pressure to produce immediately? Also, there is the important consideration of which players the club will protect in the draft. Each year there is an intra-league draft in which each club can freeze 18 players and two goalies. Everyone else in the organization—except for players in their first year of professionalism—is eligible to be drafted. Similarly, the expansion draft of 1972 allowed each club to protect only 15 players and two goalies. First-year pros, however, didn't have to be protected. The coach must be thinking ahead to these draft situations. Often, he makes deals in which he trades two or three good players, who would have to be protected, for a rookie—or a future draft choice—who doesn't have to be protected.

By the time the exhibition season begins the coach has put together the team that will carry the squad through the regular 78-game season. Perhaps there still will be one or two openings at the start of the preseason games. But for the most part the line-up is set. Some coaches like to carry youngsters through the exhibition games, even though they won't make the club. The coaches believe it's important for rookies to get the feel of big-league play, and also to be rewarded for turning in a good camp.

Not all coaches regard exhibition games the same way. Coach Tom Johnson of the Bruins didn't push his men during the 1971 preseason schedule. The Bostonians, who had posted the finest record in league history the previous season, went through the exhibition schedule with a 3-6-1 mark.

When surprise greeted these poor figures, a club official asked, "How many points did we lose during the exhibition season? None. The games don't count."

Yet, when the regular season began and the Bruins weren't sharp, Johnson realized he had made a mistake. "I should have pushed these guys harder," said Johnson, a relaxed, pipe-smoking individual who had been an outstanding defenseman with Montreal. "I thought that these guys were professional enough to realize that they should be trying on their own." Johnson quickly changed his tactics. He put the Bruins through two long workouts. In their next game they crushed the Rangers, 6-1, at Madison Square Garden—where the New Yorkers had lost only two games the previous season.

In contrast to the Bruins' preseason country club, the Rangers worked hard. Indeed, their camps have been marked by diligence and so have their exhibition games. "It's important to let the teams know, even in preseason games, that you mean to beat them," explains Francis. "It sets the tempo for the regular season. You must show them you mean business." The Rangers beat the Bruins in three straight exhibitions—then walloped them at Boston in the Bruins' regular-season opener.

When Doug Barkley coached the Red Wings during the 1971 exhibition season, he was faced with molding a complete new club. Only four players remained who had started the previous season with Detroit. Barkley also was faced with a rookie fresh out of junior ranks named Marcel Dionne.

Dionne was a 20-year-old center who had amassed 62 goals and 143 points as a junior. He was the Red Wings' first draft pick, and it was obvious people were expecting big things of the youngster. "I'm trying to make him feel comfortable with us," said Barkley. "It's important to give a youngster confidence." To help him along, Barkley put Dionne on a line with the only other French-speaking players on the club. "That's just temporary," the coach explained. "But for now I want him accustomed to playing with the people from his background."

When Bowman took over at Montreal for the start of the 1971–72 season, he found himself with the No. 1 draft choice in all hockey—Guy Lafleur. Bowman knew there was more pressure on Lafleur than any other rookie. The 20-year-old Lafleur was supposed to be the new Jean Beliveau, and the French-Canadian fans at the Forum would be pressuring Lafleur to deliver.

In the exhibition games, Bowman put Lafleur at center between two of hockey's top goal-scorers, Frank Mahovlich and Cournoyer. Lafleur became the second-leading point-scorer on the team for the preseason schedule. It was more difficult for Lafleur during the early part of the regular season. "I have to be careful he doesn't get down on himself," said Bowman. "I try picking him up whenever I can. I know it'll be difficult for him. A center in this league has to know when to fore-check." During quiet moments off the ice Bowman—who spoke English to the team during club meetings—would take Lafleur aside and have chats with the rookie in French.

Once the season is underway, the coach's work is compounded. He not only has the personnel difficulties that are sure to crop up, but also he must win games. And he must attempt to win them under increasingly difficult situations. The players' lives in today's hockey revolve around plane schedules and hotels. Before expansion, the farthest trip a team made was the overnight train ride from Montreal to Chicago. Now the teams cross a continent for one game. The West Coast clubs often find themselves on six-game or seven-game road trips. If they didn't take it all in at once, they'd be forced to do even more traveling. Some coaches tell their players to set their body clocks on eastern time when they swing west. They know the three-hour time difference takes at least a day to get accustomed to. But teams usually are on the Coast fewer than 24 hours before a game. The coach thus has mental and physical fatigue to deal with.

To offset this real difficulty in game situations, coaches have tried different techniques. Some dress only four defensemen for a West Coast game, leaving the club with 13 forwards. That means a club can put out four forward lines, giving the top lines more frequent breathers. But this strategy backfired in a game several years ago. Two of the defensemen were penalized at the same time. The club had to play with only two defensemen during the short-handed period. And if one of the rearguards had been injured, the team would have been in deep trouble.

How a coach keeps his players alert for the long season depends on his philosophy. Some coaches, like Francis, believe work is the antidote. Each of his scrimmages is a lesson. He stages one every day the team isn't playing, except on Mondays.

"You can't just throw guys on the ice and say 'okay, skate,' " says Francis. "I try to teach them something, to give them a motivation to skate." Each of his sessions is devoted to some special aspect of the game, either on some weak spot he noticed during the previous game, or something to counter the next opponent.

Two of the other most successful clubs of recent years—the Black Hawks and Bruins—have had different philosophies. Coach Billy Reay of the Hawks says, "Why bother working them so hard? The season's long enough already. I don't want them to get stale."

Consider the problems a team such as the Vancouver Canucks has. It was difficult enough for them in their first season of 1970–71. Yet, they had to travel more than 65,000 miles—compared to 25,000 for the eastern teams. The Canucks would have stretches of seven games in 11 days. Their closest competitors, the California Golden Seals, were more than a thousand miles away in Oakland. Coach Hal Laycoe had enough problems getting together a first-year team of expansion players. Somehow, he had to whip them up into a unit that could live out of suitcases and exist in hotels.

After one bad beating his club suffered, when it was outshot by 52-16, he complimented his players on their game. "Isn't it a hell of a note on expansion," Laycoe asked, "when you have to compliment your players after a beating like that?"

The imbalance among teams, the pressure of traveling, the

longer schedule—all have created more tension in the coaching ranks. "Who gets fired? The players?" Laycoe asked bitterly as his club struggled along in 1971. "The league doesn't give the expansion teams any players and the coaches are expected to produce. But you know who's going to get the ax, don't you? It'll be the coach. How many goals does a coach let in? But he's the one to go."

Laycoe was speaking a few days after the fourth coach had been dismissed in the first three weeks of play in the 1971–72 season. Sid Abel, who had been one of the best coaches with Detroit, was kicked upstairs after just a few weeks with St. Louis. Doug Barkley, who had gone to Detroit, quit when he claimed he couldn't get anything out of his players. Vic Stasiuk, dismissed the season before from Philadelphia, was the Seals' new coach after Fred Glover was let go a few days after the campaign began. And Glover went over to Los Angeles to take over the coaching from Larry Regan, who remained as general manager.

Other coaching changes involved Bowman as the new coach of the Canadiens and Shero as the new coach of the Flyers. Bowman had left St. Louis, claiming that management was interfering with his work and attempting to second-guess him.

"A few years ago there wasn't even an N.H.L. team in St. Louis," said Bowman. "The owners didn't know a thing about hockey. Now the team gets successful—and suddenly the owners are smarter than you are. I had to get out of the situation. If I'm not in control, I don't want to be part of the club."

Bill Gadsby quit as coach of the Red Wings because he, too, insisted on autonomy. Reportedly, the Wings had a direct phone installed at their bench that was connected to the box of the Wings' president, Bruce Norris. When Gadsby saw the phone he ordered it removed. Gadsby lasted three games.

Punch Imlach has always insisted that no deals can be made without his approval. According to Imlach, his contract at Toronto stipulated that he had the final say on any player movement. But much publicity was given to a story in the early 1960's when James Norris, the president of the Hawks, offered $1,000,000 to the Leafs for Frank Mahovlich. The offer came after a long night of drinking, and the Leafs accepted. In the clear light of day, the Leafs then turned down the deal. But Imlach insists he never would have stood for it in the first place.

Ultimately, games are won or lost on the ice. The coach must make a decision before the game even begins: Which line to start. If he is playing at home, then the other team must give its starting line-up in first. The next move, then, is which line to use against the other team's starters. Usually, this will be the line that will be facing the other team's starters throughout the game.

Here the coach makes his judgment based on experience. If it's the other club's top-scoring line, he generally will put out his checking line. But the visiting coach can pull a fast one. Say the visitor knows that his top line isn't doing well against the opposition's checkers. So he might try a ploy by sending out his second-best line. The home coach counters by sending out the best line. Once play starts, though, the visiting team dumps the puck in the opposition's end—and changes lines. Now the visiting coach has the match-up he wants. The other team, meanwhile, can't make a line change because it is busy defending its goal. It is important to realize that this is all taking place while play is frenetically going on. Hockey is probably the only sport in which player changes are made while play is in progress. While the coach is making his moves, he's also got to count how many players he's got on the ice. If there's one man too much, the team gets a bench penalty and skates for two minutes with a man short. It was no coincidence that the two leading clubs in bench penalties during the 1970–71 season both had inexperienced professional coaches. St. Louis, coached by Al Arbour, a former player in his first year behind the bench, had 24 minutes in bench penalties. The Red Wings were coached half the season by Ned Harkness, who had been at Cornell previously, then by Doug Barkley, who was suddenly brought up. The Wings had 20 minutes in bench penalties. These two clubs accounted for nearly one-third of the league's total of 144 minutes in bench penalties.

To keep track—or attempt to—of who is on the ice, the coach

sets up a system for having his players on the bench. Players for a line always sit together. The defensemen always sit together, too, on one end of the bench. And even which end of the bench they're on can be critical.

It doesn't seem so important, but where a defenseman sits can stop a goal. Thus, the smart coach places his defensemen closest to the goal they're defending. That means that for two periods the defenders sit on one end of the bench, and for the other period they're on the opposite end. There's sound logic in this alignment. Say one of the defensemen on the ice is tired. He wants to come off. It is important for his replacement to be as close to his own goal as possible, since he must protect his goalie. So by sitting him nearest his own goal, the coach saves the defenseman 20 feet of skating, and also enables him to get in position quicker. Conversely, the forwards are always closer to their attacking zone. When a team has a rush moving, you want to get in fresh players as soon as you can. Thus, the tired forward who wants to leave the ice can dump the puck into the other team's end. Before the opposition can bring the puck out, the new forwards can get into the play and attempt to keep the puck hopping around the enemy goalie.

Remember—the coach is making his moves while play is continuing. Of course, he's got a moment to think about it during a whistle stoppage. These are times for maneuvering, too. The home team always has the last move on face-offs. Say a visiting coach doesn't want the center on the ice to face-off against the team's opposing center. He puts in a better face-off man. The home team has the option of changing centers, too. If the home-team coach makes the initial change, the visiting-team coach is also allowed to make a change. But then the home team can make still another change.

Some of the more advanced coaches have hosts of statistics on face-offs. They know which players win face-offs in their own end, or in the final seconds of a game, or against right-handers or left-handers. Unfortunately, most clubs aren't computer-oriented. Certainly, there are dozens of statistics that aren't even available in hockey. No one has thought to use them.

Once the coach throws his players out, their two minutes on the ice is theirs. That doesn't mean they do as they please. A coach might want his team to start out defensively-oriented if his club is facing a breakaway-type club such as Montreal. He knows that the first goal, especially in the opening minutes, goes a long way in deciding which team wins. So a club that normally attacks quite well might elect to send in only the center for the puck. If he doesn't get it, then the wings are in position to come back and play defensively.

This style is seen most often when the expansion clubs play the powers. Against each other the expansion teams play a normal brand of hockey. But their style is radically changed against an established team. It becomes strictly defensive.

One of the most dramatic instances of defensive play in recent seasons came during the 1971 playoff series between the Hawks and Rangers. Dave Balon, who led the Rangers with 36 goals during the regular season, was benched for the strict defensive play of Glen Sather, who had seen action only as a penalty killer. Sather's job was simple: to act as if he was killing a penalty even when the Rangers were at equal strength. The maneuver nearly worked. The Rangers held the Hawks to two goals. But they got only one themselves.

Sometimes the coach appears to be a juggler in his attempts to get the right matches on the ice. The importance of match-ups was tellingly demonstrated during the 1969 series between Montreal and Boston. In the first two games at Boston, Phil Esposito, who had set a record for assists and points during the regular season, failed to get even one point during the first two games. They were played at Montreal, where Coach Claude Ruel could send out his checking line against Esposito. But in the first game back at Boston, where coach Harry Sinden had the last word on line changes, Esposito scored two goals and picked up three assists—for a five-point game.

Assume a game has gone along uneventfully. There have been no surprises. The coach hasn't had to do much behind the bench. But his club is trailing by a goal. What can he do to put some life into the club? He can try shaking up his lines. Often a new line

—one with a new player—might find the spark that's been miss-ing. In any event, the coach is pretty certain that the new player on the line, especially if he's a substitute, will be giving out the "110 percent" the coach wants. If this fails, there's always the dressing room between periods.

Nothing mystical occurs during the pep talks. In fact, much of the time there are no pep talks. These are reserved for special situa-tions. Usually a coach will allow his players a few minutes to un-wind before making his intermission speech. Fans would be sur-prised at how matter-of-fact the talk is. The coach probably is re-minding the players of some fundamental plays. Or perhaps he's spotted a weakness he wants exploited. Only a very few coaches go into locker-room harangues or call on the spirits of the club's de-parted players to lead the team to victory.

Toe Blake had a favorite tactic he used during his great years as the Canadiens' coach. The Canadiens have a dressing room that is lined with color portraits of former Montreal stars—Howie Morenz, Georges Vezina, Rocket Richard, and others. Above the pictures is the motto: "To you with failing hands we pass the torch—be yours to hold it high." During a playoff game, or in some other clutch situation, Blake would say softly, "Look at the pictures—do you want to let those guys down?"

Emile Francis of the Rangers employed a brilliant bit of strategy on the final day of the 1970 regular season. Because of a quirk in the rules, it was possible for the Rangers to make the playoffs if they scored at least five goals. That would have given them a higher total than the fourth-place Canadiens, who were to play a night game against Chicago. If the Canadiens lost, then the club with more goals would get fourth place, since both teams would be tied with identical records. The Rangers were playing the Detroit Red Wings that afternoon. They had been slumping for the final weeks after leading the league for half a season. Francis knew about the minimum of five goals his team needed. He also knew that five might not be enough. Yet his club hadn't been on a scor-ing spree in six weeks, when they last had five goals.

Before the game Francis stood silent for a moment in the dress-ing room, surrounded by the players. "Fellows," he began, "I've been in hockey a long time, and I've seen some funny things happen. Today is one of those times you can make a funny thing happen." Then he shot questions around the room. To Gilbert: "Do you believe you can do it?" Gilbert answered yes. Each player was asked and responded. Finally, the players made a game of it, asking one another how many goals they'd score. When they took the ice, they were flying. They won, 9–5—and made the playoffs. "That," said Francis later, "is something they'll remember the rest of their lives. Whenever I tell them again that something isn't impossible, they'll believe it."

The most "impossible" comeback perhaps was registered by the 1942 Maple Leafs. They trailed in their final Cup series against Detroit by three games to none. Only one thing could turn his Toronto club around, Coach Hap Day believed—an emotional shake-up. Day benched one of his scoring stars, Gordie Drillon, and replaced him with a utility player named Don Metz. Day teamed Metz with his brother Nick. In the fourth game, the Leafs overcame a 2–0 deficit. They won, 4–3—on a goal by Nick Metz. They have been the only team ever to rally from a three-game deficit and capture the Cup.

Imlach, a no-nonsense boss with Toronto, was trying to drive home a point to show his players the difference between winning and losing the Cup. During one series the players trudged into the dressing room. In the middle of the floor was a pile of money. "That," said Imlach, "is $1,500. It's the difference between winning and losing." His players won it.

It would be nice to think these theatrical occurrences are the rule. They're not. The coach, first of all, can't pull these dramatic tricks every game. His players would have nothing left if every contest meant they'd be reaching an emotional peak. So the coach usually shows his stuff—and earns his salary—with his bench-work during a game.

One of his most important attributes must be a feeling for momentum. Because so much of the sport depends on how "up" a player is at a given moment, a team that is sailing along is hard to stop. Everything seems to break for them.

We've all seen games where nothing slows down a team for a

three- or four-minute stretch. Eventually, you just know, the team will score. Somehow, the coach of the team that is being set upon has to slow things down. There's nothing like a play stoppage to halt a team's drive. The adrenalin stops flowing as freely, the crowd quiets, the opposition has a chance to regroup. If possible, the coach will send out his experienced players merely to play defensively for a while and hopefully frustrate the momentum. However, when a team is being pressed in its own zone the coach can't start removing players from the ice and replacing them. At times like these, he has to hope that someone on the club has the presence of mind to slow the tempo—either by throwing the puck in the stands (but not making it look deliberate, which would call for a penalty), or by icing the disk.

One coach solved the problem when his team was unable to get a play stoppage at a critical point in the game. He shouted to the referee that the door to the bench was stuck. The referee took a minute or so to find the trouble. Actually, the door had been jammed by the coach. But the extra delay served to slow the other club down. Their momentum was lost and they failed to score.

Perhaps the favorite delaying ploy coaches use is the old broken-equipment ploy. They've instructed their goalies to loosen tape on a stick, or a shoelace, or untie a shirt. Then, as soon as the whistle blows, the goalie tells the referee he needs a new stick, or has to skate to the bench for repairs. The referees know what's going on. But they usually allow a goalie to do it once. The second time they're more careful.

When Bernie Parent worked in the Flyers' nets, he abused the ploy more than anyone. As soon as the other team had a flurry going he'd invariably call time at the first whistle stoppage to get his equipment checked. One of the more amusing sights was to see the Flyers' trainer take Parent's "broken" stick, place it under the bench and then give the goalie a "new" stick. It usually was the same one. Parent became even more of a habitual bench-visitor when he went to Toronto, where the other goalie was Plante. At every crucial time Parent skated to Plante to ask advice. Coach John McLellan didn't seem to mind.

One of the major decisions a coach must make is when to pull the goalie. Virtually all teams take the goalie out in the final minute if the club is trailing by a goal. It happens fairly often. About one game in every six is decided by one goal. Yet, the removal of a goalie in favor of an extra forward rarely works. During the 1970–71 season, 44 empty-net goals were scored. That means that 44 times out of about 100 short-handed opportunities the leading team crushed the strategy. The league doesn't keep records of how many times a team has pulled its goalie and tied. But it can't be one out of 10 times. Still, it's worthwhile attempting under normal circumstances. It's difficult enough to try to get a goal at any time during the game. In the final minute, with the leading club playing defensively, it's virtually impossible unless a club has a manpower advantage.

The goalie won't be pulled when the play is at his end, of course. But once the trailing team has full control of the disk, the coach signals to his goalie. The goalie skates off. When he's within 10 feet of the bench, he legally may be replaced. However, coaches send out the replacement when the goalie's even farther out. The extra skater who replaces him generally is a center. Puck control is important at this stage, and a coach wants a proven stick-handler. The extra man goes to the slot, and all areas of the attacking zone are covered.

There is nothing automatic about pulling a goalie. If the trailing team is lucky to have a power play going thanks to a penalty, it might decide to leave the goalie in his net. But more often than not the coach will take advantage of the situation by lifting the goalie to produce a two-man advantage. If a face-off with the goalie out takes place at center ice, some coaches put their goalie back just for the face-off. Once their team controls it, the goalie skates out agian.

Bowman once defied the strategy of lifting his goalie. There were about 50 seconds to play and the Blues had a face-off in the opposition's end. The Blues were trailing by 2–1, and it was a perfect time to lift the goalie. While everyone in the stands waited for Bowman to make a move, he just watched the clock run out.

Later, he said simply, "I didn't realize there was so little time left." But that wasn't the real reason. The Vezina Trophy was on his mind. His club was on its way to an easy West Division title. If he lost the game it wouldn't matter much in the final standing. But if his club allowed another goal it could hurt in the Vezina race. So Bowman gave up a chance to win for the more certain possibility of keeping his club's goals-against average down.

There are coaches who don't bother with strategy. Such as King Clancy, the engaging former Maple Leaf star who coached the team in the mid-1950's. "King was one of the best in the world— for everything except coaching," said his former boss, Conn Smythe. Toronto didn't have much of a team under Clancy. So he substituted boisterousness instead.

His players were instructed to fight if the going got tough. "Clancy figured it this way," said Smythe. "If you lost the game by 5–1, but won five fights—well, he figured you really won the game."

It isn't often that a coach has a fighting team combined with a winning team. The exception of recent years were the Bruins, especially under Harry Sinden. They were tough and good. He carried a few spare players who knew what their job was when they hit the ice: It was to hit the opposition. Sinden gave his players their heads, and they loved him for it. They were a club that had been on the bottom a long time. They had been small and had been pushed around.

When they were at their peak—in fighting and winning—and had earned the nickname of "Animals," Sinden said (smiling), "What's everyone getting excited about just because we fight back? We don't go looking for fights. But we've got to protect ourselves."

The General Manager

Today's hockey is a multimillion-dollar operation. Yet none of the 14 general managers who started the 1971–72 season held degrees in business administration. Most are former players with an intimate knowledge of the game. All have had extensive coaching or scouting careers in the minors. These men, however, write the checks for clubs that do an annual business of up to $4,000,000. Expenses run about $1,500,000. Every club has about 60 players under contract. In addition there are travel expenses—which are considerable—and office staffs and scouts.

In addition to the business side, the general manager must make the moves that bring a respectable hockey team together. Perhaps it is easy now to see why all the general managers are hockey men, and not business men: It's easier to teach a man how to handle money than it is to teach someone how to evaluate a hockey player.

Although clubs don't own junior hockey teams anymore, it is still necessary to have a far-flung organization. Players still must be scouted, perhaps even more closely than before. The reason is the draft. A team now can get its players only by drafting them, except for trades. It must go into the amateur draft aware of the potential of the thousands of players eligible. This means the general manager has spent weeks going over battle plans with his staff—which players to take, what the opposition needs, what you need. There aren't many opportunities to overcome a mistake if you draft the wrong type of player. You've given up your turn, and you're stuck with him.

Scouting thus becomes an integral part of a general manager's life. During the regular season, when there is so much paperwork involved merely in running the big club, the general manager will travel to look at junior prospects, or to the team's minor-league professional farm clubs. Although there no longer are any junior affiliates, there still are minor-league operations, most of which lose money. But the club has to maintain teams in the Central, American, or Western Leagues. It can't keep all its players in the majors. Teams in these leagues might cost the parent club $200,-000 a year, or more. The G.M. must be in constant touch with these clubs to see who's developing. He has to know the potential talent he has in case he wants to make trades. Virtually all deals made in the N.H.L. are made by the G.M.

Where does his money come from? The single largest revenue producer, naturally, is attendance. All clubs play 39 home games. Many also stage two preseason games at home. And eight teams get the benefit of playoffs, which mean a minimum of two home games. Unlike football and baseball, the visiting teams don't share in gate receipts. The home club keeps it all. Most of the teams average capacity, about 15,000 a game. Say the average ticket price is $5. That's $75,000 a game, multiplied by a minimum of 39 home dates. The average team, then, takes in about $3,000,000 a season in gate receipts. There is also television and radio revenue, shares from concessionaires and advertisers. Thus, a $4,000,000-a-year empire is built. The G.M. has his fingers in most of these deals. He has to know how much he's taking in because he has to know how much he can spend.

On virtually all N.H.L. teams the G.M. negotiates salary with the players. There is no philanthropy here. While the G.M. doesn't want to make his players unhappy, he doesn't want to give them as much as they think they're worth. The greatest single outlay of a team's expenses goes for salary. In the East Division players average about $25,000 a man, including bonuses. In the West Division it's about $22,000 a player. This is about a 30 percent increase since 1969, when lawyers and agents weren't a major factor in hockey negotiations.

Sam Pollock of the Canadiens probably is the finest G.M. in the game. He has kept an endless flow of talent coming to Montreal. It has been only the last few years, though, that Pollock even was willing to meet with lawyers for players. Many G.M.'s believe the intimacy is missing if a middleman comes in and starts to negotiate for an athlete. Given today's taxes, salaries, and bonuses, however, it is hard to see how the average 20-year-old could negotiate the best possible contract.

Several general managers also are coaches. They insist that heated bargaining over salaries doesn't continue in the locker room. But it's difficult to imagine any general manager who can sufficiently separate his coaching role. His feeling for the player —good or bad—would have to spill over to the bench. The most bitter salary dispute since the lawyer became a factor involved the Rangers' general manager-coach, Francis. During the training camp of 1970 he suspended four of his stars—Brad Park, Jean Ratelle, Vic Hadfield, and Walt Tkaczuk—after they had hired the same lawyers, who advised them not to sign their contracts.

"I can separate my feelings," Francis insisted. "Negotiations have nothing to do with my relationship with them as their coach."

"I have enough confidence in Emile that he won't carry over any hard feelings," said Park. "He'll continue to treat me as a player, not as someone he had a business argument with."

"Are they kidding?" said one of the lawyers. "How could anyone in his right mind think a general manager could be saint enough to cut off his feelings from one area of his relationship? No one could do that. Of course the negotiations will affect his relationship with the guys."

Ironically, Francis was a tough negotiator when he was a player. Once, he was locked into a hotel room to sign a contract. Another time he had a stormy session with a general manager. The G.M. tried to downgrade Francis's ability as a goalie. "Why, you're weak on your right side," said the G.M. "The hell I am," replied Francis, dramatically removing a booklet from his shirt pocket. "Here are the statistics." And inside, the book revealed that no more goals went in against Francis from the right side or the left side.

Contract negotiations are a game played between general manager and player. One mediocre player walked into the G.M.'s office at contract-signing time with a host of facts and figures—plus and minuses, winning goals, tying goals, and so forth. "That's terrific," the G.M. replied. "But it didn't help us get into the playoffs." That deflated the player's demands.

The next season the pair met again. This time the player wasn't so well-armed. He had a poor season, and the G.M. offered the player the same salary. "But," said the player, "we made the playoffs."

One of the absurd labor-management situations cropped up in

1970 when discussions bogged down between the Seals and Harry Howell and Carol Vadnais. The Seals' negotiator was Bill Torrey. He suggested to the players' attorneys that they submit a list of arbitrators. Meanwhile, the Seals had suggested Clarence Campbell, the president of the league, and Charles Mulcahy, the Bruins' attorney and vice-president. The lawyers felt Mulcahy and Campbell were management-leaning. So the lawyers suggested Alan Shepard, the astronaut; Stan Musial, the ex-baseball star, and Dr. Jonas Salk, who discovered the anti-polio vaccine. According to the lawyers, Torrey's reply to this list was: "The list is partial."

Then the lawyers submitted another list, with one man—Earl Warren, the former Chief Justice of the United States Supreme Court.

Torrey replied: "That's ridiculous. He's not a hockey man."

Once the G.M. signs a player the athlete's role in the team and its future must be evaluated. Imlach had a theory that if you could get three or four mediocre players for one marginal player, you make the deal. This way, the new players could be made available in the draft. Instead of losing several players of quality, you lose a few extras who don't matter.

With so much expansion going on it's critical for G.M.'s to know which players they'll be protecting. Having a bunch of talented kids on the farm doesn't help if you can only protect, say, 15 players in an expansion draft. A reverse of the Imlach theory is Francis's. He believes in trading away several promising youngsters to obtain one player who can help him now. A perfect example came early in the 1971–72 season, when he dealt four young players—including three Central League stars—to St. Louis. In return he got Jim Lorentz, a left wing, and a 20-year-old rookie named Gene Carr. Since none of the young players Francis traded to St. Louis could have made the talented Rangers, he would have lost them in the 1972 expansion draft. He couldn't afford to protect them. In exchange, though, he got only one player he had to worry about protecting—Lorentz. Carr, a first-year pro, was exempt from being protected under league rules. Francis made the deal at a time his club was leading the East Division. It didn't have to look for players. But the timing was right, since St. Louis was floundering and needed quick help. After he made the deal Francis noted: "We don't have to worry about protecting those kids anymore."

The cagiest G.M. must be Pollock. It's no coincidence that he has got a flock of draft choices over the years. He's had enough talent to give to the expansion teams in exchange for future choices. In 1969 Pollock acquired the Seals' first choice in the 1971 amateur draft. As the 1970–71 season was underway, it was apparent that the most sought-after player in the draft would be Guy Lafleur, who was on his way to scoring 130 goals. Pollock, however, would only get Lafleur if the Seals finished last. That would give the Seals the first draft pick.

Some cynics insist that Pollock made sure the Seals would finish last. They point to the fact that the Canadiens traded Ralph Backstrom, a 200-goal man, to the Kings in exchange for two aging minor-leaguers. The trade came just as the Kings were beginning to slide toward last place. Backstrom got 14 goals in 33 games for the Kings. Meanwhile, Pollock took one of the players in the Backstrom deal, Gordon Labossiere, and traded him to Minnesota —when the North Stars were slumping. Neither Minnesota nor Los Angeles finished last—the Seals did. It was suggested that Pollock had bolstered up the Seals' opponents to insure a last-place finish for the Seals.

"I deny the charges categorically," said Pollock. "We made the trades simply because they were good deals for both clubs." In the amateur draft the Canadiens had the first choice. They chose Lafleur.

Expansion has created a wealth of jobs, and problems for the new general managers. An owner decides he'd like to own a hockey team. He hires a general manager to help him build one. Where do you start? Any G.M. knows that the available talent from the expansion draft won't stand up under the long haul. At the June, 1972 expansion, for example, each of the existing clubs could protect their top 15 players, plus two goalies. That meant that the best an expansion team could hope for was the player considered 16th best on any team. As the draft goes along, the talent thins out. The new clubs can take 18 players and two goalies. But of which type? General managers like to talk of "strength down the middle." That means they start with the goalie, then go to the defense, then the center.

When Bud Poile was general manager of the first-year Flyers in 1967 he simply went for "the best players available—regardless of position." Thus, if he saw that his top three choices, for example, would be defensemen—he'd take them. Some clubs wound up with a disproportionate number of players at one position. But if the players were fairly good, they could be traded off for talent at other positions. Jack Riley of the expansionist Penguins was perhaps under the most pressure of any of the G.M.'s on the new teams. His owners believed that Pittsburgh would only support a winning club. So Riley went into the 1967 expansion not thinking so much about building a club for the future as putting out a winning combination immediately. That meant he had to take proven players, and they generally were veterans. The Penguins' average age was 31 years—probably the oldest team ever assembled for any sport. Within two years, the Penguins had to clean house. They are a perfect example of what can happen to a hockey team when owners—who may not know the game—start to overrule the judgment of a hockey-wise general manager.

Poile and Larry Regan, the Kings' G.M., were the only general managers who were able to prepare for the future—both their clubs purchased topnotch farm teams. The Kings bought the Springfield Indians of the American League while the Flyers bought the Quebec team. During the season both N.H.L. teams were able to fill in gaps in the line-up. As a result, the Flyers finished first and the Kings finished second.

Poile eventually left the Flyers over a front-office clash. When Vancouver was awarded a franchise to begin play in 1970, Poile was selected as the new team's G.M.

"A guy's got to be crazy to start an expansion team twice," said Poile. "You need a good wife, and it helps to be nuts."

Poile, however, remembered well the mistakes most of the expansion clubs had made previously. "I needed a nucleus," he explained. "I looked at other clubs in expansion that had made a lot of changes, but didn't improve themselves."

Poile believes that every club needs a leader. Philadelphia hadn't had one when he formed it. But Orland Kurtenbach was available in the 1970 draft, and Poile wisely chose the old pro. Poile also beefed up the Canucks' Rochester farm in the American League. When the season began the Canucks were one of the surprises. With Kurtenbach becoming one of the league's early scoring leaders the Canucks stayed at .500 until mid-December. Then Kurtenbach was injured. The team sagged. Still, their early-season spurt proved that what Poile had done was correct.

Expansion has also meant new arenas, and several little aspects of the role a G.M. can play in an arena aren't noticeable to most fans. Before a season starts, a club can decide which goal it wishes to defend in the first period. That means it also will be defending the same goal in the final period. The team also can choose which bench it wants, and which penalty box it desires. Right away, the home club's general manager can make two key decisions.

By choosing the penalty box that is closest to the goal his club is defending for two periods, the G.M. allows his penalized players to get back into the defensive action more quickly. It is obviously important to bring the club to equal strength in your defending zone as soon as possible. And by placing the team's bench closest to the defending zone, the G.M. ensures line changes for two periods that will be closer to the team's goalie.

It is rare that a G.M. gets fired. Certainly, the coach is the first to go. The crafty G.M. knows that losses will be blamed on the coach, and that a surplus in the bank can be credited to the general manager. Lester Patrick didn't always have winners for the Rangers, but his team usually showed a profit. He saved most of his expenses by the outrageously low salaries.

"Were we underpaid?" exclaimed Babe Pratt, now a Canucks' official. "Listen—when I played for Patrick he wouldn't give a worm to a blind bird."

The Scouts

At last count, 67 scouts take credit for discovering Bobby Orr. The scouts, after all, build their reputations on who they've found in Kapuskasing or Banff or wherever else their travels take them. So when you listen to a group of scouts talking you're going to hear stories that rival those of fishermen. A scout can't show a balance sheet of profit or loss. His assets are his ability to spot talent and his balance sheet is a roster of names he's found who have made their way to the big league.

Every team has at least a half-dozen full-time scouts and dozens more who bird-dog, scouring their home territory for promising youngsters. In addition, every club has a chief scout who works closely with the general manager and coach. The chief scout must be aware of the team's needs, as well as what the opposition is looking for. The scouts form a sort of fraternal organization in which everyone is looking over his shoulder. General Motors doesn't guard its new-car designs from Chrysler any more craftily than a scout keeps his information away from rival bird-dogs.

It isn't unusual for a chief scout to log more than 100,000 miles a year. Most of the travel takes place in the winter—when hockey is played. Since the game isn't confined to major metropolitan areas it is necessary to log thousands of miles by car to small cities that don't have an airport nearby. Scouts have taken bush planes and snowmobiles to search for talent.

One chief scout, who prefers anonymity, describes his operation this way:

> "Say there's a kid one of our bird-dogs likes. He gives me a collect call and tells me there's a really sensational right wing. Now, I know the particular likes and dislikes of this scout, and I know if he tends to favor one sort of player over another. But if I'm convinced that the kid will make a good prospect, I'll call one of our regional directors and ask him to take a look at the player. Sometimes you can tell just from one game if the kid can't make it. But you can't tell from the one game if he definitely will make

it. We try to see the kid under different circumstances. You might just catch him at a time he doesn't feel well, or has an off night. So my guys will look at him at home and on the road. That's very important. Some guys freeze on the road. They choke up. Their style changes.

"We also want to know what kind of a kid he is. We don't like bad actors. You'd be surprised how many kids of 19 or 20 already are pretty bad drinkers. You know, they're living away from home, they become big heroes in the town they play in. People want to be nice to them. And the kids can wind up bad, unless they're careful.

"Okay. My regional man still likes the kid after investigating him and seeing him in several different game situations. He sends me a detailed report on the kid if he likes him. In the report I want to know some simple things right away—how old the kid is, what's his height and weight. Then I want to know his scoring figures. But after that, I want a solid evaluation: What are the boy's assets? Is he a good skater? That's No. 1. Skating. We like to say in hockey that skating is the name of the game.

"Now we get down to his other abilities. Is he a good stick-handler? How's his passing. What kind of shot does he have. Can he use his backhand. Is he a selfish player. What are his defensive credentials. Does his style of play change when the team is winning or when it's losing. Some kids are world-beaters when their team has a quick lead, you know. Then the roof falls in if the club is trailing. They start to choke and you'd swear you were watching two different players.

"I'll talk the report over with the G.M. If we're both convinced the kid's worth looking at, then I'll take a run up there and get a good look at him. Usually, I'll take along one of the scouts from the area or our regional scout.

"I don't like to let anyone know I'll be at the game. It's not unusual for our bird-dogs to be at a game, but if anyone from a rival team knows I'm there they may be wondering just who I'm interested in. So I keep things a secret as much as possible. All the scouts know one another pretty well. If I happen to run into someone at a game, I don't even tell him who I'm looking at. Let them guess. Sometimes they're not even sure I'm looking at who they think I'm looking at.

"We're pretty cagey. On my notes during the game I don't even put down the name of the kid. Sometimes I use the name of another player. Sometimes I make up a name. That's just in case my notes get stolen. I've seen that happen. But even if they're not stolen, some guy can take a seat behind me and look over my shoulder. Let him guess who I'm writing about.

"There are times, though, when everyone knows who you're looking at. Like, you couldn't keep Bobby Orr concealed. But I still don't want anyone to know my impressions of a kid. So I use my own code. Maybe I'll have the number 'one' on a sheet, with some marks next to it. The 'one' might stand for stick-handling ability.

"Next to the 'one' I use my own shorthand. I'm the only guy who knows what it means. If someone was to take a peek at the sheet, they wouldn't have the foggiest notion of what it's all about."

Shero, the Flyers' coach, recalls some of the scouting duties that took him to places like Kirkland Lake, Ontario.

"It was so far north," says Shero, "that if you opened your car window you'd be shaking hands with Santa Claus."

The vast majority of scouts are in Canada, looking over junior talent. But in the last few years more are being employed to visit the United States college campuses, where the game has had an extraordinary upsurge. And because N.H.L. teams play one another so few times these days, it is important to scout the N.H.L. opposition.

Scouting other N.H.L. teams serves two purposes—it can tell a G.M. or a coach what to expect when the clubs meet, and it can tell the G.M. some important aspects of a player he might want to trade for. Statistics don't tell the story, even on a proven player.

There is the case of Bobby Rousseau, for example. Rousseau was the rookie of the year in 1961–62, playing with the Montreal Canadiens. During the 1965–66 season he led the league in assists. In nine years with the Canadiens Rousseau scored 200 goals. He was traded before the 1970–71 season to the Minnesota North Stars. Rousseau scored only four goals during the season. Yet, when the season was over the Rangers traded Bob Nevin, who had scored 21 goals, for Rousseau. Certainly the trade was a ridiculously bad one for New York, based on the statistics. But constant watching had uncovered the following facts about Rousseau: He played on a regular line for less than half the season. He wasn't used on the power play—where the extra goals come from —after the first few weeks of the season. The North Stars had radically altered their style of play under their new coach, Jackie Gordon. Instead of being offensive-minded, Gordon wanted the team to concentrate on defense. The change was too radical for Rousseau, who had played for some of the greatest scoring machines hockey had seen. He sulked. He had played nine years for Montreal, and suddenly was in a strange city in another country, where his specific talents didn't fit in. Yet, the scouts—in this case the top men on the Rangers—could see that Rousseau still had the ability. All it needed was the proper channeling. So the Rangers made the deal. Before the season was a month old, Rousseau had doubled his previous season's output.

The cost of all this looking and scouting and telephoning and paperwork runs the average club more than $150,000 a year. In today's hockey it's not enough to be "pretty sure" of a player's capabilities. A club has to be damn sure. There are about 5,000 20-year-olds eligible for the amateur draft each year, and a club with a decent scouting system should have a line on hundreds of prospects. It gets even more involved than just the coming year's prospects, though. Many teams know who's eligible for drafting three or four years from now. The reason? A little roulette, maybe, but clubs might want to make a trade for a club's top draft choice in two years. Say a team knows that a boy it thinks will be a superstar will be eligible for drafting in two years. It wants first crack at him. If it's a top team then the chances are it will not have a high draft choice. Here's where the roulette comes in. A club's G.M. must try to anticipate which team will finish with the worst record—or close to the worst record—two years from now. Then the G.M. attempts to make a deal with that club in which it would receive the other team's top draft choice in two seasons.

If the scouts have done their job the prospect will be worth waiting for. Lafleur, for example, came to the Canadiens three years after the Frenchmen had traded Carol Vadnais to the

Seals. Sometimes, though, a player whom every scout believes is a "can't-miss" does miss. When Allan Hamilton played junior hockey, he was labeled the second-best young defenseman in Canada, next to Bobby Orr. Hamilton had size, agility, and strength. Yet, he never made it with the Rangers—and they didn't think he could. They left him unprotected in the 1970 expansion draft, and he wound up with the Buffalo Sabres.

One of the most heavily scouted players of the 1970's was Marcel Dionne of the Red Wings. Even when he was 14 the scouts knew he was a sensational prospect. One team's scouts were so high on the teen-ager that they told the club to get Dionne at any cost. This was in the day when N.H.L. clubs could own amateur teams. The club's general manager was sold on Dionne. In an extraordinary move to insure that Dionne remained his club's property, he negotiated a deal in which he purchased Dionne's entire team. A few days afterward, the N.H.L. passed the law forbidding sponsorship of amateur squads by N.H.L. teams. The G.M. had a worthless piece of paper in his pocket. In the 1971 amateur draft, Dionne was the second player taken after Lafleur.

"It's funny the way things work out," said the general manager, speaking of the team that got Dionne. "We wouldn't have taken him now. He never really grew very big. I guess that's part of the hazards—or luck—of scouting. You have to guess how good a kid's gonna be years from now. That's one of the reasons we have scouts."

4 | The Officials

The Referee

After a call that went against him, Gordie Howe skated over to Referee Frank Udvari and said, "Frank, you're the second-best referee." Somewhat pleased, Udvari inquired, "Well, who's the best?" Howe replied: "Everyone else. They're tied for No. 1."

In no other sport does the chief official come in for as much abuse as a hockey referee. And in no other sport is the tempo—or tenor—of the game decided so much by the referee. Because of the simple word "intent" the fate of players and a game rests in a referee's whistle. Who's to say how much a factor emotion becomes in dictating the way a referee calls a game? Or the fan reaction? Often, it is easier to spot a penalty from the stands, where all the action unfolds in front of you, than it is in the hectic ice-level world. Fans are constantly seeing infractions go unpenalized. In frustration, they'll boo a referee who has spotted one of their heroes throw a punch in retaliation—but has not seen the enemy throw the first blow.

"Sure, that often happens," says Scotty Morrison, the league's referee-in-chief. "You'll miss the first punch, or the high stick. But you hear the fans scream. So you try to look at what they're screaming at. And then you see a player throw a punch. You can't guess that the opponent threw the first punch. You can only call what you see."

This is an essential factor in refereeing, and one that many fans don't appreciate: A referee can't guess, or assume—even if logic and his experience enables him to make an educated judgment. That is why, by rule, a referee must blow the whistle and stop play immediately if the puck is gone from his view.

We've all seen a goal scored a split second after the disk has been lost in a pile of players and the referee has blown his whistle, ruling the play dead. Yet, the fans continue to boo, thinking the ref has blown the goal. He hasn't. He has followed the rules. That fact doesn't deter the coach, the players, the fans from drowning out the referee's reasons.

Because so many calls a referee makes during the game are really a matter of judgment—a deliberate trip versus an accidental trip—he must constantly explain himself. If he did it to every player who had a question, he'd never get on with the game. To ease his path, the league requires that in order to question a referee on his decision, only a team captain or alternate captain may speak to the official. Thus, we have the "A's" on uniforms. Each team is allowed three alternate captains, and before each game the referee is advised who they are. However, theoretically a referee may not be questioned about his call of a penalty. He may only be questioned about his interpretation of the rules. And only the captain or alternate on the ice at the time of a referee's disputed decision may question the referee. The captain, for example, may not come off the bench to ask a question. That calls for an automatic misconduct penalty.

The league's rules suggest that a club shall have a captain, or alternate captain, on the ice at any given moment. This is one reason why defensemen often wear the "A." They see more ice time than forwards. A coach, however, wouldn't make defensemen who play together each alternates. That wouldn't give him enough A's to go around when that particular defensive tandem was off the ice.

The referee does more than watch out for infractions. He is the final word on every aspect of the play. He begins the game with a face-off, and faces off again after any goals and the start of the second and third periods. But he does not participate in the face-off at other times. He used to have that job. But now the linesmen drop the puck at these times, with the referee positioned so he can look around for any infractions that might be committed during a face-off. The referee also has the last word on whether a goal has been scored, regardless of what the goal judge says. The referee also reports to the official scorer the number of the player who has scored—but he does not tell the scorer who received the assists.

It's interesting to hear the different receptions referees receive in various rinks. When Art Skov's name is announced in Boston, the fans roar in anger. In New York, there's hardly a ripple. When John Ashley's name is announced in New York, the fans boo. In Boston, there's barely a murmur. It all goes back to some real or imagined slights a particular referee once committed against a team. The fans don't forget. From that day on, the referee can do no right. Surprisingly, referees have feelings.

"The public has no compassion for these men," says Morrison. "You know, they're washed up when they're 41 or 42—in the prime of life. They have stress constantly, and they can please few people. Sometimes I wonder why they take it. They put up with so much abuse. I guess it's because they're men with pride. They enjoy a job well-done."

No one at the age of 16 or 17 says to himself, "When I grow up I want to be a referee." Most skating youngsters want to be players. Realistically, that can't happen. So, many try to latch onto the sport as an official. Most of the 16 referees in 1971 were would-be hockey players. They'd learned early in their careers that they lacked the ability to make a living at playing and turned to officiating. Referees are scouted—just as players are. Initially, says Morrison, he looks for young people. That is the first consideration. After that, his men must meet three criteria: "They must be in good condition, have good judgment, and good common sense. Common sense is at least 60 percent of a referee's duties."

If a referee has potential, he can become a trainee in, say, the Central League. After three years in the minors he is eligible for spot assignments in the National Hockey League. The referee must perform his duties knowing that for virtually every call he makes he is sure to antagonize someone. Almost every penalty brings a complaint (supposedly illegal) from the penalized player. If it's a hometown player, thousands of fans will join him. Fans imagine every check tossed against one of their players is illegal, and the referee in a rough game receives the abuse constantly.

There are good reasons, then, for him to feel the pressure. He travels between 70,000 and 80,000 miles a year, works in 70 big-league games and another 10 in the minors, and has to make more judgment calls than officials in any other sport. An experienced referee earns more than $20,000 for the seven-month season. They also have the same pension plan as the players: At age 45 they may receive $300 annually for each year of service, or they can take $1,000 annually for each year of service at 65. To get the referees in shape, there is a preseason training camp.

Camp doesn't prepare referees for the emotional rigors of the long season. A few years ago Morrison demoted one referee to linesman. Morrison explained that the official was keyed-up and unhappy before a game. He'd break out into hives. He wouldn't be able to sleep or eat. The referee, who had so much potential, made mistakes in clutch situations, forgetting rules, forgetting his role. He is happier now as a linesman.

When Vern Buffey was a top referee in the 1960's he followed a ritual that he hoped would ensure impartiality, and avoid giving him headaches. He never bought the newspapers in the city he was working that night. He wouldn't even read them the next day.

"I don't want to know who's on a streak, who's fighting, or what they're saying about me or other referees," he explained. "If I pick up a paper and I read that some club is coming to town and there are some fights to settle, I might tend to be watching for fights too closely, and blow a quick whistle at the least contact. And I don't want to read about a game the following morning in case some coach or player has something to say about me. If I don't know about it, my judgment for the team can't be affected."

Buffey, more outspoken than most officials—who are not permitted to talk to the press, except to explain a rules interpretation —admitted that referees sometimes are outwitted. "We call what we see," he said. "Now you take Gordie Howe. You see he's tangling with some guy in a corner. The puck comes out, and you start to follow the play. Then you turn around and you see the guy who was with Howe is lying on the ice. Howe is so strong and tricky. He's got a dozen little moves he can make with his stick and elbow. You know Howe did it, but how can you prove it?"

Although a referee's decision isn't infallible, it is completely official. No matter what mistake he might make, and be fined by the league or cautioned, no referee's decision can be overruled and no game can ever be replayed because of a referee's mistake. Even if a referee admits later that a goal should have been credited—or shouldn't have been allowed—the final score stands, as does the decision he made at the time.

Obviously, it's essential for the league to stand behind its referees. That means if an official is even touched by a player the league deals severely with such action. The question of how much support the league gives is one that may be entirely personal on the part of the referee. Red Storey, for example, quit as the top referee in 1959, claiming that Campbell didn't stand behind the referees. Storey claimed on a radio show in Toronto that in one game at Boston late in the season, the referee-in-chief, Carl Voss, went to the officials' dressing room and told Storey: "There's one team out there fighting for a playoff spot—the Rangers. The other team, the Bruins, aren't going anywhere. I want you to be sure that any penalties you call against the Rangers must be good penalties."

Storey said later that he interpreted that to mean to go easy on the Rangers. "I have no doubt in my mind that what Voss meant for me to do was ease up on New York. If they were eliminated from the playoffs, it wasn't going to be because of a poor call."

This statement also brings up the question: Do referees' standards vary depending on the game they're calling? In other words, are they less than 100 percent objective in certain situations?

Storey claimed that referees used double standards when calling games in Montreal. Before the rule was changed ending a power play as soon as the team with the man advantage scored, a club with a power play such as the Canadiens easily could score two goals within two minutes. "Our instructions were to be careful what penalties we gave to the visiting team. Make sure it was a good one because we might ruin a good game," said Storey. "Let's say you didn't look at the visiting team like you looked at the Canadiens."

It must be remembered that these are after-the-fact statements by a man who believed he was abused by the league. Yet, it makes you wonder. One club owner reportedly told Storey, "We own this league and you'll run it the way we tell you."

If there was intimidation, it never got to Mickey Ion, a great referee who made the Hockey Hall of Fame. "Tough is the only way to referee," said Ion. One of the probable apocryphal stories concerning Ion happened in a game with the Canadiens. Toe Blake was one of the club's stars, and Ion hit Blake with a two-minute penalty. "I don't want to get another penalty," said Blake with a scowl. "But you can guess what I'm thinking." Ion replied: "I have guessed—and you get another five minutes."

Reading people's minds usually isn't part of the judgment calls a referee makes. Penalties are. If there are 11 penalties called in the average game, then about 90 judgments have been made that weren't translated into penalties. Campbell estimates that the referee must make about 100 decisions a game—whether to call or not call, whether a goal was scored, whether there are too many men on the ice, or too many sticks on the ice, or if a change was made legally, or if he was cursed sufficiently to warrant a penalty, or if the game has been intentionally delayed.

One of the trickiest calls is the new rule that makes it a penalty for a goalie to deliberately shoot the puck "outside the playing area." For a long time the league didn't enforce the rule. It was worried about lawsuits. As a matter of course, goalies had shot the puck into the stands, or the benches, to stop play when the other team was attacking. If the rule had been in the books, said league officials, it would have given a fan who was injured by such a batted puck a better legal case. The fan could have claimed that the goalie violated the rules of hockey and thus caused injury. It would have been a deliberate violation on the goalie's part, and not simply an accident. But Cheevers of the Bruins so angered opposing teams with his tactic of lofting the puck into the stands to avoid trouble that the rule finally was passed in 1971.

"It's strictly judgment," admits Referee Bruce Hood. He had called the violation in one game against a goalie who had cleared, by a few inches, the photographer's box at ice level. If the shot had gone a foot to the right, it would have hit the protective glass and not called for a penalty.

"You have to figure that because the goalie took a few steps and brought his stick back before hitting the puck, he was trying to lift it," Hood explained. "Of course, there are some goalies who can lift the puck with a simple wrist shot. That's the hard part—determining whether it was an accident or deliberate. And in some rinks the glass is 10 feet high, in others it's only seven feet high."

Morrison gives this advice to his referees: When in doubt, call it in favor of the player.

Adding to the considerable pressure in recent years has been the instant replay. Morrison estimates that 90 percent of the replays vindicate his officials' calls. Fans, though, tend to remember the calls that a referee blew.

Morrison's three supervisors blanket the United States and Canada with constant coverage to ensure the referees are doing their job. On any given night, the officials will have most games covered. They sit in the stands and take notes. As soon as a game is over, or sometimes between periods, they'll talk to the referee about mistakes he might have made.

Starting in 1970, Morrison began an extensive breakdown of the type of penalty each referee in the league called. The statistics were revealing. They disclosed that some referees are prone to call cross-checking or high-sticking. Others call more boarding or charging. If these statistics are in wide variance with the averages of all penalties, then Morrison talks to the referee to determine the reason. Once a referee gets known around the league for permitting certain types of infractions, the players pick it up and are certain to try to get away with them.

A look at a box score tells Morrison a lot. If he sees a game in which there are few penalties in the first period, then more in the second, then still substantially more in the final period, Morrison begins to wonder: Is the referee setting his standard early enough in the game?

"If that pattern goes on for a few games," says Morrison, "it means the referee has been clamping down late in the game to avoid having it get away from him. On the other hand, when I see a lot of penalties in the first period, then progressively less as the game goes along, it means the referee has pretty good control of what's going on."

A week-long training camp, followed by three weeks of exhibitions, prepares the referee for the long grind. Conditioning takes up most of their camp time. The referee receives a wake-up call at 6:15 A.M. and he's on a football field by 7. Then he runs a half-mile. A half-hour of calisthenics follow, and then it's another half-mile around the field. After breakfast, there's a question-and-answer session, followed by lunch.

In the afternoons the official goes through a two and one-half-hour session on the ice in which skating drills and exercises are stressed. Morrison allows his men to have a little fun by letting them do some stick-handling and shooting. But the major reason for this week is to get everyone in shape. Referees are as susceptible as players to groin pulls early in the season. Two evenings during the week are devoted to rule discussions. And for two afternoons the officials play a little touch football and soccer.

Every little bit helps if a referee is to keep his composure and his health. It's all necessary. As Ion used to tell his men: "Remember. From the time the whistle blows until the last buzzer, you and I are the only sane men in the rink."

The Linesmen

They are the most faceless men on the ice, and usually the least noticed. Perhaps once or twice a game they're hooted when fans believe an offside has been blown. Most people think of linesmen only as those two fellows who call a play or a pass offside, or who call icing. If their job was that simple, they'd have the easiest of times. But there are many other facets to their duties, and they have many rules to work by, only a few of them appreciated or understood even by the players.

When the game is ready to begin we see the linesmen skate out with the referee. One linesman goes to one end of the rink and checks the netting on the goal post, while the other linesman does the same ritual at the opposite end. For the first half of the game, each linesman will have that half of the rink as his responsibility. In effect, they split the ice in half. One side, from the center line to the goal is one linesman's; the other half belongs to the other linesman.

During the course of play, the linesmen station themselves close to the boards. They cover the area from blue line to blue line, leaving their posts only on icings. Their angle of vision must be near-perfect to determine whether a pass or a player is offside. A player, of course, may not precede the puck into the attacking zone. But how do you determine how much he precedes it by? The majority of fans aren't aware that the determining factor is the position of the player's skates, and not his stick, that makes a man offside. Both skates must be over the blue line for a player to be considered offside. If the linesman hasn't a clear view of the action, and if he isn't on the blue line, he runs the risk of blowing the play or of being fooled by his depth perception. It is similar to judging the finish of a horse race. If you stand at an angle behind the horses, you might think the outside horse won. If you stand to the right of the finish line you could think the inside horse was first. If you stand laterally with the finish line, though, you've got the best chance of judging the winner.

In determining whether a pass is offside by virtue of having gone two lines, it is the position of the puck—and not the player's skates—that matters.

Most of the linesmen's time is taken with making offsides—players and passes—calls. But he also calls for icings. Generally, the back linesman makes this call. The front linesman's job is to determine when the puck has crossed the goal line on either side of the net and a defensive player has touched it, causing an icing.

Virtually all the 60-odd face-offs in a game are handled by a linesman. The referee drops the puck only to start each period, and following a goal.

"A face-off shouldn't be a game of chance," says Morrison. His linesmen are drilled in proper face-off technique. They are taught to station themselves in a squat position, and to hold out the puck clearly in front of them, 12 to 16 inches off the ice. The opposing players must see the puck. When the linesman is satisfied both players are prepared, he lets it go with a quick, short wrist action.

The linesmen go practically unnoticed during one of their most important functions—breaking up fights. They receive specific training in how to handle brawling. The instruction starts at their preseason camp. In no other sport—except for boxing, naturally—is fighting taken for granted. Campbell, the league president, has called a man-to-man fight a "safety valve" for releasing players' tensions. But few people like an all-out brawl, or to see anyone receive an injury. In training camp, linesmen prepare to halt fighting in several ways. There is one drill in which linesmen pair off and stage arm-wrestling competitions, as though trying to pull a player away. They also stage make-believe fights, with pushing, wrestling, and punching. Then the other linesmen practice their routines.

Ideally, a linesman should follow this technique: He should wait until he and his partner get to the scene of the action. It's not a good idea for one linesman to go in alone. He is taught never to approach a player from behind, or to pin his arms. Two things can happen. If a player feels someone behind him, he might take a swing at the person. Or, if a linesman pins one player's arms, the other player can begin pummeling his opponent unmolested.

A little psychology is helpful for a linesman. They're instructed to talk to the battling players to calm them down, saying such things as "okay, you've had your fun," or "take it easy," or even a warning: "You can get kicked out if you continue."

The reason that it's the linesmen who break up the fights is to allow the referee to note who's doing what to whom. If the referee got in the middle of brawls, he wouldn't be able to get the complete picture of which players should be penalized. So while the linesmen are in the middle, the referee stands back and tries to get the numbers of the players involved, and the severity of their penalties. He also has to be on the lookout for any violators of a new rule which makes expulsion mandatory for any third player to join in a fight. The league has found that the third man in usually sets off mass fisticuffs. Officials generally are advised that if two players are fighting, and it appears neither will be hurt, then the fighting should be allowed to continue for a few seconds and then broken up. Most of the hard blows will have been landed early, and after a few punches the players are amenable to being separated.

Linesmen now are permitted to call a few penalties. Why, the fans usually ask, don't linesmen call a tripping or a boarding infraction that the referee doesn't see? It's a matter of having a consistent standard. If each of the three officials were permitted to call any penalties they noticed, there'd be chaos, as well as variance. But linesmen today may call a penalty for a team having too many men on the ice, or for any articles thrown from the bench. They also report to the referee if a team has deliberately displaced its goal post. That rule was put in following a play in the 1971 Cup finals between Montreal and Chicago, when a Chicago defenseman deliberately lifted the post off its mooring just as a Montreal player shot. The puck went in, but the goal was disallowed because the cage wasn't in place. The linesman could see the defenseman pull the cage, but the referee missed it.

Linesmen also are used as consultants if a goal has been scored and the referee missed it. It is remarkable how rarely during a season a referee will not be in position to accurately determine whether a shot went in. If the referee isn't sure, he doesn't go only by the goal judge. He consults his linesmen.

To make sure the linesmen are using proper face-off techniques, and are stationing themselves properly for calling offsides, Morrison regularly employs a television tape recorder in his office. Periodically, he calls in his linesmen for discussion of proper technique.

"I emphasize the positive aspects of what they're doing," says Morrison. "You've always got to try to encourage the officials."

The Minor Officials

Except for the goal judges, the minor officials are virtually lost in the crowd. Yet, there's nothing minor about the duties of the six officials—the two goal judges, the scorer, the game timekeeper, the penalty timekeeper, and the statistician. The only reason they're called "minor" is to differentiate them from the "major" officials—the referee and two linesmen.

There is something almost folksy about hockey's method of determining who its minor officials will be: it allows teams in each city to submit the names of the minor officials it would like. The procedure works something like this: Each summer the supervisor of officials in a city presents the names of the minor officials to the team. The club's general manager looks over the list and sends it on to the league office. Theoretically, if a team doesn't approve of an official who may be judging it, it can turn the name down. This doesn't happen, though. It is pretty much of a rubber-stamp affair. Once the league approves the list of minor officials, these men work all the regular-season home games for that team. It seems a strange system—the hometown team being judged in large measure by hometown officials. Yet, the overall quality of the officials is high. And to ensure against a potential "homer" bias, Clarence Campbell takes an extremely active interest in the roles these people play.

During the regular season the minor officials receive no pay for their services. According to Campbell, "we want men of sóme standing in their communities, and men who love the game." During the playoffs, though, neutral minor officials are used. In the playoffs the men receive $60 a day expense money, and also get first-class transportation to the cities they're working. Under regular-season conditions they generally receive two tickets for every game, plus a nominal expense for parking and supper.

This unsung corps has its share of problems, pressures, and responsibilities, not all of them appreciated. Here's a closer look at just what they do.

The goal judges are the men in the glass booth, in the stands directly behind, and slightly above, the goaltenders on either side of the ice. They have only one job: to signal when they've seen the puck go completely over the goal line. That's the key: the puck must be completely over. Halfway in doesn't count, and if it touches the goal line it doesn't count. Anytime that puck crosses the line, the red light goes on. It's a goal if, for example, a goaltender takes the puck in his glove and draws his arm back—over the goal line—to throw the puck in play.

Although the league doesn't like to admit it, the goal judges have their blind spots. Not every judge's location is in exactly the same spot in each rink. Some might be higher than others. The most common blind spot has to do with perspective. It is virtually impossible for a goal judge to determine whether the puck is touching the line if it is only a fraction of an inch over the line. The judge would have to be over the cage, looking down, to see whether there's daylight between the puck and the line. One goal judge made an experiment in 1971 to see at what point he could actually see space between the line and puck from his vantage point. He couldn't tell until the puck was an inch clear of the line.

Another blind spot has to do with the physical structure of the cage. The top of the cage has a crossbar parallel to the goal line. It is supported by a vertical bar that runs the center of the top to the back support. If a puck rises and strikes underneath the vertical support and bounces out, the goal judge often can't tell whether the puck actually crosses the goal line.

Despite these difficulties, goal judges are amazingly accurate. Each sees upward of 20 shots a game, most of them coming at high speed while the fans are bellowing inches away from the judge. Many shots come in and go out so quickly the average fan hasn't even seen them pass the goal line. Indeed, many players don't even see such goals. One of the most bizarre flare-ups occurred because of a shot that hit a metal support in back and ricocheted back in play so swiftly the players believed the puck couldn't have made a goal.

It happened in a game in 1965 in New York. The Red Wings took a shot and the puck came back. The goal judge, Arthur Reichert, flipped the red-light switch indicating the goal had been scored. Emile Francis was the New Yorkers' general manager then, and he had a seat in the side arena. Francis refused to believe Detroit had scored. He dashed over to Reichert to argue the call, while Ranger players pounded their sticks on the protective glass that separated Reichert from the players. While Francis berated Reichert, two fans sitting nearby began to get on Francis, telling him to shut up. Soon, Francis was fighting with the fans. When the players saw what was happening they went in to help out Francis. The quickest way to get there was to scale the glass wall. And that's what they did. Half the team climbed over the glass in a bizarre scene.

By this time Reichert was merely a spectator. Players and fans were brawling, and Francis came out of it with a black eye. After the game the Rangers' president, William Jennings, was particularly angry. He said he was going to bar Reichert from the rink. The next day, however, the game films showed that Reichert had been correct. The goal had been scored. Jennings was told by Campbell that the league would decide if an official was to be relieved of duty, and Reichert remained. Six years later, the fans in the brawl were awarded $35,000 in damages from the Rangers.

Goal judges aren't always able to keep their jobs. The irascible Eddie Shore, the dictator of the Springfield Indians of the American League, ran his team and arena as he pleased. The visiting Cleveland Barons once scored a goal and Shore objected. He fired the goal judge on the spot. Shore, the iconoclast, replaced the judge with a state trooper who had walked in to keep warm. Shore was fined $1,000 by the league, but he never paid it. He never used the goal judge again, either.

It is impossible to recall any such goings on in the N.H.L.'s modern era. But in 1933, according to one story that may be legend, the now-defunct New York Americans tried to get "their man" as a goal judge against the Wings. The Americans were owned by Big Bill Dwyer, a bootlegger. Dwyer had bet heavily on his club for this game. He wanted to make sure his team won. So he installed one of his lieutenants as a goal judge, with the instructions that anything that touched the goal line would be considered a goal.

A dutiful employee, the goal judge was trigger-happy. But he signaled a goal for one shot that so obviously wasn't even near the line that Alex Connell, the Detroit goalie, stormed over to the judge. In those days, the judge wasn't separated by the protective glass. Connell punched the goal judge in the nose. That was a mistake. From out of the shadows grim-faced men emerged, hats pulled down over their eyes, prototypes of movieland mobsters. It took a police detail to take Connell safely away from the Garden and back to his hotel. The police remained with the player until he boarded his train for the ride back to Detroit.

Precautions are taken today that makes favoritism a thing of the past. Still, when it comes to goal judges it is a matter largely of faith. To try to achieve the fairest system, the league in 1970 required goal judges to switch stations every other game. Before the rule, judges would always work from the same end of the arena every game for years on end.

"I think the change is a good one," says one goal judge. "Where I used to sit I used to get the home team attacking on my side for two periods. Now, in one game I'll get them for two periods and the next game I'll get the visiting team for two periods. If there's any unconscious bias on my part, it'll work itself out."

The vast majority of goal judges are what might be termed "cage watchers." Their eyes are riveted on the cage during the action. "We used to be able to be 'puck watchers,'" says the goal judge. "But the slap shot changed all that. You just can't follow the puck when a fellow takes a slap shot at 100 miles an hour, and then some guy in front of the net tips it and changes the direction."

No matter which style is followed, the goal judge must be quick on the trigger—but not too quick. If a judge has a habit of keeping his finger on the switch that signals the red light, he might push it out of nervousness.

"It's best to stay away from the switch," says one goal judge. "This way you have the split second to think about what you've just seen. Then, if you're satisfied a goal has been scored, you reach out and flip the signal. You still can signal fast enough, but you've got a little extra time."

This goal judge keeps his hand on the switch only in the closing seconds of a period, and that only for a practical matter. Once the period ends, at the 20-minute mark, the red-light signal is locked. Of course, if a goal's scored with one second remaining it still counts—even though the red light might not be activated in time. But to avoid disputes, the goal judge is especially ready in the final seconds. If there is a score, he wants his goal signal to precede the buzzer that signals the end of the period.

The Maple Leafs have one of the senior goal judges in Eddie Mepham. For years he quietly and efficiently did his job. Then he blew a goal for the Leafs in a playoff game. The Toronto management tried to get him dismissed. Apparently, they hadn't noticed his "failings" until he missed a score for their side. The league, of course, refused to fire Mepham. By the next season the Leafs had forgotten their anger against Mepham and routinely submitted his name to again act as goal judge.

How accurate are the goal judges? Says one: "In 20 years I've been overrruled by the referee just twice. And one of those times I'd swear he was wrong."

The work of the official scorer, says a man who has been doing the job for 30 years, "is Mr. Campbell's baby." There are few areas of hockey that receive as much personal attention from the league president as the scoring summaries. It is one of the most difficult aspects of the sport. While there may be only a few occasions during the season when a goal judge has the only clear view of what has happened, in the vast majority of cases the referee and other players have seen the puck go in. But the official scorer has many more "iffy" decisions to make. He is in charge of properly crediting the goals, as well as assists. With so many sticks on the ice, and so many pairs of skates, it is a job demanding a high degree of concentration and judgment.

For example: The left wing passes to the center. The pass is slightly tipped by an opposing player, but the center is able to control the puck. He shoots and scores. Does the left wing receive an assist? The clue here is how significantly the opposing player touched the disk. It must be significant enough for the play's course to be altered, even if the opposing team doesn't get control. If, however, the deflection doesn't change the play, if it continues its course, then the official scorer should award the assist.

With so much going on at once, it seems an impossible task to remember who gave the puck to whom. But the official scorer cheats a little. He keeps notes. Actually, it's simply a series of numbers—the numbers of the players. Most of the scorers work this way: They write down the number of the player winning the face-off. The puck is passed to a teammate. His number is recorded. Another pass finds another teammate. That player's number is noted. Then the opposition intercepts.

A line is then drawn under the number of the last player who had the puck before the interception. Under the line the player for the team now in control has his number put down. The procedure is repeated. When a goal is scored the official scorer is the last word on who gets the goal. Once he has credited a player with a score, he merely rechecks his notes to determine which teammates, if any, receive assists. Little things such as numbers on sleeves make the official scorer's job easier. The chances are he knows all the players on his team. But if he can't spot the number on the back of a visiting player, he often can see an arm and get the number from there.

"It was easier before expansion," said one official. "We'd see the other teams seven times a year, and you pretty well knew what the line-up would be. It was easy to remember who was who. Now a few months can go by before you see a team. And if it's a new team, the chances are they've made a lot of personnel changes."

On a goal that the scorer might have missed—a tip-in during a pileup in front of the net—the referee will tell the scorer his version. Sometimes a player will notify the scorer who got the goal if the referee was screened.

No matter who gets credit, once the game is ended and the referee signs the scorer's sheet, no changes may be made. That's the way the goals and assists remain. Three copies are made of the scorer's sheet—one goes to Campbell, and one each to the opposing coaches. The sheets are official and not subject to change—even if films show a mistake has been made. The information it contains includes the name of the goal-scorers, the assists, the time of the goals, and how many home players and visiting players were on the ice for each goal.

The official scorer also is responsible for receiving the official line-ups—the starters and all other players eligible to see action—for both clubs before the game. Also, the line-ups must indicate which players are the captains and which ones wear the "A." The scorer then presents the line-ups to the referee.

During each quarter of the season, the scoring is analyzed. The league breaks down the ratio of assists to goals for every team on the road and at home. A club should average 1.65 assists for every goal it gets.

"Sometimes," says the league's executive director, Brian O'Neill, "a team gets heavy with assists at home. We bring it to the scorer's attention."

The league says a 6 percent variance in assists-ratio is acceptable. There have been many unsubstantiated stories about assists in

Boston and Montreal being awarded indiscriminately to local heroes. If that's happened, it doesn't happen very often. The league would crack down.

The occasions when a wrong goal is credited are virtually nonexistent. When a player has scored, he knows it. Usually, he can convince the referee or scorer. There is the odd time when a player won't say he's tipped in someone else's shot. But it would have to be a real special occasion—the other player going for a three-goal night, or a 30-goal season. Otherwise, players harbor their goals and assists and don't particularly like to give them away. If it's early in the season a player wants to make sure his goal counts. He may have a bonus arrangement with the club (say, $1,500 if he reaches 20 goals) and there's no way of knowing early in the campaign if he'll score 19 or 20.

The official scorer, of course, is aware of how important points are to a player and the league. The Art Ross Trophy goes to the overall point leader (goals and assists). It can be worth up to $2,-000 to one player. The overall winner receives $1,000. In addition, the leader for each half of the season earns $500 apiece.

"I don't mingle with the players," says one long-time scorer. "I've been asked out by the guys, but I avoid it. I don't want to be influenced, and I don't want the players to think they can influence me. As far as they're concerned, I'm just a guy in the stands who they don't know."

Common sense is all that separates opponents when they're in the penalty box. The box is the domain of the penalty timekeeper. In many cases he's working in older rinks where the penalty benches for both teams are separated only by an aisle. In those arenas that have penalty benches in separate areas, he usually has an assistant working in the visiting box.

The first thing the penalty timekeeper does when a penalty has been called is open the gate to let the penalized player in. Then he notes on his official sheet the name of the player, the infraction committed, the duration of the penalty, and the time of the penalty. The scoreboard displays the number of the player penalized, and the duration of the penalty. But the penalty timekeeper uses a back-up system. He has a stopwatch provided by the league. As soon as play resumes, he starts the watch.

During the penalty he is not too busy. He is, naturally, keeping an eye out for the players. In Montreal, opposing players sat a foot from one another. Besides the penalty timekeeper, a policeman was used to maintain order.

In the closing seconds of a penalty, the timekeeper alerts the player to be ready, and keeps a hand on the gate. The player must remain in the bench area until the penalty is over. Once the infraction has been served the player can return to the ice. Some slippery players, such as Mikita, try to get a foot over the side with one or two seconds remaining.

"You learn after a while which ones to watch," says a penalty timekeeper. "Most of them are pretty good about it. Occasionally, you'll get the guy who tries to grab some extra seconds."

Actually, players who are penalized are usually out of the action for a bit more than their prescribed time. Since the length of the penalty must be served in the box, it might take them a few seconds to get to where the action is. They must return to the ice —or to their bench—when the penalty is over. A team cannot make a substitute from its bench and direct the penalized player to remain in the penalty box.

Misconduct penalties and coincident major penalties aren't recorded on the scoreboard for the fans to see. Players who are caught for these infractions are not permitted to join the game when their time is up, unless there happens to be a play stoppage. The penalty timekeeper notifies the players when the end of their penalties is approaching, since they have no way of knowing. If, for example, a five-minute penalty has been served, but the puck is kept in play for 90 seconds after the penalty is over, the player must wait the entire time in the box.

There is only one time when a penalty timekeeper is concerned with the scoring. That is during a penalty shot. It is his duty to record in the penalty records any penalty shot awarded, the name of the player taking the shot, and the result of the shot.

To avoid ugly incidents because of mistakes on the scoreboard, the penalty timekeeper also is responsible that the penalties posted for the benefit of the public are correct. If they're wrong, he must report the mistake to the referee.

After the game, the penalty timekeeper's record is distributed to the official scorer for transmission to the league, and to the opposing coaches. The official sheet is used by the league in its statistical breakdown of penalties called by each referee, and to determine fines. Although the players don't relish being fined, they want to make sure the money turns up in the right place. All fines go into the Players' Emergency Fund, which is enriched by more than $30,000 a year.

Each third of the season the league compiles an exhaustive list of figures that it distributes to the news media and the clubs. The list is the same for newsmen as it is for the teams, with one exception: the plus and minus statistics. These figures go only to the teams. Although the clubs aren't hiding anything from the opposition, for some silly reason they don't want the figures made easily available to the public. Perhaps the clubs believe that if a player sees he's minus, he'll begin pressing, especially if everyone else on the team is plus. In any event it seems absurd. Since a player becomes plus or minus by what he does on the ice, then it's simply a question of doing some paperwork to arrive at the man's average. However, the average newsman doesn't always have time to stop and figure who's on the ice for a goal. He's busy taking notes on such things as who scored, the type of shot that was taken, the crowd reaction.

But the statistician has the time to make the proper notations. That's his job. He's in charge of the plus and minus figures—he notes the numbers of the players for each team who are on the ice for a goal. He's also in charge of recording and tabulating the players who take shots on goal.

If that were all there is to the job, any high school kid could do it. But it's more complex. It takes a good deal of judgment to decide whether a player has gotten off a legitimate shot on goal. Just because a goalie stops a shot doesn't necessarily mean a player receives credit for a shot. For example, if the puck is shot to the side of the net and the goalie deflects it away it is not a shot. It has to be in the 6 by 4 rectangle. By the same token, a high shot the goalie gloves isn't considered a shot "on goal."

Strange as it seems, not even all shots that a goalie stops—that would have gone in had he not been there—are counted as shots. If a player is killing a penalty, for example, and dumps the puck from his end 180 feet down ice, the statistician probably won't award a shot even if the puck is flush on goal. Also, if a player attempts to make a pass to a teammate, but the pass is too long and winds up hitting the goalie, the player won't be credited with a shot.

At one time, the league used the word "save." Every shot that would have gone in was credited as a save to the goalie. However, there was some confusion and some meaningless statistics. If a defenseman accidentally deflected the puck toward his own goalie, the goalie would be credited with a save. If a long pass happened to wind up on goal, it would also count as a save. But if, for example, the goalie left the crease and a defenseman backed him up and stopped a shot, there was no way that shot could be credited. Certainly, the goalie couldn't be credited with a save. So that shot went unrecorded.

The "shots-on-goal" statistics, then, are more meaningful. And also more accurate. A goal counts as a shot. But a puck that hits the post and doesn't go in doesn't count as a shot. It wasn't, after all, a shot that was good enough to have gone in. If a puck caroms off another player and hits the goalie, the shot doesn't count. But say a man takes a shot from the point. It hits a defenseman, who accidentally knocks the puck past his own goalie. Since a goal was scored, a shot must be credited. It goes to the man who shot the puck. In this case, the player at the point. But if the shot from the point hit an offensive player—even on the skate or the arm—and went in, then the player who deflected it in, even accidentally, receives the shot-on-goal credit.

Keeping track of the players on the ice is no easy job, but it's essential for the proper crediting of pluses and minuses. At any given moment, the statistician has recorded on a work sheet the numbers of the players on the ice for both squads. When there's a line change, the players who left are crossed off the sheets, and the numbers of the new players are added. Even when a goalie leaves the ice on a delayed penalty or in an empty-net situation late in the game, his number is crossed out and his replacement added.

During the playing, the statistician notes if the sides are at equal strength or which club is short-handed at any given moment. Then, if a goal is scored, he makes an appropriate notation. Some scorers use a circle to indicate a power-play goal, or an "X" to show it was a short-handed score.

When there's a bench-clearing fight situation, the referee doesn't always remember who was on the ice and who hopped off the bench. He has to know in order to mete out the appropriate penalties. A player who leaves the bench to fight is subject to a fine and a penalty. But if a player already is on the ice, he can only be penalized for any fighting he might engage in. So often the referee will consult with the statistician to get the names of the players who were legitimately on the ice when a brawl erupts.

"A lot of people aren't aware of how busy we are," says a statistician. "But I'll tell you—there's a lot of hustling involved in this job. Especially when you get a couple of quick goals. You're busy writing down the shot, the numbers of the players on for the goal. And just when you're ready to relax a little bit, the play starts, you've got to start writing who's on the ice, and then suddenly you've got another score to enter. It's not so simple as it seems."

Like the other minor officials, there's more to a game timekeeper's job than the title alone would indicate. He's got several important responsibilities.

The first—and perhaps only duty—we think of with this official is the operation of the scoreboard clock. Seconds can be critical in a game and it's essential that playing time be halted as soon as the referee's whistle blows. There have been a few instances in some rinks where the timekeeper is two or three seconds behind the play. A timekeeper for a home club that's winning could allow a precious few seconds to elapse toward the end of a game when a referee halts play for any reason. You don't hear of that happening much anymore. However, there was a major scandal in Montreal when a game timekeeper was coerced by a betting syndicate into allowing the clock to run under certain conditions. There is heavy betting in Quebec on the time a goal is scored. If the bookmakers found they had an unusually large number of bets on, for example, the 18-minute mark, they'd instruct the timekeeper to let the clock run for a few seconds if a goal was scored at that time.

Today's timekeepers have a set routine. His is the official time, even for the time of day. Thus, before a game he alerts the referee and each club how much time remains before the game should begin. Once the game is underway, time begins from the moment the referee drops the puck. We all see the seconds tick away on the electronic scoreboard. But the timekeeper also keeps a stopwatch running in case of a breakdown.

After 19 minutes of play—with one minute remaining in the period—it's the timekeeper's responsibility to notify the public-address announcer that the clubs are in the final minute of play. When a period ends, most rinks have an automatic buzzer or bell that sounds. But if a rink isn't so equipped, or if the machinery fails to function, the timekeeper is responsible for signaling the end of the period. Most timekeepers keep a battery-operated foghorn around for such emergencies.

The timekeeper also is responsible for the proper intermission time. In 1971 the league required all rinks to post intermission time on the scoreboard. It's a good idea and it keeps the fans informed how much time they've got left to get hot dogs or make phone calls or comb their hair. Once the period ends, the timekeeper punches the proper buttons and the scoreboard shows 15 minutes of intermission. It is the scorekeeper's job to make sure the intermission doesn't run beyond the 15 minutes. With three minutes remaining in intermission, he notifies the major officials and the clubs. With about a minute remaining, he again tells the officials and teams how much time they've got.

At the end of the game the timekeeper has to be pretty quick. Once the last second has been played, he must lock the timing device. This also shuts off power to the goal judges' cages, and prevents the goal light from flashing. Once the period, or the game, ends, a green light goes on, next to the red goal light. It is essential to have a visible light. Players and coaches can see when the game has ended, and can't complain if a puck goes in once the green light has flashed.

5 | What You Don't See

Training Camp

For one month each autumn, towns such as Guelph, Kitchener, and Oshawa become big-league cities. They are the training-camp sites for N.H.L. teams. Only three American clubs—Chicago, Detroit, and St. Louis—stage their camps in the United States.

There are several reasons why the remainder of the N.H.L. clubs—most of them based in the States during the regular season—go to Canada to rehearse for the long season. Virtually every city of any size in Canada has a rink with big-league dimensions. They usually have big-league accommodations, too. Americans would be surprised to see how well-maintained the local rinks are north of the border. After all, for many small towns the local junior team is the equivalent of a major-league football or baseball team.

Another factor that draws clubs to Canada is tradition. Since everyone else is training there, you might as well go, too. It's easier to schedule exhibition games if you're close to one another. In 1971, for example, six teams were within 100 miles of each other.

A third consideration is this: It's easier to keep tabs on players in small towns. There are fewer diversions. The players stay together. If teams trained in their hometowns, it could be difficult to control all the players. Even when a club does prepare in its own city—Toronto does—the Maple Leafs stay in the same hotel. They use it as their home base for the duration of camp.

One general manager says: "I've got spies all over town where we train. Bartenders, waiters, people like that. They feel they're part of a hockey organization if they can tip me off about what some guy's doing wrong. Actually, I don't even need the spies. People are funny. They'll come running to you when they hear a rumor or see someone breaking training."

More than 60 players report to camp, most of them in car pools. Wives, of course, aren't permitted. That's not to say that in some cases they don't come and are deposited at a nearby motel. One star player even took his girl friend along and shared a room with her. To compound matters, he took her swimming at the motel pool. Luckily for him, the coach never went near the water.

The players arrive the day before camp opens. The only equipment they have is a pair of skates, which are club property. In today's hockey, all the players have done some preparation for camp by skating the preceding few weeks. Many players work at summer camps instructing youngsters, so they're in shape. Others will rent out a rink along with other players—even on opposing teams—for a few hours a week to prepare for the training-camp grind. The first thing to know about a training camp is that it isn't a health farm. Players are ordered to report in shape. Most clubs distribute an exercise and diet plan when the season is over, and the players are told to follow a specific regimen over the summer months.

The first day is banal and time-consuming, having little to do with the game of hockey. It is given over to picture-taking and medical examinations. The photographs usually are taken at two different places—a studiolike setup for the "head" shots, and the rink for the simulated action pictures. The first-day activities find the players posing for their head shots. A clue can often be found here. The general manager doesn't want to waste expensive color film on players he doesn't think will make his squad. So he usually instructs his photographer which players should be shot in black-and-white as well as color, and which players in black-and-white only. If a player sees the photographer shoot with two different cameras, then he's got a pretty good idea that the general manager believes he can make the squad.

The photographs are used in the team's yearbook, which contain the black-and-white shots. The color pictures are reserved for the club programs, or perhaps magazine requests. The complete squad's photos are shipped to all the newspapers and television stations in the team's area, as well as the league's office. During the course of the season the club will distribute hundreds of photographs to various organizations. Whenever a player speaks before any group, he takes along a few dozen photographs to hand out.

The medical examination includes an X-ray, taken at a nearby hospital, and a urine analysis. Cheevers of the Bruins says that he and several teammates cheat when it comes to preparing a urine sample. They take from other players. One season one player provided three others with urine samples. Their specimens came out negative, but the player was ordered back for a retest when his own sample didn't pass inspection.

That first night there generally is a team meeting, at which the coach, the general manager, the scouting staff, and the players get together. Nothing really dramatic takes place. The coach must apprise the players of curfew rules—usually 11 P.M. He tells them such things as: get an alarm clock, don't give broken sticks to kids (thousands of youngsters will start bothering the players), be well-groomed. Whenever clubs travel players must wear suits and ties. And of course the coach will talk about "desire being 90 percent of the game," and "we want players who give out 110 percent."

It isn't unusual for half the players to report to camp without being signed. Under a new ruling, all protected players and those who appeared in 50 or more N.H.L. games during the previous season may not be in camp if they're not signed. During camp, then, the general manager is a busy man. He's arranging appointments for dozens of players to discuss contract. Those players who are signed receive a flat payment of $600 for the exhibition schedule of 10 games—or $60 a game. Camp may not begin more than 30 days before the team's first regular-season game, and protected players and those who appeared in 50 games the season before may not be kept in camp longer than 28 days. Many clubs used to have a training table, at which they'd receive all their meals. But so many players complained about the quality, and lack of variety, that the Players' Association was able to do away with the table. Instead, each player receives $12 a day in meal money. At Canadian prices—a filet mignon costs about $5 in a restaurant—it's an adequate allowance.

The Players' Association is pretty suspicious. Perhaps it has reason to be. Before 1971, every player received $100 for an exhibition game played against N.H.L. opposition in an N.H.L. city. But for all other games, the players would receive only $25. The association charged that coaches or general managers often kept its proven players out of the $100 games. Supposedly, the players were paid only $25 in other games because those contests didn't bring much money. But many exhibitions have been staged in the 12,000-seat arena in Winnipeg, and sold out. The majority of players benefitted from the new exhibition ruling. In 1971, for example, the Kings played only three $100 games. Under the old system, the players who saw action in all 10 games would have received only $475, compared to the new rate of $600.

On the eve of the first practice, the workout schedule is posted. If it's a big camp, there'll be as many as three different groups, each working two shifts a day. The first group, about 30 players, will consist of the regulars, top minor-league prospects, and top junior prospects. These are the players with the best chance of making the team. The second group is composed of players from the high minor leagues, or holdovers who aren't accorded a chance to make the club this time around. The third group contains players from the low minors, low draft choices, and amateur players seeking tryouts.

A typical schedule will have the first group on the ice from 7:30 A.M. to 9 A.M., then from 1:30 P.M. to 2:30 P.M.—90 minutes in the morning before breakfast, an hour in the afternoon after lunch.

The morning of the first day of camp is an adventure for the kids of the town. It is a drag and dreary for the veterans. It is a nerve-racking time for the rookies. Even though school is open, dozens of youngsters troop into the arenas. Most of the buildings are strictly functional. They are steeply sloped (almost like a cock-fighting amphitheater) and small. There are perhaps 5,000 seats. Usually, city officials will attend the workouts, as well as a score of policemen and firemen and mailmen. It is a tremendous source of civic pride to land a National Hockey League club, even for a short while. In 1970 the Rangers spent a few days in Brantford, Ontario, late in the season, preparing for a big game against Detroit. More than a thousand school-age children—half of the city's school system—cut classes to attend the workout. They were all excused if they could show they had cut to see the Rangers.

When the Jones & Laughlin Steel Corporation of Pittsburgh wanted to thank the residents of Kirkland Lake, Ontario, for their help in working a major iron ore mine, the company thought of a suitable present to give the town: A seven-ton stainless monument to the 35 N.H.L. players who hail from Kirkland Lake. There are only 15,000 residents in the city. Obviously, Jones & Laughlin knew what turned them on.

But when it comes to training, one town looks just like another as far as the players are concerned. After entering the chilly building, the first thing they do after getting undressed is step on the scale. It is their first ritual.

The coach has a good idea of the weight he wants his players to report at. Chronic weight problems can be dealt with severely. Some marginal players have been cut outright if they haven't shown the coach that they tried to contain themselves during the off-season. When Boom Boom Geoffrion was an assistant general manager with New York, one of his duties was scale-watching. As each player stepped up, the Boomer jotted down the player's weight. He was a hard taskmaster. Players would argue over a few ounces. If the scale showed a shade over 190, Geoffrion would put down "191."

Sometimes a player would lean on the wall with one hand and hope to shave a pound. "They can't fool me," said Geoffrion. "I used to play, too. Remember?"

There's a rush of applause as the players take the ice for the first time. In the dressing room they appear lean and not very big. In their uniforms, wearing their skates, they seem almost monstrous. The shift will be broken down into two squads—the whites and the blues. For a normal 30-man shift, each club will have 15 players. There will be two goalies, four defensemen, and nine forwards. But they're not ready to play just yet. First come the exercises.

The most common muscle problems early in camp are referred to quite charmingly as "the groins." The groin muscle is most easily damaged when a skater isn't used to stretching. So the players start off slowly, all the while under the tutelage of their coach. Occasionally, a team might employ a physical-education instructor. The Maple Leafs under Imlach once recruited a Royal Canadian Air Force fitness teacher, who instructed the players from a platform. One day he fell off the platform and broke an arm. The Leafs went back to the old methods.

There are some traditional loosening-up exercises. In one routine the players move forward, raising first one leg to chest level then the next. It is almost a drum majorette's step, a prance on ice. And the first moans are heard. There are other exercises, including one in which the players wave their sticks over the ice, bending forward, as though searching for a contact lens. Through all the moving exercises they keep their sticks with them. Soldiers with their guns. Every movement on the ice is made with the sticks in their possession. The sticks get dropped to their sides, though, for the calisthenics. These include hip rotation, stretching, toe-touching, and push-ups. Many of the players slump back, exhausted. But the day is young. Now they must do some real skating.

If there is one basic exercise in hockey—one that is carried through the entire season—it is the end-to-end rush. Consider that a rink is 200 feet long—nearly 70 yards. The players must dash to one end—and come back again. And they must do it as if they mean it. It is in such situations that the rookie, or the mediocre player, can show he's trying a little harder. The skaters are sent off in waves: first one line, then another and another, then the defensemen, then the goalies. All the while they're holding their sticks. The younger players are trying to show up the older ones, whose jobs they covet. They know the scouts in the stands, and the coach at ice level, will be watching them, alert for that "110 percent" effort.

"You always feel that they're watching you," says Sheldon Kannegiesser, a young Pittsburgh defenseman. "It's as though you got to prove something just by skating. But you better do it. If you don't, someone else will be trying to show you up."

Andre (Moose) Dupont, a rather large, beefy defenseman, had a ridiculously high number of penalty minutes in the Central League. He didn't have much finesse, though. He knew it, too. "I know why they bring me up," he said. "They want me to hit." In training camp Dupont didn't bother hitting forwards. He zeroed in on defensemen. "They're the guys whose job I want," Dupont admitted. "What good does it do me to look sensational hitting a forward? I must make another defenseman look bad."

On the afternoon of the first day there are more drills. On many teams, the players still haven't touched a puck. It is held in abeyance by the coach, a reward. When the players weigh in again after their first workout, some have lost as much as five pounds. And that's without body contact.

By the second day, the coach will allow the players to shoot the puck. It isn't done in helter-skelter fashion. The "blues" take one half of the ice and the "whites" the other half. The shooters station themselves at the blue line, the goalie gets set in his cage. Down the line, machine-gun fashion, each skater takes a shot. The veterans know that they must keep their shots low. There's no sense in injuring your own goalie. It takes a few days before a goaltender gets accustomed to the blasting. Rookies often disregard the orders of the coach. They want to get goals.

Slap-shot exercises may be followed by the first line rushes of camp. In the dressing room the coach has posted the alignments —for forwards and defensemen. This is the first inkling the players have as to who they might be playing with. The rookies especially are curious. If they're teamed with seasoned players, they can look that much better.

It is still difficult for a rookie to break in. But he isn't subject to the mental torment that used to greet first-year men. In the days of a six-team league there weren't that many jobs to go around. About 120 players were in the big leagues. Each selfishly protected his position. A rookie had to be something special to crack the line-up. Because of the simpler times, the regulars were a much closer unit than they are today. There were virtually no outside financial interests. After a game or a workout, they'd pal around together. Because of train travel, they were thrown together for extended stretches. Players also married later, so there were a considerable number of bachelors on each team.

"I remember when Edgar Laprade came to the Rangers," says Shero. "He was the best player in camp. But you would have thought he was an outcast. The other players were forever bumping into him. Even when he went into the locker room, the players would elbow past him. He was a rookie."

When Lafleur cracked the Canadiens' starting line-up as a rookie in 1971, he became the first player with Montreal to make the jump from the junior ranks since Henri Richard accomplished the feat in 1955. Players from the juniors just didn't make it as a regular. But in the 1971–72 season, the top five draft choices made the leap successfully. Because of expansion, the teams need more bodies.

Despite their press clippings, though, the rookies still must prove themselves. When Juha Widing came up for a big-league tryout he was attempting to take away Orland Kurtenbach's job. Widing was born in Finland and played his hockey under international rules, where there was less checking.

"In every league I played in since I came to Canada they were always testing me," said Widing. "I used to skate with my head down. I learned pretty quickly to keep it up. They would hit me. Everything here is hitting. These kids have it put into their heads when they're seven years old."

During the first scrimmages of training camp, Widing's line was pitted against Kurtenbach's. At every opportunity Kurtenbach took a run at the rookie. He couldn't catch him, though. Widing was younger and faster. He made the team.

The scrimmages don't begin in camp until the various lines have had the opportunity to play together. Usually, the coach will send out a three-man line rush against a pair of defensemen. It's a 3-on-2 situation and the forwards should be able to look good in this sequence. The coach gets an idea of how the line shapes up. With 3-on-2 the forwards can move unhampered, and it's easy to see if the three players can keep up with one another, and how they handle the puck in relationship to each other.

The coach also can gain some insight into the workings of his defense. He looks to see how the defenders react to being out-manned, especially if the rookies are keeping their heads and making the right plays.

By the third day the players ache. The cure is more work. This is the point where skating no longer is fun. Every year the players know that the third day means pain—probably more discomfort than they'll have at any time during the year. But it is also the first day of real scrimmaging, when the blues and the whites will be playing games and the staff in the stands will be writing down impressions and filling in columns of pluses and minuses, shots, face-offs, and saves. Scouts smile when they see players brawl in training camp. "That's what you like to see," says one. "It shows you that they're trying."

Except for the proven lines and defensive tandems, the coach will experiment. If a player looks good with one center, the coach might try the player with a different center. If a rookie defenseman appears sharp with a veteran, the young defenseman might be placed with another rookie to see if he continues to look good.

It's surprisingly fast, but after the fourth or fifth day of camp the coach has a pretty good idea of his team. The first exhibition game usually is staged a week after camp opens and it is remarkable to see how well the players perform after four or five months (depending on whether the club was in the playoffs) of living away from the ice. There are few surprises in game situations. The scrimmages give the coach and staff a good idea of who can do what. Perhaps that's why the scrimmages are so tough, and the scouts coo when they see someone taking a run at a teammate, or even fighting. Perhaps there is something to be said for "desire" and those other intangibles hockey people are forever talking about.

The Routine

The reporter was sitting in the press box in May, covering a Stanley Cup game. Outside it was 80 degrees. Inside the ice was melting. "What the hell am I doing here at this time of year?" the reporter wondered. Imagine how the players felt.

Hockey's season probably is the longest in sports. For a team that goes to the playoff finals it is eight months long, including training camp. For many teams, the only day off they give their players is Monday. And even a Monday doesn't mean a complete day of rest for a team that has just played a game on either coast and then is traveling home. Say the Seals play a Sunday game in Boston. They'll usually sleep over, and leave the next morning. Even benefitting from the time difference, they're not in their homes until the early afternoon. If a club is returning home from the West Coast after a Sunday game, it also sleeps over. It doesn't arrive home until late Monday afternoon.

According to League rules a team may not leave for a game the same day, except in special circumstances due to weather. The one exception is the short trip between Philadelphia and New York. This means that every club leaves the day before for a road game. Say it's a Tuesday and the Canadiens are going to meet the Bruins the next night in Boston. The Canadiens will stage a workout at the Forum in Montreal. Then they'll have lunch. They'll meet at the airport a half-hour before departure time, usually in late afternoon, and take the plane to Boston.

By the time they arrive in Boston it is suppertime. Their curfew is 11 P.M. That means that, according to the rules, the most entertainment they can hope for is a movie. They usually have breakfast at 9:30 the morning of a game. In 1970 their daily meal allowance on the road was $16. By 1973—74 it will go up to $18. If the club provides a meal on Game Day, the allowance is cut in half. After breakfast there'll be a team meeting at the rink, followed by an optional skate. When Toe Blake was coaching, players rarely exercised their option. Everyone showed up. On most teams the second-stringers and rookies are certain to skate in these light sessions.

Sometimes the meetings are boring. Sometimes the players learn something. It isn't unusual for a coach to go over shooting strategy against a particular goalie. Some netminders are weak on their glove side, some on their stick side. Some goalies can't stop high shots, others may have poor footwork on the low drives. Players say that under heated game conditions they can't always aim the puck. Sometimes they just swipe at it. But if a player has a breakaway he can have time to shoot to the goalie's weakness. Also, when a player shoots from the point he has a bit more time and can try to follow his coach's advice.

Coaches don't try to psych up their players at these noon meetings. There's too much time before the game begins and the effect would be lost. But they do try to establish a sort of game plan, as much as it's possible to achieve one in the fast sport. For example, if a club is going to try a defensive style—only sending in one man with the puck—it doesn't decide to do it on a whim. The strategy is discussed in advance.

One coach likes to use money as an incentive. Before a game a few years ago he offered an interesting bonus: If the Canadiens' Tremblay lost his helmet that night, the player who knocked it off would receive a $100 bonus. Now, the coach didn't come right out and say "Let's bully Tremblay." But the players received the message.

After the meeting the players have what they refer to simply as "the steak." That means lunch. During critical situations, such as the playoffs, the team usually will eat together in a private room of their hotel or motel. Other times, however, they're on their own. The steak is followed by a nap. Somehow the players manage to sleep the afternoon of a game, a ritual they've followed from their junior days.

Ninety minutes before game-time they meet in the lobby for the bus ride to the rink. A half-hour before the game begins they go on the ice for their 15-minute pregame warm-up. When the game is over, they take the team bus to the airport for their next destination.

That's it. They've been in a town a little more than 24 hours and probably don't have one recollection about it, except for the game. Their life has revolved around the hotel. Their impressions of the city have been gleaned from the waitresses or autograph-seekers in the lobby. In that 24-hour span they've taken two substantial flights, been in three hotels, three airports, and, for the most part, have been bored.

Perhaps the loneliest member of the club is the coach. Many of them are former teammates of the men they now control. They used to socialize. But once a coach leaves the playing ranks, he must keep his distance. When Doug Barkley coached the Red Wings, just a few years after an eye injury had cut short his Detroit career, he found himself the boss of several close friends, including Howe and Delvecchio.

"It's a lonely life on the road," Barkley admitted. "On the one hand you know some of the guys real well. You used to go out with them. Suddenly you're in a different position. You can't let yourself get too close with the guys."

Imlach often calls up reporters traveling with the team and asks them out to lunch, or for a postgame drink if the club is staying over. Billy Reay of the Hawks is another who sees more newsmen than players away from home. Reay, an easygoing sort, is also careful to avoid embarrassing his players. Sometimes when he goes into a bar he'll ask a reporter to take a peek in first to see whether there are any players around. On one occasion the reporter looked in and discovered one of the club's skaters dancing on the bar. Reay was ushered elsewhere.

Some coaches also will ask someone to walk into the hotel lobby first if it's past curfew. They don't want to be in the position of discovering a late player and then fining him. There are coaches, though, who keep spies around—the trainer, or a scout —to sit up late in the lobby and note who strolls in past curfew. One coach had a bad drinker who he could never seem to catch. About 2 A.M. he was awakened by the security guard. The guard led him to the office, where the player was standing in his underwear.

"I finally got ya," screamed the coach. "What the hell did you do this time?" The guard interjected: "No, you've got it wrong. His room was just robbed and he ran out to catch the burglar. He caught him, too."

At home the players' lives are quite different. For one thing, they live in their own homes or apartments. Since most players are married, their curfew is self-imposed. How many couples, after all, stay up until two in the morning during the week? Of course, the situation is different for the bachelors.

Let's take an example of a few days at home: The club has just finished a Sunday night game. If they're in Montreal or Toronto they're spread out, many of them living in permanent year-round homes. But in a city such as New York, practically all the players live in Long Beach, Long Island. It's a summer community on the water. That means that houses are available for winter rental. Okay, the players have Monday off. There is an exception—if the club has really floundered Sunday night and miffed the coach, he might want to stage a rare Monday practice. But that's highly unusual. So the club next skates on Tuesday. These workouts usually begin late morning and last for 90 minutes.

The severity and length depend on the coach and his methods. During Ned Harkness's short tenure as coach of the Red Wings, he expected his players to whoop it up in the locker room —before practices.

"You can't pull that kind of thing with pros," said Frank Mahovlich. "Maybe that worked with college kids at Cornell. But who ever heard of shouting it up before a practice?"

Before Harkness took over, the easygoing Sid Abel was the coach. Abel was still the general manager when Harkness arrived. Harkness spoke to Abel about practice. "Don't worry—things fall into place," Abel assured him. "Well," said Harkness sometime later, "things don't fall into place. You have to work damn hard to make sure they do." Part of Harkness's technique was something he called "constant motion." He demanded that his players in workouts always be moving, always thinking ahead to the next possible play. And with it he tried to bring along the college spirit that had made him the most successful collegiate hockey coach in history. It didn't work out, although in fairness to Harkness it should be noted that he didn't have the club for that long to find out whether his ideas would work. Before the season was a month old Abel told management: "Either he goes or I go." Abel went, and Harkness moved up to the general manager's post.

Some skating workouts are held almost as classroom exercises. Red Kelly, for example, is continually halting play to stress key aspects of the game, or to point out mistakes a player has been making. Francis is another who believes teaching is a key element to success. "Sometimes I get bored listening to the same stuff all the time," says the Rangers' Rod Gilbert. "But I guess it's good for the new kids. It really sinks in after a while."

There are some coaches, however, who merely believe a workout is just that. The players skate, take some practice shots, and that's it. Boston and Chicago have operated that way for years, and are tremendously successful. If it works, it must be right for them.

When the Tuesday workout is over, the players again go their separate ways. That is one reason why a few coaches believe it's easier to keep a team together on the road. Some players also say there's less pressure when you're away from home. Since hockey players are young marrieds, they have young families. That means 4 A.M. bottle feedings. It means all the things that having a family obligates the breadwinner to do—errands, shopping, home repairs. On the road there are no family squabbles and few distractions.

"The average fan isn't concerned about whether you've got a cold or if you had a hard day at home," says Reg Fleming. "You can't go to the middle of the ice before a game and shout, 'Hey, I'm sorry, folks, I don't feel well tonight.' All the fan knows is that he's paid his money and he wants to see you play your best."

On the day of the game some home-team coaches prefer their players to grab their afternoon nap together in a hotel. The coach will stage a light skate at noon, have the meeting, send the players out to lunch, and then shepherd them under the same roof. This procedure may be varied if a club returns home from a game one night and has another game the following night. The team might not even spread out and return to its individual homes. It often heads straight for a hotel.

When the players arrive at the rink they expect their uniforms to be bright and clean, their sticks in the proper slot, their skates with a fine edge. It has all been attended to by the man with the most hectic routine on the club—the trainer.

Ironically, the "training" or physical-conditioning aspects of the trainer's job are among the least of his duties. There is a doctor in attendance at every big-league rink and all clubs have at least one physician on a retainer.

The trainer fills several major roles, though. Often he is the confidant, the buffer who will listen to a player's problems. He is the mother hen watching over his brood and he can pick up a player's quirks, or unhappiness, faster than the coach can. The trainer is always with the players in the locker room, where he can sense a shift in mood. The coach usually appears in the room only for pregame or intermission talks.

By the time a team appears for a game at night, the trainer already has spent a full day at the rink. Let's say that the club played the night before on the road. When the game was over the players stuffed their road uniforms into outsize satchels, which contain enough room for the skates, the padding, the protective gear, and the uniforms. The trainer and his assistant are charged with getting the 20 bags, as well as the sticks, on board the bus then onto the plane. When the club arrives home, the trainer gathers up the substantial load and takes it over to the rink, where he stores it. Then he goes home for a night's sleep.

The next morning, however, he's got some things to do. First, he launders all the road wearing apparel. All rinks are equipped with washing machines, and many have dryers. Then he hangs out the club's home uniforms. These have been thrown in the dryer after the previous home games. He counts the number of sticks for each player. The number of the player is on each handle, and the trainer wants to make sure there are at least three of a player's model on hand. The trainer also is aware of every player's particular stick model. In case he runs out of one player's stick, he can substitute the stick of a teammate who has the identical model.

Then there's skate-sharpening. Every rink is equipped with a blade sharpener, and this is a particularly critical job for a trainer. At the speeds the skaters move, a rough edge on a blade can have disastrous consequences. Many trainers bring their own sharpening gear on the road for any little emergencies that might crop up. But all trainers do the sharpening, or leave it to a trusted aide. In hockey's more primitive days it wasn't unusual for a rival trainer to chop up the blades on the other players' skates. The trainers today don't take chances.

A trainer also is busy with needle and thread. Darning is an important aspect of his job. When players collide along the boards, it's easy to snag a shirt. When there's a fight, there's certain to be a major sewing job required.

Late in the afternoon, just before the players arrive, the home-team trainer performs another ritual: He freezes the pucks. About 20 will be used during the game and they must be cold in order to achieve a truer bounce. Just a few years ago a dozen pucks were enough for a game. But the slap shot came along and the force of its ricochet often carries the disk into the stands and into the hands of spectators.

As he waits for the players, perhaps the trainer checks out his kit, an elephantine doctor's satchel. It opens to reveal a bizarre and wonderful assortment of patent medicines, home remedies and tools. The kit weighs more than 20 pounds. One trainer has some bottles quaintly labeled "pain" and "shits." There are muscle salves and creams, jellies and lotions. There are liquids that prevent you from sweating, there are some to bring heat to an injured area of the body. There are rolls of bandages and tape, scissors and pills in blue, green, and pink.

One of his most important tools is a tongue forceps, which the trainer keeps in his pocket at all times. Because of the jarring collisions on the ice, players can be hit so violently that they swallow their tongue. The tongue forceps is used to retrieve the tongue.

As the players troop in, the trainer is quick to gauge their mood.

"There are times when you know you can joke around," says one trainer. "But sometimes you can see the guys are dead serious, like for some special game. You don't want to set the mood yourself. You've got to follow it. So if I see the guys are kidding with each other, then I'll join in. If I see they want to be left alone, then I'll leave them alone."

In these pregame situations the trainer also is aware of an important phase of their lives—superstitions. "Now take my goalie," says the trainer. "He doesn't want me to get his stick. He doesn't want anyone to touch his stick. Just him. I don't even want to go near the stick. But the funny thing is, there are some guys on this team who think it's good luck for me to handle their sticks. In fact, they'll tell me to hand it to them for luck."

There is an unwritten rule about superstitions: You don't tamper with them. Some players like to be the last to leave the room, or to leave the ice. The other players don't intentionally linger. "I make sure my guys are out of the room before this particular player, who insists on being last. Why should I let anything bother him? I don't think it makes a bit of difference. But he does, so that's good enough for me."

During the course of the game, the trainer must know where everything is. He's got a collection of high-energy liquid drinks in plastic containers which have a straw connected to the top. He's got a bunch of towels. He's got enough extra sticks handy so that every player has at least two replacements. The sticks are arranged numerically in a rack. They're easier to find this way.

In the intermission period minor scratches, aches, and equipment repair are attended to. "I've got one guy who insists his skates always need sharpening," says one trainer. "During the intermission I take his skates in the next room, so he can't see me. Then I turn on the machine. But I don't do a thing to them. Then I bring him back the skates. The guy looks at them and says 'fine.' They're absolutely the same, but he thinks I improved them for him and they don't bother him. What's the harm?"

When a game is over the trainer rarely has even an hour to get everything put away for the club's next game. If it's leaving for a road game the differently colored road uniforms have already been packed. He usually adds a few extra jerseys, though. There might be a player trade, or perhaps a replacement will come up from the minors.

There is one part of the routine the trainers don't have to worry about—putting on the uniform. It is a laborious task that players have mastered. The goalie has the most time-consuming job of all. Including workouts, he probably spends 200 hours—the equivalent of 25 working days—putting on and taking off his uniform from training camp to the playoffs.

The goalie's equipment is the most expensive in sport—it costs about $550. It includes a $70 pair of skates and a $100 fiberglass mask, and a chest protector, overstuffed pads, special reinforced inner and outer jocks. It's no wonder that it takes a goalie anywhere from 30 to 45 minutes to get dressed. Because he is standing so much, the goalie's skate blades are flatter than the other skaters'. They use a semi-rocker blade which is important for turning but not so good for standing in place.

The average forward or defenseman can get dressed in as little as 15 or 20 minutes. He is, after all, only wearing $300 worth of equipment. Many players today wear helmets, and a good one costs the club $20.

When a game is over, they're able to peel off the layers of

leather in nothing flat. But they're not quite ready to receive the press. Most coaches close the locker-room door for five or 10 minutes when a game is over. Especially after a defeat. A loss drains a player in hockey, perhaps more than in any other sport. The coach wants his players to unwind. He also wants to make sure the bothersome job of equipment-collecting is taken care of before newsmen come in, upsetting the routine. More than one coach has said, too, that he wants a rest period so his players can compose their thoughts. In the excitement following a game a player might say something he'll regret later.

The postgame routine works something like this: The coach will be the first outside the dressing room, usually within a few minutes. He'll talk to the newsmen for five or six minutes, and then tell them it's okay to interview the players. Some players spend all their postgame time in the shower room avoiding newsmen. Bobby Orr stays in the trainer's room on many occasions, waiting until the reporters have gone.

Most of the players accept the questions as a part of hockey life. But after the questions the players face another obstacle between themselves and a night's rest: the fans. Autograph hunters somehow have a grapevine from which they learn the hotels players are staying at, or which exits from the arenas players use. Yet, a player such as Bobby Hull will stand for a half-hour after a game giving autographs.

"It's part of being a public figure," says Hull. "Where would I be without the fans?"

The Media

Perhaps because hockey is an alien game in the majority of the cities it's played in, the quality and the extent of the coverage given the N.H.L. varies so widely. But first, it is necessary to make some differences known: "Media" merely crops together all the news-disseminators. It includes the reporters who work for morning and afternoon newspapers, the magazine writers, the sports journal writers, the television game broadcasters and the television announcers, the radio men who cover the game, those who report the scores, and those who work for 1,000-watt FM stations. All these men have distinct functions, and all have different relationships with the players, the coaches, and management. Often, the various "media" people have no relationship to one another, physically or spiritually. Indeed, they're often at war.

The most uneasy relationship between players and media men is that between athlete and daily newspaper reporter. They share an unreal world. They see lots of one another on the road, often eating together. They take the same flights together. Yet, the relationship always is guarded, especially on the players' part. Ultimately, the writer is there to interview and to write about how well the players performed. The writer always is—or always should be—a critic.

When Terry Sawchuk reported to training camp on the first day, a reporter extended a hand and introduced himself. Before he could finish saying his name, Sawchuk waved him away, saying "No questions. No questions."

The fact that he must ask questions, at a time when the player doesn't always feel like answering them, puts the daily newspaper reporter in the sometimes difficult position he finds himself. No one likes to be questioned after they've made a mistake. Imagine how a hockey player feels after a hard loss to be asked what happened, or why he blew a certain play. This leads to the favorite retort of angry players or coaches: "That's a dumb question." Actually, there are few dumb questions. It's just that in the context of the moment they might seem trivial. For example, a goalie gets a shutout. "How does it feel?" is the question most often asked. Think about it. Is it really so dumb? The public wants to know how the goalie feels.

The difficulty in writing about hockey is that virtually all reporters in the United States came to it late in their careers. For many of them their first exposure to the game came as a working newsman, when they had to write about a game they'd never seen before and barely understood. So they're going to make mistakes, and they're going to appreciate the wrong things and look over aspects of the game that should be reported. On the other hand, this doesn't mean that every writer in Canada is an expert just because he's covering his country's national game. Certainly no one believes that every writer in the States who covers football, basketball, or baseball is an expert just because he's grown up with these pastimes. But there is a suspicion on the part of Canadian players when they appear in United States cities that the reporters there don't know as much as their own newspapermen.

Players also used to complain about the amount of coverage newspapers in the States gave hockey. They forgot one simple fact: hockey vies with football and basketball for most of its season, and now overlaps baseball. The public would rather read about those other sports. Hockey is the fourth most popular sport in a four-sport nation. In Canada, what other major sports are there? Only the Canadian Football League, which has fewer than a dozen clubs. Toronto, for example, doesn't have a major-league basketball or baseball team. But Chicago has major-league teams in every sport, including soccer.

Because hockey players usually feel more comfortable with Canadian writers than those in the States, some strange situations develop. There is one N.H.L. coach, for example, who wouldn't dare tell his city's writers, many of them new to the game, the same things he tells Canadian writers, or others who have been around. Once he made a trade for a marginal defenseman, but quickly boosted the player as one of the finest available. The only people fooled were the writers in his own city. In other words, he could "snow" the fellows who weren't so knowledgeable.

To help promote hockey coverage many clubs pay the way of newspapermen covering the team. One wonders how a reporter can remain responsible to the public and still permit the team to take care of his expenses. The clubs not only pay the transportation, but also take care of hotel bills and give the reporters "walking around money." Some of the largest papers in the United States accept this free ride. One major newspaper had a reporter who was habitually drunk, and he knew nothing about hockey. As a matter of course, the club would bring along its public relations man on the road, who would knock out the reporter's story. The club even paid the costs of Western Union transmission.

Very few of the reporters covering a hockey team even get to training camp, in contrast with the regulars who cover baseball, football, or basketball. Perhaps because of the distance—most of the camps are in Canada, and far removed from the cities where the team will play during the season—most newspapers give short shrift to training-camp coverage. That's unfortunate. Training camp is where a newcomer to hockey can learn more about the game in two weeks than a whole season of coverage. He's able to get to players in relaxed moments, he sees a club being formed, there's time to talk to scouts and management.

But what happens if he hasn't been to training camp? And he doesn't go to workouts? If he writes for a morning newspaper, it usually means his deadline is approaching pretty quickly after a game. It means he doesn't have time to go to the dressing room for clarification. He's got to write what he thinks he saw, without benefit of investigation. Or perhaps he's just got time to talk to the coach, who are past masters at allowing neophytes to know just what they want them to. How many times have we read hometown stories complaining about the officiating—against the hometown team? A coach can blame a referee for a missed infraction. He throws in a curse word or two, and it makes a good quote. He's quoted in the paper and the reader accepts the fact that his team was jobbed. Newspaper readers generally don't recall if what they had read was a quote, or was written as a fact by the reporter.

For some reason players believe the hometown writers are—or should be—on their side. They believe the newsmen should revel in the club's victories and be saddened by defeat. Brad Park once complained of "our own writers" laughing on the plane following a loss. There are subtle ways that writers become part of a team. Less sophisticated newspapers allow reporters to write about "our Bruins," or "our Black Hawks." It's as though the reporter were leading a cheering section for the fans. But there also are monetary awards for obliging reporters. All N.H.L. teams have programs. Many of the stories written for these publications are done by the writers covering the team. They receive from $25 to $50 a story. There also are radio and television appearances between intermissions that can be quite beneficial. The Bruins, for example, give away a half-dozen shirts, each costing $16, and a stereo radio for one TV appearance. Clubs have exercised their own form of censorship. If there's a writer who's been unfavorable to the club, or controversial and the team thinks he's hurting it, he can be denied access to the programs or broadcasts. There was a silly situation recently when a club was unhappy with a columnist. This writer was a regular at the games and was used in a rotation to select the "stars of the game," a feature of every N.H.L. contest. The fans consider the stars of the game awards important, and in most rinks the majority of the fans wait around after the game is over to applaud the players selected. The players themselves covet the awards. It is instant recognition for a job well done. And in many cities, gifts accompany the awards.

When the columnist gave his selections to the public relations aide, to be delivered to the announcer, it was noticed that the writer had selected two visiting players as stars, and only one home-team player. Without notifying the writer, the official changed the stars—adding another local hero and taking out one of the visiting players. There is an unwritten rule fans should be aware of when the stars are chosen: If the home team wins a close game, the selector chooses two home players and one visitor. If the game is a complete rout for the home side, three local players can be chosen. But if the visitors score an easy victory, one home player generally is selected as one of the stars. Some reporters refuse to select stars. They believe their function is not to advise fans at the game who they like, but to report it in the papers. The vast majority of reporters, however, have no qualms about making their selections known.

In contrast to the reporters, radio and television announcers make no secret about where their sympathies lie. This doesn't mean they can't be objective and critical. The good ones are. An announcer can be a fan—and still be objective. That is, he should be pointing out good plays by the opposition, and making the public aware of bad playing by the team he's covering. Of course, he'll revel in a victory and that's what fans expect. Did you ever hear a fan object because the home announcer was too favorable to his team? But you often hear fans berate other clubs' announcers as "homers."

It is essential to remember this when discussing announcers: All are paid, or approved, by the club they're covering. We are talking about the play-by-play announcers and the color men, not the incidental newscasters or sportscasters. So if you want controversy when listening to or watching your favorite team, you can probably forget it. No announcer is going to take up a campaign to fire the coach, or trade away a certain player. And some announcers can rationalize this quite well: "Look, I'm being paid to report the games," says one personality, who has handled the network game-of-the-week telecast, as well as done extensive broadcasting for one team. "It would be silly for me to think the club hired me as a crusader. I think I can still be honest in the framework I've selected. If you want truly harsh judgments, or second-guessing, then you go to your newspaper. Who would I be fooling if I became a hard-nosed announcer? I'd be out of a job soon, and what good would it all do? I'd be cutting off my nose to spite my face." Precisely.

On some clubs, the announcers are paid directly by the team. On others, the radio or television station hires the announcer after the club has given him its blessings. Even the announcers on weekly telecasts are approved by the league. If any member voices too-strong objections the chances are an announcer's name will be vetoed.

Because in a sense the announcers are club employees, the relationship between them and the players is more open than the relationship between players and newspaper reporters. The player doesn't have to worry about being misquoted. The announcer is his friend. After all, when the player makes an appearance over the air, he is doing the talking, not worrying whether a middleman will write exactly what he said. And the tone of the questioner is usually more friendly.

Indeed, if there is one generalized statement that can be made about an announcer interviewing a player it's that the questions are friendly—or at least more acceptable to the player. The player won't scowl or sneer when he knows a million people can see or hear his reaction. And the circumstances are friendlier. It's before a game in the announcer's booth, or between periods (if a player isn't dressed), or after a game if the player has won. Except for Stanley Cup play, how often has anyone seen a losing player interviewed?

Another key to the easy relationship between broadcasters and players is that questions off the ice can be asked of players without the athlete worrying about giving a guarded response. It's just conversation. Does the athlete, however, ever know if a reporter is asking him a question for publication or just to make idle talk? He doesn't. So announcers and players become social friends, going out together, drinking together, seeing one another's families.

The club exercises a form of control over its public image only through television and radio coverage it owns. This is not to say that it tells its announcers how to handle their chores. Virtually every announcer and color man insists they've never been told what to say or what not to say. This is admirable, if true. But if a coach or general manager goes on for a 15-minute between-periods interview, he can often reach more people than the newspapers can. He can justify a bad trade—or a good one—and he can boost a player for all-star recognition and he can make other statements that will not be questioned. The announcer, after all, isn't there to debate the coach.

Where the club can truly be a censor is by approving or denying who the air-time guests will be. Red Fisher, a long-time and respected Montreal columnist, became a nonperson as far as television was concerned in 1971, when he released a secret, damaging report on expansion from Campbell that he had acquired through devious means. Scott Young, a probing columnist in Toronto, lost a pregame show when he described a million-dollar deal for Mahovlich as a "hoax." Whether Young, a newspaperman, should have been working for the Maple Leafs in the first place is another story. He claims it didn't hinder his objectivity. This concept of public image is a sore point with teams. When the Rangers planned a postgame television interview, Emile Francis wanted only his players interviewed, no matter how well any opposition player might have performed. To the credit of the station, the request was denied.

Since the development of the miniature tape recorder, everyone's a newsman. It isn't uncommon to see two dozen men walking around with $20 machines at all-star games or playoff contests. Many work for small, suburban stations and are able to get five minutes of air time with an in-person interview. The tape recorder has enabled even the smallest stations to bring famous personalities to their listeners. Gump Worsley, the goalie, refuses to talk into a microphone unless it's a live radio or television mike. "Once I did a tape-recording interview with some guy," he says. "I didn't know the guy from a hole in the wall. He stuck the thing in front of me and I just started talking. Well, I figured he'd edit out the curse words. But he didn't. He edited them in. Then he chopped some words out, and put a whole interview together that wasn't really what I said. The thing became a collector's item."

The unofficial mouthpiece of the National Hockey League is *The Hockey News,* a weekly tabloid with a circulation of more than 80,000. Its writers are from each of the big-league cities in the United States and Canada, and they write about their teams. Although the league has no formal connection with the paper it grants its tacit approval by allowing it to be sold in the rinks. Don't look for controversy in *The Hockey News.* Indeed, one writer was bounced on orders by the club he was covering. Often, the weekly is a forum for coaches, who can make certain points about their teams without fear of contradiction. *The Hockey News* writers are perhaps the poorest paid of any journalistic group in North America. Each story brings a writer $15 or $20. Very few newspapermen would be willing to work for that kind of money. However, since it's published every week of the year, it can mean an extra $1,000 over 12 months.

One of the paper's most important functions is its statistics. The National Hockey League makes them available each week to newsmen. But the public doesn't get the chance to see them, and it doesn't have the opportunity to get the late results if a game is played on the West Coast and the fan is in the East. The paper prints the scoring summaries for every game played the preceding week. It also has a table listing the scoring leaders, giving such breakdowns as power-play goals, short-handed goals and game-winning goals. In addition, there is a fairly extensive roundup of the minor leagues, with the leading scorers in each league.

The paper also presents two awards that are significant to the game: the coach of the year and the minor-league executive of the year. Over the course of the season fans can learn most of the information they desire. The balloting of the various polls is presented, and a rather complete listing of all the weekly game-of-the-week telecasts, as well as call letters for all the radio stations around the league.

But if the average fan wants the most complete records he can get, four publications are available from the league at its office in the Sun Life Building in Montreal. These are the books the newsmen refer to most often and are indispensable. Not everyone—not even the experts—know off the top of their heads such facts as the record for most points in a game by a defenseman, or the longest home losing streak. The first of the publications, and the most important one for anyone in the media, is the *NHL Guide*.

The guide, priced at about $3, comes out each year, usually the first month of the season. It contains more than 500 pages and helps make reporters very smart. For example, the year-by-year record of every player active in the pro ranks is listed, as well as his N.H.L. totals. The players' playoff performances also are listed, as well as notations of any awards the player might have won in any season, or any league-leading performance by the player.

The year-by-year record of every team in the N.H.L. is listed, as well as leaders for each year. And every record the league keeps track of, individual and team, is available.

There is also the most complete selection of the previous season's statistics: the game-by-game results of all games played, the records of every player who appeared during the season, a complete breakdown of goalies' performances, and a set of playoff statistics. If you're curious how Boston fared against West Division teams, there is a team breakdown in which every club's record is shown for home and away games, and against its own division and the other division. There are also brief histories of the general managers and coaches currently in the league.

An important adjunct to the guide is the league's playoff publication called *The Stanley Cup,* available in March for under $2. The rosters of every Stanley Cup champion are given. The scoring summaries for each of the previous season's playoff games—from first round to the finals—are listed. So are the records for Cup play, as well as team-against-team performances.

The N.H.L. schedule (free) and the N.H.L. rule book (50 cents) are other valuable tools. These books are in breast-pocket-size form and are carried by every coach and general manager. The schedule not only lists the date and site for every game during the season, but also contains enough room for the fan or newsman to jot down the score. It also contains the previous season's statistics. The rule book contains every conceivable rule, from the dimensions of the goal cage to the amount of money a player should be fined for certain infractions.

A busy man named Ron Andrews is the editor of these publications. Andrews is the league's director of information and statistician. He has only one assistant, Norm Jewison, and one secretary. Yet, his office disseminates more than a million pages of press releases a year, in addition to the books.

Each week Andrews is responsible for mailing 1,800 separate releases, which are not available to the public. These are the current statistics for every player in the N.H.L. They go to every official on every club, as well as to newspapermen and broadcasters. To get this information together, Andrews and Jewison alternate working Sunday nights. One of them arrives at the office at 10 P.M., when the first group of games is ending. They transcribe all the weekend results on computer cards, including such information as game-winning goals, game-tying goals, and penalties. This keeps them busy until two in the morning. Then they walk across the street with the cards to the league's computer center, which digests the information. At 6 A.M. the computer is finished. They bring the information back to the office. From there, the statistics are sent by Telex to the various news services and all the N.H.L. teams. Another 1,800 copies are made to be mailed.

The league has often been accused of moving at a Neanderthal pace. Certainly it moved slowly in many areas before expansion, due to the closed-corporation nature of its structure: it had only six teams. These clubs usually played to capacity. If the league was unreceptive to the public it was because it didn't have to bother pleasing people. Andrews, for example, is only the second press relations man the league has ever had. Before Andrews joined the league in 1963, it never released such statistics as shots-on-goal percentages. Under Andrews the league now compiles short-handed goal figures, penalty-killing statistics and power-play percentages.

For each third of the season, Andrews's office provides a detailed accounting for the media of every player's performances. The list includes such items as a player's "proximate" goals—those scores that bring a club to within one of tying. The fact sheet also lists game-tying goals, score-tying goals, winning goals, the first goal of the game, the leading goal, the insurance goal. With the exception of the last two, these goals are called "important goals." At the end of the column each player's percentage of important goals to total goals is listed. They are significant and revealing. They might be called clutch goals.

Until 1972 the league kept the plus-minus figures on these sheets only for club officials. But now they will be sent out to the press each third of the season, under a new, more meaningful, form devised by Andrews. Now a player will not be merely "plus" the number of goals scored by his team while at full strength with him on the ice. He will be plus or minus a percentage of the team's goals. Early in the 1971–72 season, the Rangers' Brad Park was plus 25, the highest figure in the league. His club had scored about twice as many goals as the opposition. Perreault of the Sabres, however, was minus 9 for a team that gave up 50 more goals than it scored. Park, in other words, was plus 34 over Perreault. However, Andrews tried a different way of figuring, one which would avoid the pitfall of measuring a player for a poor team against one for an outstanding club. He took the percentages of goals scored when each player was on the ice compared to the total number of goals scored. Then he subtracted the percentage of goals scored against the team when each player was on the ice. The figure reversal was remarkable: Perreault wound up with a plus percentage of 15.1, while Park had a 13.1.

It works this way: If Perreault is on the ice for 50 of his team's goals, and it scores 100 goals, he gets a 50 percent. If the opposition scores 80 goals, and he's on the ice for 20 of them, he gets a 25 percent. Then the 25 percent is subtracted from the 50 percent to arrive at his figure.

As an indication of the thoroughness that Andrews brings to the job, there is the Babe Dye–Cy Denneny anomaly. Dye, a star of the 1930's, had been listed in the guide as the player with the highest career goals-per-game scoring average. For years the figure of .798 had been accepted. Denneny, another old-timer, was second at .737. However, Andrews discovered that a historian had credited Denneny with four more goals than appeared in the guide, and that Dye had actually scored two less goals than the guide gave him credit for. Andrews went through the game-by-game results for the two stars and discovered the guide was in error. The correction was made and Denneny took his rightful place. He was elevated to a percentage of .767 while Dye dropped to second at .738.

The press and the broadcasters aren't the only ones interested in the statistics coming out of Andrews's office—the players are fascinated by it. At any given moment, a player knows the statistics most important to him. He also is aware of how well he's doing in relation to a teammate who plays the same position. In any locker room you'll hear the defensemen bantering about which has the most goals among the defensive corps.

While Andrews's job is primarily to ease the newsmen's path, and be the official record-keeper for the league, another man in New York, Don Ruck, is in charge of the league's public image. Ruck, a vice-president of the league, is also president of National Hockey League Services, Inc., the arm of the league that trades in on its name.

There are more rinks in the United States than in Canada. But until expansion gave hockey a more striking American image the rinks were havens more for figure skaters than for body checkers. The explosion of the sport created a virtually new hockey industry in the States, and attracted manufacturers that had never considered hockey tie-ins with their products. It is estimated that hockey equipment will have the greatest percentage increase of any sports gear by the end of the 1970's. After the Blues came to St. Louis the town became hockey-wild. One year more hockey sticks than baseball bats were sold in that city.

As a result of such interest, manufacturers have besieged the National Hockey League with products, paying for the league's crest on their items. There are such nonsports products as vitamins, pillowcases, watches, and glassware. Whenever such products are sold, the league receives a fee. It has generated enough money to pay for the upkeep of the Hockey Hall of Fame in Toronto and the annual Lester Patrick Awards Dinner in New York.

Ruck was brought in in 1965, at a time when the league had announced it was going to expand. One of his primary duties was to set up a television deal. Television was an essential ingredient in expansion. It had produced extraordinary revenues for the National Football League—and indeed the TV advance money helped get the A.F.L. started. Since the National Hockey League no longer was to be confined to the eastern United States, it had a bargaining point for extracting more money for network telecasts. It was also essential to the league to have a network show to help promote the product—hockey. More areas meant new markets for

N.H.L.-endorsed products, which would mean more revenue coming to the league.

Ruck's start in the sport was greeted by a less than enthusiastic reception by the Canadian press. Because he was to have his office in New York, many Canadian newsmen believed this was the beginning of the United States' takeover of their sport. The six new expansion cities, after all, were to be in the United States. One Toronto reporter, who had never met Ruck, wrote, "The National Hockey League is seeking a new image, and they hired a Madison Avenue huckster named Don Ruck to promote it." This was typical of the reception he received.

Unquestionably, network television brought hockey to areas of the United States that previously had never even thought about the game. The N.H.L. was—and still is—faced with a problem in these weekly telecasts. It never has been quite sure how much the play-by-play announcer should take for granted. Obviously, the game is being seen by people who don't have the first idea what it's all about. However, the die-hard fans also are watching it. So the problem is: How do you announce a game while explaining what's happening, and yet not offend the knowledgeable viewer? It's a difficult assignment. Canadians especially were quick to put down the announcers of the first network telecasts, who would explain something so simple as an offsides pass. Eventually, a happy medium was found. Announcers today won't simply say, "That was offsides. An offsides pass occurs when the puck travels past two lines." They'll say something like, "The puck went over two lines, so it's offsides." It's a subtle, but effective, difference.

Although the quality of the telecasts improved markedly, the show has never produced the "numbers"—ratings—that basketball or other big-league sports are capable of. As a result, the league's network revenue is the smallest of the big four sports. It comes to under $1,000,000 a season for weekly coverage from January to May. This is split among the United States teams. The three Canadian clubs—Vancouver, Montreal, and Toronto—have their own private Canadian television deal. Vancouver alone receives more than $600,000 a year, while Toronto and Montreal each take in about $1,000,000. Canada's Saturday night telecasts, known as "Hockey Night in Canada," are the country's top-rated shows.

Meanwhile, the weekly telecasts continue to look better. At first, the cameramen were completely unfamiliar with hockey. The game probably is the toughest to televise. Combine that with a director and cameramen who are unacquainted with the sport, and it can come over as a constant blur. The Canadian telecasts, however, were held up as a model of how it should be done. Over the years, though, the coverage in the United States has improved to the point where, at its best, it equals that of Canada's.

There is an uneasy truce between television and fans at a game. Once network television began, it meant there would have to be commercials. Since the league didn't want the TV viewers to miss any of the action, play would be held up so a commercial could be finished. The commercials would never start when play was going on. They'd begin as soon as there was a natural play stoppage—a face-off for an offsides, a goal, a penalty. Most advertisers favored the minute-long commercial. However, most play stoppages didn't last a full minute. So the fans at the game would sit in anger as play was held up. The television became a monster for some, who claimed that even a five-second delay when a team is ready to go can halt momentum. Certainly it stopped the natural flow of play in a game that prides itself on being nonstop, quickly paced, and action-filled.

Fans complained lustily (during one game home viewers constantly heard a chant that went, "C.B.S. stinks!"). The press also blasted the league, and television, for tampering with the game. Of course, this distressed Ruck. He was in charge of ordering when commercials should be shown. Since he admittedly came to hockey with little knowledge of the game, he didn't always call the right signals. He would order a one-minute commercial at a time when there would only be a short natural play stoppage. Eventually, he learned more about the game and its patterns. He would notice that when a player argued with an official over a penalty, the discussion would usually take the minute. When there was a major fight, it would take at least 60 seconds for all the penalties to be assigned. If he saw a goalie complain of equipment damage, he discovered the delay would be significant.

Still, the situation wasn't perfect. Sponsors demanded a minimum number of commercials each period. Some hockey games just don't lend themselves to interruptions. And there are many periods that just fly by, with five-minute stretches without one stoppage of play. That meant the advertisers wanted their commercials squeezed into the other stoppages. Ruck had long talks with advertising agencies. He asked that they cut their commercials from a minute to 30 seconds. Most of the agencies balked. Traditionally, they said, the most effective commercials lasted a minute. But Ruck was able to strike a compromise: During each period there would be one 60-second commercial. The others would be shorter.

This turned out to be a happy medium. The fans have grown accustomed to the occasional disruptions, although they've never completely accepted them. The league remains acutely aware that misplaced commercials can hurt the game. One of Ruck's assistants now attends every game-of-the-week telecast. His job is to determine the propitious moment for a commercial. The linesmen are equipped with a beeper hidden under their shirts. The assistant, meanwhile, is in the TV booth. When there's a play stoppage, and the aide wants a commercial, he signals the linesman with a "beep" that a commercial has begun. The official then waits until he receives another beep signaling him that the commercial is ended. Play is then resumed. For the majority of commercials these days, there are no significant interruptions. On some of the one-minute spots, though, time lags. These are the occasions when the fans notice that the linesman is delaying play.

Although this observer often found fault with television and the league for permitting the interruptions, the commercials have now arrived at the stage where they are acceptable to most fans at a game. It never will be perfect. However, what must be measured is the greater good: Would the fans prefer no television at all, or are they willing to accept the sometimes frustrating inconvenience of commercial time-outs? If there were no commercials, there'd be no telecasts.

When the contest is ended, the star-of-the-game announcements are treated dramatically on Canadian television. The camera zooms in on the player selected as No. 1 and superimposes his picture over a shot of the applauding crowd. This picking-the-stars business is serious work in Canada. Perhaps the best (although not necessarily the most accurate) story about the selections concerns Rocket Richard. The game was over and Richard was asked to explain his selections:

"Well, I chose Henri Richard not because he's my brother, but because he's always driving. He was always trying tonight and so he was the No. 1 star. Then I picked Jean Beliveau as the second star, because he's an inspiration to Montreal. Without him, they wouldn't have been in the game at all. I know some people will think I chose these two because they play for my old team. Well, it's not true. Because as the third star I pick Gordie Howe—if it wasn't for his three goals the Red Wings wouldn't have won by 3-0."

Money

No wonder a hall-of-famer such as Maurice Richard is constantly knocking today's players—most of them make more money than he did in his best years. Much of his jealousy and his harping about the quality of play probably has to do with the fact that today's hockey players want what's coming to them. There's nothing wrong with that. It's not so much that today's stars are overpaid —it's just that yesterday's stars were underpaid.

The Rocket never approached the $40,000-a-year figure, and he saw action into the late 1950's, when his baseball counterparts, Ted Williams and Mickey Mantle, were earning $100,000 a year. Another Canadiens' hero, Boom Boom Geoffrion, played well into the 1960's, when football and basketball also had its $100,000 men. The Boomer never earned more than $35,000 with Montreal.

When Red Sullivan was the Rangers' coach in 1965, he was earning less than $16,000 a year. Not one of his players was in the $30,000 category. It is likely that only Howe and Hull earned more than $50,000 that season.

What was going on? Were the owners a bunch of tight-fisted rascally know-nothings? Were the players mere sheep who took what was offered and went about their business? A little bit of both is true. And in most instances involving money, there is even some good to be said for both sides.

In the first place, professional hockey has always dealt sternly with its dissident players—and especially with players who threaten to strike for more money. As far back as 1910, the National Hockey Association, the N.H.L.'s forerunner, banded together to halt demands by players who wanted a union. The players claimed their salaries weren't sufficient. The N.H.A. then voted itself a ceiling on salaries—no club could pay a total of more than $5,000 a season to the entire team. It was ludicrous. Art Ross, the star defenseman, had earned $2,700 the previous season. Now the players were being told they would average $500 a man for a 10-man team. When the players balked, the public suddenly rose against the athletes (a situation repeated many times since for holdouts in all sports). Management had some justification for the price ceiling. The Ottawa club, for example, grossed only $25,000 the previous season and paid out $15,000 in salaries alone. It didn't make a profit. The league threatened to cut all players who hadn't agreed to sign, and suggested it was going to scavenge through the amateur ranks to induce players to turn professional. Ross was moved to write a remarkable letter to the *Montreal Herald*. It read in part:

> While playing hockey the players run the risk of injury and probable loss of time which is almost bound to effect advancement in business. All these things have to be taken into consideration when assessing the value of a professional hockey player. Hockey isn't a gentle pastime. If it were, people wouldn't pay to see it and there wouldn't be any need for salary limits, because there would be no paid players. All the players want is a fair deal.

Within a few weeks, the dissident players signed under the league's terms. A few years later, Ross was at it again. Another wage ceiling had been imposed, and Ross began to sign teammates to play for an outlaw league he was going to start. Ross promptly was suspended from professional hockey. The N.H.A.'s owners had a sudden change of heart, though. They believed they had acted too harshly, and reinstated Ross.

It was nearly 10 years before another major labor-management flare-up took place. The players for Hamilton refused to take part in the 1925 playoffs. They argued, with logic, that they had signed two-year contracts the previous season, when the schedule was only 24 games long. On the second year of the contract, though, the schedule was increased to 30 games. They wanted more pay. The president of the N.H.L., Frank Calder, didn't bother to negotiate with the players. He merely suspended the whole team, telling the players they couldn't compete in the playoffs. When the following season began, Hamilton still was under suspension. Rather than meet the players' demands, Calder simply disbanded the entire club, making the players free agents.

With this extraordinary action, a pattern was set for hockey: You play for the owners, at their terms, or not at all. Since the urge to compete in the N.H.L. is so strong among Canadians, there were few dissidents. Certainly the idea of unionism was virtually dead. When Conn Smythe took over the Toronto club in 1926 (and changed the name from the "St. Patricks" to the more patriotic "Maple Leafs") he set about looking for players who were "sportsmen." Smythe believed the game (and country) came first, and monetary rewards came second. Smythe, in fact, turned down the prospect of picking up the legendary Babe Dye because "Dye was more like a union man than a sportsman."

After World War II there was another move to bring the players under a union-type umbrella. Was it coincidence, therefore, that in 1948 the league started a pension plan? The cynics say the plan was started to thwart the proposed union's raison d'être. League officials say it was merely the logical step of a progressive league moving forward into a new era of labor-management relations. In the 1950's, though, a new thrust was given to a union by the energetic Ted Lindsay, one of the Red Wings' stars. Lindsay was soon traded to the Black Hawks. Coincidence again? The same year Lindsay was traded the pension plan was upgraded considerably and a substantial amount of money was added to the playoff purse.

But the great expansion of 1967 once and for all brought hockey players into the athletes' new era of affluence. It came at the same time the Players' Association was formed with Alan Eagleson, a Toronto lawyer, at its head. Great goalies such as Glenn Hall and Terry Sawchuk, picked by new expansion teams, suddenly retired. They knew they finally had a wedge for bargaining. If the new clubs didn't pick them, there would be no experienced goalies. Each was "coaxed" out of retirement with $20,000 raises. Meanwhile, virtually every player in the league signed up with the association.

One who didn't was the Leafs' Frank Mahovlich. The Big M was a supreme performer, but a worrisome sort who let his problems well up within until they exploded.

His coach was Imlach, who in time was to get a bad rap as being "anti-union" (which he was, but not necessarily for red-necked reasons). When the recruiting for the association was at its height, Mahovlich failed to show up for two practice sessions. Imlach finally collared Mahovlich before the club's next game. Mahovlich told his coach that he was one of the few players who had refused to join the union, but the other players had badgered him, telling him that they needed a player of his magnitude to increase their bargaining power. Mahovlich also had been receiving a stream of letters from the association, asking that he join. Unable to handle the situation, Mahovlich simply refused to show up for workouts.

Before the game that night Imlach raised the roof in the dressing room. "There's not one of you in here who's half the player Mahovlich is," Imlach told his team. "If I ever catch any of my players bugging someone by soliciting for the union, that player's gone." Later that night the team spent the night in the sleeping cars of a train that was to take them to Detroit in the morning. At 5 A.M., Mahovlich left the train and went straight to the home of a doctor friend, asking that he be admitted to a hospital. He spent the next month in the hospital.

Whatever its deficiencies, the association made the players aware that they weren't alone, that they could use muscle to get what they considered was a fair salary. Each training camp more and more players held out. Salaries suddenly began leaping. For some, the salaries weren't enough. The first major confrontation between players and owners took place in September, 1967, the training-camp period before the first season of expansion.

Many of the game's stars stayed away from camp, under the impression that their contracts were ambiguously worded. They believed they didn't have to report if they weren't signed. However, management contended that contracts ran from October 1 to September 30—thus the players who weren't in camp were contract-breakers. Later, many of the players were to complain that they had been misled by the union. In any event, Eagleson established a strike command post at, of all places, the Rangers' camp. He used Arnie Brown's hotel room to make phone calls—and receive them—to players all over North America. The Ranger camp was the most significantly struck. Five players refused to play, including Brown, Rod Gilbert, and Orland Kurtenbach—three of the club's stars. They were dealt with severely, each receiving a $500 fine. Those were the highest tariffs in the club's history. As Eagleson sat at the phones he bolstered the players' confidence, telling them such things as "we're all in this together," and "don't sign for anything just out of fright." That day the Flyers' top draft choice, Ed Van Impe, was a holdout. So were the Penguins' top two choices, Earl Ingarfield and Al MacNeil. Tim Horton, the anchor of Toronto's defense, didn't show up. Neither did Norm Ullman, Detroit's star, nor Pat Stapleton, Ken Wharram, and Pit Martin of the Black Hawks.

Hockey survived the uprising. But it was apparent the old ways were finished. Eagleson, who had come to prominence in the sport by representing Bobby Orr, paved the way for other lawyers. After 50 years of virtual authoritarian rule, the N.H.L. was forced to deal with a union and with players' attorneys. That didn't mean the owners all liked it. Later that season Ullman was traded to Toronto, and at least one general manager not involved in the deal said it was made "because Ullman was a strong union man."

By the second year of expansion salaries began to rise dramatically. The average for East Division players went to about $21,-000 while in the West it was $18,000 a man. Not great, but certainly much better than before. Bobby Hull was receiving more than $80,000 a season and it was believed that Gordie Howe became the sport's first $100,000-a-year man. Still, the rookies did rather poorly. The vast majority received a bonus of $1,500 to turn pro, while in football and basketball players were signing multi-year contracts calling for hundreds of thousands in bonus money. Hockey, of course, had no rival league to worry about. Players might bargain, and argue for a bigger bonus, but in the end they usually signed for just a bit more than what the club originally offered.

Meanwhile, the sport was riding the crest of a wave of public acceptance. Players suddenly were in demand for endorsements and speaking engagements in the United States. These outside activities could sometimes double a player's salary. Certainly when a player could receive $3,000 for doing a shaving commercial, say, he was going to think twice about accepting a salary for only $20,000. The salary didn't look so large to him anymore. Hockey schools began to sprout up in the United States, too. Slowly, subtly, but surely, the players' vistas were broadened. Hockey still was the great goal, but players discovered they could be their own men. They stopped looking at themselves as mere chattels.

Players broke the $50,000 barrier with regularity. Horton, who had been happy with $45,000 a year, was jumped to $80,000 a season when he had decided to retire from the Leafs. In 1971, he was coaxed out of retirement again with a $100,000 offer from the Penguins. Rookies, too, began making money demands. The

Sabres signed Gil Perreault for $30,000 a year on a multi-year contract and the next year Dionne got the highest rookie contract ever—more than $60,000 a season.

However, not everyone was ecstatic with their money. At a time when he was one of the biggest gate attractions in the sport, Derek Sanderson of the Bruins was pulling down $14,000 a season. He had already established himself as a 20-goal man and had won the rookie-of-the-year award. But he was in a three-year contract that "escalated" from $12,000 in his rookie campaign to $14,000 in his third season. When he complained about it publicly, the Bruins, perhaps for the first time, made a player's earnings public. They claimed that actually he had earned $39,000. The Bruins were guilty of a bit of sophistry. True, they did give him a $10,000 bonus. But the other earnings came from the Bruins' high finish in the standings and playoff victory. All other players on the club earned the extra money, none of which was directly received from management. The Bruins also said, with justification, that Sanderson was an unknown when he broke in. If he couldn't have made the club he would have received the salary even if he had been sent to the minors. Both sides had taken a chance, said the Bruins, who don't believe in tearing up contracts and issuing new ones simply because a player becomes a star.

The multi-year contract also affected the team's top players— Orr and Esposito. During the 1970–71 season each was in the final year of a contract calling for about $40,000. But each had already established scoring records that should have put them in the $100,000 category. So they played the season, each setting more records, for a relatively small amount. But in 1971 they both signed long-time contracts worth more than $150,000 a season apiece. They may have been the greatest raises in sports history. As an indication of how sensitive players are to the big figures, and how well they realize that the public is impressed with a player—and bases an opinion on how good he is—by the player's salary, Esposito was disturbed when speculation about the contracts came out. The Boston papers estimated Orr's salary at $180,000 a season, while saying that Esposito had received only

$125,000 a season. "In everyone's mind, that makes Phil a lesser player," said a friend of Esposito's. Actually, the two players' salaries were nearly similar.

Because of the high salaries on the club, and the fact that several other players had achieved outstanding seasons, Campbell went so far as to speculate that it might be in the Bruins' interest to trade one of their stars. "I don't know if the Bruins can afford the team," said Campbell. Cynics saw it as a ploy by the league to attempt to keep salaries down. Yet, the Bruins, who make a good deal of money, were faced with a problem. They'd have to keep raising the price of admission to keep their profits up. There'd come a time when a point of no return would be reached.

The most bitter, and most publicized, contract dispute concerned the Rangers and four of the team's top players—Jean Ratelle, Brad Park, Vic Hadfield, and Walt Tkaczuk. It exploded during the 1970 training camp when the four were suspended from the team and sent packing. The most interesting part of the controversy was that the players' lawyers made the salaries public. From an ethical point of view it wasn't the wisest decision. And it led to acrimony between the lawyers and the team management. But it also may have helped get the players what they believed they deserved.

It started over the summer, when Emile Francis had heard that his four heroes had got themselves some lawyers. Park, an all-star the previous season, had played for about $12,000. Tkaczuk, the leading scorer on the club, had also received about the same. Hadfield, the senior member on the team in point of service, was under $30,000, while Ratelle, generally acknowledged as the finest player on the club, was at the $30,000 plateau.

Francis sent out his salary offers, but specifically made them low to see what the players' reaction would be, as well as to bring the lawyers out into the open. When the contracts arrived, the players were insulted.

Tkaczuk and Park each received offers that would still keep them under $20,000. Hadfield was offered a negligible raise, while Ratelle was offered a somewhat better deal. Park fumed when he saw the offer for $18,000. Francis countered with: "It's a 50 percent raise." The lawyers replied, "Fifty percent of nothing is still nothing."

When the public saw the figures that the Rangers offered, it was surprised. Ratelle, for example, was earning less money than the sixth man on the Garden's basketball team, the Knicks. Every starter on the basketball team earned twice what Ratelle was receiving. Hadfield, meanwhile, had been offered a lucrative deal from the Spalding sporting goods people. A golf pro, Hadfield was an astute businessman. He could have earned as much from Spalding as from hockey. He was ready to quit if his terms weren't met. Ratelle, a sensitive fellow who has always abhorred the violence inherent in the game, had been a long-time follower of the stock market. He, too, was insulted with the contract offer. He was ready to leave the game out of pride if he didn't receive a fair salary.

Francis was convinced the lawyers were making a package deal —using the four as a wedge against the team. His neck stiffened. He took Park's skates away, refusing to allow the defenseman to work out, claiming the skates belonged to the team.

In one of the discussions with Hadfield, Francis claimed that he wasn't offering the left wing much of a raise because Hadfield had had a poor season. He had been minus while his linemates, Ratelle and Gilbert, had been plus. The lawyers tried to get a copy of the plus and minus statistics. Francis refused to give them one. This was the kind of pettiness that occurred.

But the players remained firm. Eventually, they all signed, but not until the regular season had started. Tkaczuk and Park nearly tripled their salaries, while Hadfield and Ratelle received substantial raises.

By the end of the season, Campbell said that the average salary in the East Division had jumped to $26,000 (including bonuses) and to $23,000 in the West Division. The players formed their own licensing company, in direct competition with the league's. The contract wasn't extraordinary by other sports standards, but it was a start—a five-year deal worth half-a-million dollars.

Other off-the-ice activity flourished. Even mediocre players were in demand for speaking engagements, often for fees ranging from $100 to $500 or more, depending on the player and the type of organization he was speaking to. Players' pictures began to appear with many products. Perhaps the average fan may not have noticed, but most players appear without their team uniform. Often, they'll be wearing an outfit of similar color, but without the team's name or crest. There's a good reason for this: Whenever the team's name appears in an ad or a commercial featuring a player, the team takes a one-third cut.

For most players, though, the majority of their extra money comes from making the playoffs. Under the 14-team setup, that meant that more than half the players in the league were assured of some playoff money, since four teams in each seven-team division got into the postseason tourney. Of the league's total of $827,000 in award money paid in 1972, $567,000 went to playoff performers. Even members of a fourth-place club were guaranteed $2,000 a man. Fourth place is worth $500. If the team loses its first-round playoff series, it still earns $1,500 apiece.

Thus, while most observers say the finish during the regular season is unimportant, that it's the Stanley Cup that really counts, that's not quite true from a monetary standpoint. The team finishing first picks up $2,500 a man. Second is worth $1,250, third $750, and fourth $500. In 1971, however, there wasn't that much incentive for the Minnesota North Stars to finish third. They would earn only $250 more than if they finished fourth—and would have to face the powerful Chicago Black Hawks in the opening round. But if they finished fourth, they'd meet the St. Louis Blues in the first round. The North Stars finished fourth, and defeated St. Louis. The Flyers, who finished third, were swept out of the playoffs in four straight games by Chicago. This isn't to suggest that the North Stars deliberately lost their three final games to drop to fourth. But the suspicion was there. To give incentive to a club to attempt to finish as high as it possibly can, the league changed the playoff format for 1972. The first-place team would play the fourth-place club, while the second-place team would meet the third-place club in opening-round play. Presumably under the new system, no team would want to finish fourth and meet the division champion. Besides the money, and the chance to play a weaker team by finishing higher, there is another advantage: that of the home ice. The team higher in the final standing gets the extra game at its home. And in interdivisional play, when the clubs cross over in the second round, it still remains important to have the highest regular-season finish. During the crossover phase, the team higher in the standing gets the odd game. If the clubs were tied—say both finished second in their respective divisions—then the team with the better record receives the extra game.

This is significant. Say a team has first place locked up in its division. It wants to coast the remaining few games. But if it knows that the first-place club in the other division also has a fine record, it will attempt to keep its record better than that team's. It wants the extra-game advantage, so conceivably it will be trying and putting out its best effort, even for the last few games of the season. Football was taken to task for its playoff structure in 1971. The Baltimore Colts made the playoffs although dropping their final regular-season game and falling to second in their division. The loss meant the Colts would meet the Cleveland Browns, instead of the powerful Kansas City Chiefs, in the playoffs. Some people said the Colts weren't trying to win their final game, that they were better off playing Cleveland. And there was no monetary incentive for Baltimore. They didn't get a dime for finishing second, and they wouldn't have got a dime for finishing first. Many observers thought that pro football should have an awards incentive, as hockey does, for regular-season finish.

Until the 1972 playoffs, the Stanley Cup money was poor compared to the other pro leagues. The most a Cup winner could earn was $7,500—compared to $25,000 a man for the Super Bowl champion, $18,000 apiece to the World Series victors, and $11,-000 each for the basketball titlist. But a few days before the 1972 playoffs in hockey were to begin, the league dramatically upped the payoff—the winners would get $15,000 a man, while $7,500 would go to the losers.

It was the least the league could do (the Players' Association was asking $25,000 for each member of the victorious Cup squad). Under the former payoffs, players received approximately their regular-season wages. The playoffs can last five weeks—it could go 21 games. Under the $7,500 maximum payoff system, that only comes to an average of about $25,000 for the season. Yet, in the playoffs ticket prices are raised about 50 percent. In other words, the owners received increased revenue while paying the players regular-season wages.

In addition to final-standing and playoff money, there is money for a host of other awards and accomplishments. The single most valuable award is for making the all-star team's first squad. This is worth $2,000 to each player. The all-star team selection is in the hands of the Professional Hockey Writers' Association. Three writers in each league city receive ballots just before the end of the season from the league office in Montreal. They vote, in order of preference, for the top three goalies, centers, right wings, and left wings. On defense they vote for the top six.

Because of the scheduling that brings visiting teams in only three times apiece, much of the voting is based on statistics rather than a close look at the players. Since most of the writers don't travel with the teams, the only look they have at opposition players is when the teams visit their cities. This isn't an ideal way to make selections. In the first place, teams don't do as well on the road, so a writer in Chicago, for example, is always watching the Pittsburgh Penguins at a disadvantage. In 1971, for another case, the Montreal Canadiens paid only one visit to New York the entire second half of the season. Many writers had only one look at Frank Mahovlich as a Canadien. How intelligently could they judge whether he should be the all-star left wing over Bobby Hull?

How good a defenseman was Tim Horton with Pittsburgh in 1971–72? The Penguins paid their final visit to New York by mid-December. Horton played in only the third game—he had been out with injuries the first two.

Over the long run, many mistakes—if any—won't be made. The top players are virtually certain to be elected. But many decisions are made strictly after consulting the statistics sheets, or after reading out-of-town newspapers. If Hull doesn't do well in the season series against Montreal, would the Montreal writers leave Hull off their ballots? Hardly. They know what Hull can do. Still, the system leaves something to be desired. At one time, when there were six teams and a 70-game schedule, writers saw opposition-team players 14 times, 20 percent of all games they appeared in. Now they see them six times in 78 games, or 8 percent.

Often, emotion and statistics get in the way of logic. John Bucyk made the first-team all-stars over Hull in 1971. Bucyk played for the Bruins' juggernaut, and he scored 51 goals and amassed 116 points. A truly remarkable season. But Hull played for the strictly defensive-oriented Black Hawks. He got 44 goals and had a 96-point total. If any coach in the N.H.L. had to start one game and needed a left winger, would he take Bucyk over Hull? It's to be doubted. The Bruins scored 122 more goals than the Black Hawks did during the season, yet Bucyk had only 20 more points than Hull. The Hawks' star, moreover, had 11 game-winning goals, compared to five for Bucyk.

Hull had a consolation, however. As a member of the second team he received $1,000.

There is also an all-star game, which has nothing to do with the all-star selections. The game now is staged at midseason, between the best players of the two divisions. Ballots are sent out in mid-December for the contest, which is held in late January. The format is radically different from what it had been. The first official all-star game (there had been a few previously, as charity affairs for injured players) was held in 1947. It pitted the all-star team as selected the previous season against the previous season's Stanley Cup champion. The game was held at the beginning of the campaign. There were many things wrong with this system. For one, many of the all-stars were members of the Stanley Cup victors. They couldn't play against their own team, of course, so players were substituted. Secondly, the game was held at a time when interest wasn't high—the season hadn't even started. But since there were only six teams, and only one division, the league couldn't figure out any other acceptable way. In 1951 and 1952 it tried something different: the first all-star team would face the second all-star team. This didn't work out, either. Teammates wound up playing against each other, since some clubs had a few players on the first team and some on the second team.

In 1967 the game was changed to midseason, which conceivably could make it more interesting. However, players were appearing who had been all-stars nine months before. The current stars, or rookies, couldn't make the team.

Expansion solved the all-star dilemma. There were two divisions—a natural all-star rivalry.

The voting took place in midseason, when true all-stars—that is, the current all-stars—would be selected. The first contest under this system was staged in 1969 and it turned into a surprising 3-3 tie, despite the fact that the East Division had, on paper, all the power. The voting system was also changed. Three writers in each city voted only for the players in their division. This was a good idea when it began. The schedule was imbalanced, and writers, naturally, saw more opposing players from their own division than the other division. But the expansion of 1970–71, when Vancouver and Buffalo were added, created a balanced schedule again. Thus, a writer saw East Division and West Division opponents equally. Unless the schedule is once more radically imbalanced, it doesn't appear necessary to limit writers' ballots only to teams in their division.

Another all-star tradition was broken in the 1970 renewal. Previously, all games were staged in the Cup defender's city. But since the defender no longer played an all-star team, the site was illogical. Also, few cities in hockey had ever seen an all-star game. The Montreal Canadiens and Toronto Maple Leafs had won so many Cups that those two cities usurped the all-star game. The best solution was a rotation system. This had its drawbacks, however. When the league changed the game format to east versus west, only three West Division cities were assured of good attendances—St. Louis, Minnesota and, perhaps, Philadelphia. Pittsburgh, Oakland, and Los Angeles were drawing poorly. The league was leery of rotating the game and winding up in Oakland, with only a few thousand people in the stands. It just wouldn't do to have a showcase draw poorly.

The league arrived at what it hoped was a solution. It began the all-star-game rotation at St. Louis. The second was scheduled for Boston, the third for Minnesota, the fourth for New York. Each year the divisions alternated. By the fifth year, 1974, the league figured, hockey would have arrived sufficiently in its marginal cities to attract a good crowd.

Players complain, rightly it would appear, about the amount of money they receive for all-star play. Each member of the winning team receives $500. The losers receive $250. In the event of a draw, each player gets $375. But at today's salaries, $500 isn't that significant a figure, and it certainly isn't an awful lot more than the loser receives. That is perhaps the major reason why the all-star games have generally been dreary affairs. The superstars especially have played as if they didn't care, or as if the risk they were taking just wasn't worth it to them.

"You're asking me to win for a $250 difference," says Phil Esposito. "That's ridiculous. That's no money today. Why don't they make it $1,500 to the winner? Then you'd see something."

Actually, the players do get a bit more out of the game than the winning or losing shares. All the receipts for the contest are returned to the competitors in one way or another. The money is used for the game expenses, for the all-star team awards, and for administering the pension plan.

The pension plan is a good one. It was the first in sports when it started in 1947, and it has improved steadily. Now the owners pay all pension money (before 1969 it had been split between owners and players). Any player can take his pension at the age of 45 or 65. If he takes it at 45, he receives $300 a year for each year of service. If he elects to take the pension at 65, he receives $1,000 for each year of play.

It is the here and now that concerns most players, though. There are many other awards besides all-star team money. The Art Ross Trophy can also be worth as much as $2,000 to a player. This is the award given to the league's leading point-getter.

The overall winner gets $1,000. But the leader for the first half of play receives $500 and the leader over the second half also receives $500. Thus, if a player leads all the way he earns $2,000. If there is a tie in total points, then the player with more goals gets the honor. If there still is a tie, it goes to the player with fewer games played. If that doesn't break the deadlock, then the player scoring the first goal receives the money. The runner-up in the overall scoring earns $500 and the runner-up in each half receives $250.

There are several other $1,500 awards, the most noted of which is the most difficult to define—the Hart Trophy for the most valuable player.

According to the wording of the award, it's for "the player adjudged to be most valuable to his team." But most selectors make their picks as to who is the best player in the league, or which is the scoring champion. For example, of the 16 winners starting in 1956, the league scoring champion was named most valuable nine times. A goalie, Jacques Plante, won it only once. And a defenseman, Bobby Orr, took it only twice. One of the years Orr won it, he was the scoring champion. The other time he captured it he had 139 points. Another interesting fact about the Hart winners over that 16-year span: Seven have come from teams that finished first.

In other words, if your team didn't have a high finish, if you're not among the scoring champions, if you're a goalie or a defenseman—then you don't stand much chance of winning the award. This is not to say that the winners over those years didn't always deserve it. But certainly there were teams with mediocre records who might have had abominable records if it weren't for one key player. Yet, no one notices players for the also-rans. Most writers select the easiest route—the proven, the well-publicized, the star who sticks out.

Some players who come to mind who've never been among the tops in the balloting are: Cesare Maniago of the North Stars, Dave Keon of the Maple Leafs, Ed Giacomin of the Rangers, Pat Stapleton of the Black Hawks. Where would those teams have been without these players? Nowhere near as high, one guesses. Maniago and Giacomin are goalies. Stapleton is a defenseman.

The runner-up in the most-valuable-player balloting receives $750. Predictably, it has gone to the same type of player who has finished first.

The Vezina Trophy has nothing to do with voting. It is an automatic award to the goalie or goalies playing at least 25 games for the team that has given up the fewest goals. This is another potential $2,000 prize—$1,500 for the overall winner, $250 to the leader at each half. The league has always maintained that this award is, in effect, a team award. That is, the goaltender with the best average doesn't necessarily receive it, but the team with the best average does. At one time it was academic. Only one goalie played for each team. But now there's a two-goalie system. That means that there can be cases where one goalie can post the best goals-against average in the league and not win the Vezina if his partner allows considerably more. The situation happened during the 1970–71 season. Jacques Plante of the Maple Leafs was the only goalie in a significant number of games who posted a goals-against average under 2. His 1.88 average for 40 games was easily the best in the league. Yet, the club's average of 2.70 was only fifth best in the league, and Plante won nothing.

Starting in 1965, the Vezina has been split between two goalies every year except one. There has been agitation in recent years for a rearrangement of the Vezina. Perhaps it should go to the netminder with the best average. Or, if the league doesn't want to alter the award, perhaps a separate trophy should be given to the goalie with the finest average. With two goalies now sharing the award, there isn't a ready public identification with the trophy. But for other awards given to individuals there is more excitement since it comes down to a personal basis, easier for the fans to relate to.

For example, the public will be much more concerned if the Vezina is a race, say, between Plante and Giacomin—rather than between Toronto and New York. It would also make possible the exciting prospect of confrontations between goalies. Generally, hockey games aren't considered as a man-to-man affair between netminders. But under a system in which the goalie with the best average comes in for an award, a new dimension could be added. Of course, a problem could arise. A goalie might be leery of facing a high-scoring machine if he thinks his average could be adversely affected. Today's goalies can become ill and not worry where help is coming from. But since the game is predicated on integrity, it should be assumed that a goalie will not back out of a game merely to protect his own selfish interests.

Another interesting award, which should be purely subjective, is the Lady Byng Trophy. It is worth $1,500 and goes to the player who combines "sportsmanship and gentlemanly conduct" with a high degree of skill. There is a certain amount of class in this award. After all it is given to someone playing perhaps the most violent of games. It has a nice ring to it, anomalous almost —Lady Byng.

For many years this award was looked upon as a goody-goody prize. No real he-man could possibly win it. From 1925 until 1965, every winner had fewer than 20 penalty minutes with only six exceptions. Good players won the award, but the best players didn't. In the award's first 40 years only one player who was also named most valuable captured the Lady Byng, and only one Lady Byng winner was also the league's scoring champion.

Bobby Hull changed all that. In 1965 he received the Lady Byng and most-valuable-player awards, amassing 71 points and getting 32 minutes in penalties. That was a rather high penalty total—the highest for a Lady Byng winner since 1927. But the selectors also took into account the fact that Hull was in the era of the shadow, and he kept his temper under remarkable control. Hull was a symbol of power, and the fact that he won the award that had carried a somewhat effete connotation gave the Byng a new image.

Two years later, the pugnacious Stan Mikita won the Lady Byng. He also won the scoring title and the most-valuable-player award. Ironically, the year that Hull had won the Byng award Mikita had the outlandish total of 154 penalty minutes. But by

1967 Mikita had cut down the number of minutes to a remarkable 12. In 1968, Mikita also won the three awards.

Thus, in the space of four years, the Lady Byng was captured by the most valuable player three times and by the scoring champion twice—after 40 years in which only one scoring champion and one most valuable player gained it.

Except for Hull, who was so outstanding he couldn't be overlooked, most selectors won't even nominate anyone who has more than 20 minutes in penalties. In the six years following Hull's award, no winner had more than 16 minutes. It is unfortunate that a player such as Beliveau was never given serious consideration. It is hard to think of a player who demonstrated more "sportsmanship and gentlemanly conduct." But it always seems to go to players who have a very high ratio of points to penalty minutes.

The Calder Trophy, for rookie of the year, has perhaps the most lobbying by management. The player gets $1,500. But the award also demonstrates how smart the coach or general manager is by finding the rookie and playing him, realizing that the youngster had potential. In recent years, starting in 1967, the selections have been exceptionally good, and have proven themselves— Bobby Orr, Derek Sanderson, Danny Grant, Tony Esposito, and Gil Perreault.

While Esposito was developing at Chicago into an outstanding netminder during the 1969–70 season, the Rangers had a rookie they thought should be considered No. 1—Billy Fairbairn. The Ranger right wing was well ahead of the other rookies in scoring, and was on his way to setting a record for total points for a first-year man. The Rangers were first, the Hawks were fifth when the clubs met midway through the season. After the game the rival coaches were asked, of course, about their respective rookies.

"I don't know anything about Esposito beating out Fairbairn," said the Rangers' boss, Emile Francis. "All I know is we're in first. Where is Chicago, even with Esposito?"

"Of course Francis has to say he likes Fairbairn over my guy," said the Hawks' coach, Billy Reay. "After all, Fairbairn plays for him."

Meanwhile, the Flyers were boosting their young center, Bobby Clarke. He was leading the team in scoring, but the Flyers were such an unimposing squad, frightening no one, that Clarke wasn't getting any publicity. The Flyers sent out press releases suggesting that the voters remember their star rookie.

By season's end, Fairbairn had gone into a slump. He didn't set any rookie records. And Esposito not only played most of the Hawks' games, but also turned in 15 shutouts—a record for any-one, veteran or rookie. Also, the Hawks finished first, comfortably ahead of the fourth-place Rangers. Esposito, the Vezina winner, was the easy winner of the rookie award. Fairbairn was second.

The next season Francis had the good rookie goalie, Villemure. The new Buffalo Sabres had Gil Perreault. Now Francis was say-ing that it's harder for a rookie goalie to make it than it is for a forward. All the arguments he had used the previous season against voting for Esposito he suddenly turned into positive state-ments for Villemure. There were other good rookies—the new Vancouver Canucks had Dale Tallon and the North Stars had Jude Drouin. It was a tossup the first half between Villemure and Perreault. But Villemure didn't have quite the same campaign the second half. Perreault, who set a rookie record for goals and total points, finished first. Drouin, who established a rookie assist mark, was second. Villemure was third.

The 1971–72 season was barely a month old when Hal Laycoe, the Canucks' coach, had a rookie candidate. It was Jocelyn Guevremont, a defenseman. He hadn't even played 15 big-league games, but Laycoe said, "I don't see how you can fail to make him the rookie of the year."

Of the 22 selections made after 1950, six top rookie awards went to goalies. They are the most visible players and their jobs are generally considered the toughest. In order for a rookie goalie to make it, he must be exceptional. Few coaches want to go with an untried netminder. They'd prefer taking a chance with a mediocre one who's got experience.

Of all the trophies, none has been dominated by so few people as the James Norris Trophy to the top defenseman. In the 18 sea-sons after it was first awarded in 1954, it had been captured by only seven players. Doug Harvey won it seven out of eight years, including a four-year stretch, Pierrre Pilote won it three straight times, and Orr took it four years in a row. Three players, then, took it 14 times in 15 years. The trophy is worth $1,500.

There can be no quarrel with the choices. The players selected were all sound. Pilote's selections, however, may have been made on the basis of his point-getting ability as much as for his defensive work. It certainly didn't hurt when he set a record for assists by a defenseman. What is strange is that Tim Horton's name is missing from the list. When Harry Howell, who had been around for 15 years, finally won the award in 1967, it demonstrated to some people the importance of being on a team that people noticed. The Rangers that year made the playoffs for the first time in six years. Howell won the trophy, yet Pilote got more votes for the all-star team.

The league's newest monetary award is the Conn Smythe Trophy, for the playoffs' most valuable performer. Unlike the other $1,500 prizes, this one has no money for the runner-up. In contrast to the regular-season most-valuable-player awards, the Smythe winners have been top-heavy with goalies and defensemen. In the seven years following its inception in 1965, only two forwards captured the trophy. Goalies won it three times, and defensemen won it twice. It is an indication of the heavy premium put on defensive play in the Cup games. And one of the forwards who captured the trophy, Keon of the Leafs, was awarded it as much for penalty killing as for his scoring. Two of the seven Smythe winners played for the runner-up. The other five played for the Cup champion.

Perhaps the most dramatic example of how award money can swell a player's salary is Bobby Orr's 1970 take: His team finished second ($1,250); his team won the Stanley Cup ($7,500); he won the Hart Trophy ($1,500), the Ross Trophy ($2,000), the Norris Trophy ($1,500), the Smythe Trophy ($1,500); he was a first-team all-star ($2,000), he played for the winning side in the all-star game ($500). That year, Orr earned an additional $17,750. That included $9,000 in trophy money.

The dramatic jump in living conditions for hockey players was acknowledged by Red Berenson, the head of the Players' Association, in 1971, in the association's first newsletter, which is called "Face-Off." Berenson is a strong union man. Indeed, he claimed that the reason he was traded from St. Louis to Detroit during the 1970–71 season was because of his union activities. In his message to the players, Berenson wrote, "Remember what salaries were five years ago." That ought to help keep the association strong.

6 | Exploring the New World —Expansion

"Parity doesn't mean the same as quality," said Clarence Campbell. "Certainly the teams are more nearly equal today. But that doesn't mean the product is as good."

The league definitely is moving toward parity. But parity in 1968 meant something different from its connotation these days. With the expansion to 16 teams in 1972, the N.H.L. had 10 expansion clubs and only six "established" teams. The majority of teams are nearly equal. But in hockey's first season of expansion, the word parity meant that someday the expansion clubs would be as good as the established teams.

It is easy to fault the expansion of the National Hockey League. The games are not so consistently good. And this isn't being written by an old-timer who believes that yesterday's players were superior and today's athletes are merely a bunch of upstarts. It's written by a fellow who first covered hockey in its very-modern era—1965. Yet, in a few years the game has radically changed. The sport went along with a six-team format for 25 years. It was successful overall, although the power was concentrated in the mitts of Montreal, Toronto, and Detroit. Neither Chicago, Boston, nor New York finished first even once during that quarter-century. Over that span, only Chicago of the three weak teams won the Cup—just once. In other words, three teams won the Cup a total of 24 times in 25 seasons, and the first-place finisher every year was one of the Big Three.

Expansion was inevitable, and not simply because the three losers wanted someone they could beat. A threat of a rival league, based in western Canada and the United States, sprung up in the mid-1960's. A rival major league meant bad things: raiding parties, salary wars, an undermining of the N.H.L.'s strength. It would mean, too, the testing of hockey's reserve clause. Although management is certain the clause would stand up in court, why bother testing it? It's simple enough to say a reserve clause is bad, as many critics of established hockey have done. But unless a better substitute is found, the sport probably couldn't exist without it. Quite simply, the reserve clause in effect binds a player to the team he has signed with—for life. Are there inequities in this system? Sure. You can run into a situation in which a player is really unhappy in a city. Emotionally, he's down. Can he be traded? Only if his boss says so.

A progressive management, however, will not keep a player against his will. The trouble is, the decision often rests with management. There is a notable exception—the case of Toronto's Mike Walton. Clarence Campbell interceded, after a psychiatrist's report determined that Walton could not produce in Toronto because of a host of emotional difficulties he encountered there. Campbell was responsible for getting Walton traded after the Leafs had adamantly refused to deal the potential star.

In any event, hockey people look upon the reserve clause as their pillar—they talk of chaos following if players jumped from club to club, going to the highest bidder. So they solved the problem of a rival league with the 1967 expansion.

There were other considerations in expanding: TV, a broader market for N.H.L.-endorsed products, greater media coverage—and money. A club would have to pay to enter the N.H.L. The difficult part of expansion was figuring out a system that would work. There were six teams. Four made the playoffs. If, say, two new teams were added they'd be finishing seventh and eighth for so many years—with no chance of making the playoffs—that fans in the new cities would lose interest. The league wanted competition. It knew that baseball's expansion had failed from an artistic viewpoint—it took the New York Mets, for example, almost a decade to finish higher than ninth place. The league's expansion committee, whose prime movers were David Molson, the Canadiens' boss, and William Jennings, the Rangers' president, hit upon a novel scheme: Create a brand-new division of expansion teams. With six clubs in the division, four could make the playoffs, heightening interest.

No professional sports league had ever expanded in such a bold manner. The idea was sound. Hockey has always been extremely proud of its product. It has had consistent public acceptance, over the long haul, that is unmatched by any sport. Having the idea, the league now had to find the cities.

In 1965, Campbell made the announcement: The league was going to double in size for the 1967–68 campaign, adding six teams. The price for each club: $2,000,000. Any city that wanted a franchise had to have an arena that could seat at least 12,500 people. The league had a fairly good idea of which cities it wanted. Certainly, it desired West Coast teams—in Los Angeles and San Francisco. That would effectively knock out the rival league.

As far as other cities were concerned, well, the league was ready to listen to anyone who had the arena and the money. Pretty soon, it boiled down to the following: the Minneapolis–St. Paul area, Los Angeles, the San Francisco Bay area, Philadelphia, Pittsburgh, Vancouver. Interestingly, no one from St. Louis was making a bid. One day, the league announced it was holding St. Louis open—even though no one had applied for a franchise. The reason? The Black Hawks owned the St. Louis arena, an old, dingy cavern that couldn't pay for itself. It was, however, the only rink of major-league size in the city. If a hockey club played there, it would have to use the arena. So the league waited for someone to make a bid for St. Louis, and the Hawks contemplated, happily, the prospect of unloading their white elephant.

Meanwhile, Buffalonians sulked. The very wealthy Knox Brothers, perhaps that city's first family (the Woolworth chain, Marine Midland Bank, and so forth), had been turned down in their bid. James Norris, the Hawks' owner, had said, "I don't want a town named Buffalo playing in my building." But nomenclature wasn't the real reason Buffalo was denied in 1967. The Maple Leafs didn't relish having a rival N.H.L. club 100 miles away. The reason: television. Buffalo received the telecasts of Maple Leaf games. But if the Buffalo club was on television the Leafs could conceivably lose a TV viewing audience of more than half a million people.

By the same reasoning, the Canadiens and Maple Leafs didn't relish the idea of having another team from Canada break up their tight little monopoly of national television. Vancouver, with a spanking new arena, was denied.

Eventually, the Salomons of St. Louis made a bid for their city, and it was accepted. The Black Hawks sold them the arena for $3,000,000. So the new make-up would be: St. Louis, Los Angeles, the San Francisco Bay area, Minneapolis–St. Paul, Philadelphia, and Pittsburgh. Actually, the San Francisco team was based in Oakland. But the league didn't like the sound of a hockey team named Oakland. It wasn't big-league enough. Yet, they couldn't call the club San Francisco. A compromise was reached: It would be called California.

Canadians were furious. This was their national game, it was getting bigger (and maybe better) and, suddenly, it no longer was theirs. Canadians weren't that wild about the United States in the first place. The country suffered from a Big Brother syndrome, always in the shadow, trailing behind. In the 1960's sweeping changes came over Canada as it searched intensely for its identity. While it looked, the French faction in Quebec spoke about separatism. The country was going in two places at once: it wanted a unity, an identification as a whole nation, while certain forces wanted it divided between the French and the English. But the league's board of governors knew that for its commercial (television) success, the league had to get into as many new geographic areas as possible. So the northwestern United States (Minneapolis–St. Paul), the Far West (Los Angeles and Oakland), the South (St. Louis), and two big eastern cities (Philadelphia and Pittsburgh) were tapped.

Unless one was in Canada at the time of expansion, it is impossible to realize what an insult the 1967 expansion was to that country, whose people were looking for a reason to feel that once again it had been stepped upon by huge United States machines.

People in the United States didn't concern themselves with Canadian egos, however. They were happy, and were barely aware of any difficulties north of the border. There was a hockey season to play. That first season had an equitable arrangement. The schedule was increased from 70 games to 74. A team would play 50 games within its division—each opponent would be met 10 times—and would play 24 games against the other division—four games apiece with those teams. The imbalanced schedule could create two important situations: the new clubs would play most of their games against one another, which could give some of them respectable records, and would make for separate divisional identities.

Campbell had hoped for the new division to take 25 percent of its possible points in meetings with the established teams. But a funny thing happened. The expansion clubs gained about one-third of the possible points. Parity, said the owners, was coming quicker than anyone had hoped. The owners, and the league, had forgotten something, though. Most of these new clubs were so fired up when they faced the established teams—all of whom had let these players be drafted—that they often played above their heads, winning on scrambling and desire alone. As we noted earlier, it is impossible to discount the psychological edge in hockey. Teams get fired up for one reason or another and suddenly play the game as it's supposed to be. Consistency is the key to what makes a hockey club good.

Unfortunately, the new owners wanted even more competition with the Establishment. It wasn't that they thought they could beat them with regularity—although their first-year record gave them false hopes. They wanted more East Division competition because it meant greater attendance.

Attendance had been abominable at Oakland, Pittsburgh, and Los Angeles. How to hype it up? Not by getting better, but by getting Bobby Hull, Bobby Orr, Rod Gilbert to visit more regularly. The East Division teams had paid only two visits apiece to the new cities. The new owners wanted more of them. So in 1968, the schedule was changed. It was made 76 games long, and now the teams would play 40 games in their own division and 36 against the other. Each new team, then, would face each established squad six times—which meant the good clubs would visit three times apiece.

The game changed overnight. Expansion became part of the vocabulary, since established teams were facing the new clubs almost as regularly as their old opponents. Fans used to see their team play one of five other clubs 14 times during a season. That would mean they'd see them seven times at home. Old rivalries had been built up. There was familiarity. But a sort of culture shock set in. Now the Bruins' fans, for example, would see the hated Canadiens only four times. They'd see a club called the Pittsburgh Penguins three times. Yet, they had to pay the same prices.

Instead of seeing improved West Division play, the fans saw worse. In the second year of expansion, the new clubs earned only 30 percent of the maximum points from the East Division teams. The play deteriorated. Desire had given way to a formless scramble. Traditionalists were appalled at the quality. Soon, the word "expansion" became a synonym for ineptness. Yet, hockey people made believe everyone was enjoying the play. The established teams refused to put down the new opposition, even after fans could tell that the established teams couldn't get "up" for the games, and lapsed into the same formless style as the newcomers.

The third season of expansion, the 1969–70 campaign, saw a further lessening in West Division effectiveness. Of the 216 games played between the division, the West won only 41—and gained only 28 percent of the maximum possible points. The situation was never more evident than in the Stanley Cup finals. Ideally, the two strongest teams in the N.H.L. were supposed to meet for the championship. The playoff system was strictly intra-divisional. When the division winners emerged, they met for the Cup. This is a fine system for two balanced leagues. But everyone knew that the winner of the West Division, no matter which club, was probably poorer than four or five of the East Division teams. West Division owners, however, had insisted on this format. They wanted to be represented in the final, and who could blame them? It gave their fans something to hope for—a Stanley Cup champion. But in the first three years of expansion, only one club—the St. Louis Blues—ever posted a winning record in any season. No other new team had even been at .500. The Blues played the final each year, and each year were eliminated in four straight games. The Stanley Cup was becoming a farce. The silver chalice was tarnished.

And yet, who was at fault? The new club owners wanted recognition. The league wanted equality. Would things have been better if done differently? It appears the major mistake was artificiality. It was wrong to even the schedule simply for the sake of bringing in greater attendance. In time, winning would have brought in the fans. If a club is floundering in last place, not even Bobby Hull will draw fans. Oh, he might the first few times, even the first year. But then the club will have to make it on its own. Another error was in the Stanley Cup organization. But since the league began with an artificial premise—that the division winners would meet for the Cup—the results were a fiasco.

All was not lost, however. The league was going to upgrade the West Division. How? By further expansion. It sounds illogical, but had sound principles. First of all, the Canadian Parliament hadn't forgotten about the snub its country had suffered. In the halls of Parliament there was talk about legal actions against the league. Chauvinism was brought in. In short, the league was under intense pressure to admit a Canadian team, although, ironically, the two Canadian clubs already in the league weren't crazy about the idea. Essentially, the National Hockey League was forced to admit another club. That, however, would bring the league to 13 members, an unbalanced number. It would have to bring in another team.

Meanwhile, it was wrestling with the problem of what to do with the West Division. This idea was hit upon: Take an established club out of the East Division, move it over to the West, and add two more new expansion teams to the East. That would create two seven-team divisions. Now it had to find a club to shift to the West. During the 1968–69 season, the Chicago Black Hawks had finished last in the East Division. No improvement appeared to be in sight. But if the Hawks, the division's weakest club, were moved to the West Division, it would have a chance to improve itself. At the same time, it would bring new stature to the new division. The Hawks had Bobby Hull, they had Stan Mikita.

The league would make its new expansion effective for the 1970–71 season. It took in Vancouver and Buffalo. The new teams were added to the East. Chicago went to the West. But the Hawks didn't go in as losers. They had staged a remarkable comeback in the 1969–70 season, and finished first in the East. They went into their new division as champions.

The 14-team setup meant a new schedule. It was increased to 78 games. But perhaps more significantly, it was perfectly balanced. Every team would face every other team—regardless of division—six times apiece. That meant that each club paid three visits to a city. It also meant that now clubs were playing more games against teams from the other division than their own. A team cannot play itself. So in a seven-team division, it plays six divisional opponents 36 times. But it plays the other division's seven opponents a total of 42 times.

Fans weren't overjoyed at this alignment. Often, two months could go by before a winning team came to town. The public was seeing more expansion hockey than established hockey for the first time. They didn't like it, especially in the traditional cities.

Vancouver and Buffalo paid $6,000,000 apiece to join the league. Was a hockey team worth three times more than it had been only three years before? "Certainly not," Campbell admitted, but he added: "Maybe it's not that the price of $6,000,000 is too high, but that the original price of $2,000,000 had been too low."

There was another type of inflation brought on by expansion: Records. Virtually every scoring record has been wiped out since expansion began, and especially since the schedule was made more nearly equal, when the established teams meet the expansion teams regularly.

In all of the N.H.L.'s history, no one had ever gained more than 97 points in a season. But during the 1968–69 season, when the schedule was only slightly imbalanced between East and West, three players eclipsed that mark and one tied it. Phil Esposito broke the record with an extraordinary 126 points—29 points higher than the previous mark. At the age of 41, Gordie Howe had his most productive season with 103 points. The additional expansion in 1971 had predictable results—four players went over the 100-point mark, including a defenseman, Orr, who accomplished the feat for the second straight year. Johnny Bucyk of the Bruins, who was 36 years old and had never amassed more than 69 points in any season, wound up with 116 points.

The easiest thing to do is to denigrate the records, especially Esposito's. He had 152 points that season. He had 76 goals, breaking Hull's mark by 18. Sure, expansion led to these exorbitant figures. But the important thing to keep in mind is this: Every player in the league had the same chance to do as well—and didn't. All sports records can usually be measured most effectively only against the opposition at the time a record was set. It would be ridiculous to say, for example, that Hull's 58 goals were harder to come by than Esposito's 76. What can be questioned, however, is the number. The figures for hockey records have become so gross that they are meaningless in comparison. Before Orr came along the record for most points by a defenseman was 59. He has more than doubled that figure twice.

Before expansion came along the standard of quality was the "20-goal man." They were in short supply. If a club were lucky, it might have four of them, and would spread them around on different lines. In the 1966–67 season, the last one before expansion, the six clubs produced a total of 19 players who had 20 or more goals apiece. For argument's sake, make that an average of three a team. But here's what happened following expansion:

1967–68: The league doubled. The number of 20-goal men jumped to 34, but the average fell to under three a team. The reason? The expansion clubs didn't produce many 20-goal men, and the schedule was sufficiently imbalanced so that the established players didn't get much chance to fatten up.

1968–69: There were the same number of teams, 12. But the number of three-goal players jumped to 52, more than four a team. The clubs played a nearly equal schedule, old versus new.

1969–70: There were 50 players who got at least 20 goals. Status quo.

1970–71: Hold on. There's further expansion, and the schedule becomes equal. With 14 teams, the league produces 68 men who produce at least 20 goals apiece. That is an average of about five a team.

A new standard became necessary: the 30-goal man. Before expansion most fans could tell you the names of the 20-goal men. Now a 20-goal scorer falls into the mediocre category—not too good, not too bad. During the 1970–71 season, no fewer than 20 players scored at least 30 goals. Among those who broke the barrier were the Sabres' rookie, Gil Perreault, whose 38 was a record for a first-year man, and the Canucks' Rosaire Paiement, a virtual rookie, who amassed 34.

To its credit, however, the league did change the Cup playoff system, insuring that two of the strongest—if not the strongest—clubs would meet for the championship. After the first round of play, the clubs crossed over. They played teams from the other divisions. No expansion team got in, and the Hawks wound up facing the Canadiens in the finals. It was a satisfying windup to a bizarre campaign.

But the last of expansion hadn't been heard from. As part of its agreement to let in Vancouver and Buffalo, the league had agreed that it wouldn't change its setup or expand until 1974, at the earliest. This was done to protect the new teams, who would probably be finishing near the bottom, and would be able to get high draft choices in the annual amateur draft. Also, the league wasn't ready for more expansion. The product had become so diluted it only occasionally resembled the great sport it had been a few years before. It was so adamant about not expanding again that it passed a rule: In order to expand before the 1974–75 season, a unanimous vote would be required. Normally, only a three-quarters vote was needed. Expansion hadn't worked out the way hockey had hoped it would. Many general managers had unwisely traded away their draft choices for the here and now. It would take years and years before most of the new clubs could hope to compete on an equal footing. Campbell even suggested that an embargo be placed on deals between established clubs and expansion clubs that had involved the newer clubs' losing draft choices. The East Division wouldn't hear of it. Some of the teams, such as Boston and New York, contended that when they were in the dumps through most of the 1960's no one had helped them. They claimed that a good general manager could build a team, that incompetence shouldn't be rewarded. Minnesota, Los Angeles, and Oakland had traded away their No. 1 choices until the early 1970's.

Suddenly, in the summer of 1971, a group of men calling themselves the World Hockey Association was formed. The people were among the founders of the American Basketball Association, which went into business as a rival to the successful National Basketball Association. Why not hockey, too? they reasoned. Before long the W.H.A. announced it was giving franchises to New York, Atlanta, Los Angeles, San Francisco, Miami Beach, and other major United States cities, as well as cities in Canada. They were ready to start play in 1972, they said. The prospect of a rival league, situated in many of the existing N.H.L. cities, didn't appear to upset Campbell unduly.

"We wish them well," he said diplomatically. "I'm pleased that hockey is so successful that other people want to get into the business. But if they encroach upon us by trying to steal our players, then we'll fight them from the ramparts."

This is what it was all about, really. The stealing of players. And not only players from N.H.L. teams. There were the amateurs that had been the sole possessions of the N.H.L. Although the league didn't own the amateurs, they got them in drafts. The league also paid more than $1,000,000 a year to keep Canada's amateur program going. But the amateurs were under no obligation to go to the N.H.L. If they wanted, they could sign up with the W.H.A. and the N.H.L. couldn't stop them. Certainly, the league couldn't stop contributing to amateur hockey. That would be self-defeating. Then no one would get the players, since there wouldn't be any players developed.

Perhaps it was coincidence, but the N.H.L. scheduled a meeting in New York in November, 1971 to talk about further expansion. The meeting was to take place a week after the W.H.A. held its first major meeting—in New York.

The W.H.A. meeting attracted a remarkably large turnout, and there were more than newsmen there. Hockey had grown so quickly in recent years but was still relatively small. It was tough to get into. Many people—businessmen, small-time coaches, fringe players—were interested in how well a new major league could do. They wanted to be part of it. Optimism was rampant. The backers of the various teams appeared to be substantial people. The problem was that their arenas, for the most part, were nonexistent or too small to accommodate the kind of crowd that a major league required. Another problem was this: The league needed a New York franchise. It granted one to a lawyer named Neil Shayne, a buff who knew more about roller hockey than the ice version. Shayne, however, worked diligently to get a place to play. He and the league knew that a New York outlet was essential to every sport, and especially to one just starting up. New York is, of course, the communications center of North America, if not the world. The three television networks are based there, the major magazines are there, the foreign and national correspondents are there. Shayne knew, for example, that the A.F.L. probably would have taken longer to become a meaningful rival to the N.F.L. if it weren't for Joe Namath being based with the Jets in New York. Namath certainly wouldn't have received the publicity if he had been in Buffalo.

But Shayne was having difficulty getting an arena. A new one was being built in Long Island, called the Nassau Coliseum. The county officials hoped to stage major-league basketball and hockey in the arena, and set their sights on an N.H.L. franchise—perhaps by 1973, they hoped.

Of course, an N.H.L. franchise would intrude on the 50-mile territorial rights of the Rangers. The Nassau people had to get someone who could bring in backers of a club, then deal with the Rangers. They got William A. Shea, an old hand at bringing in teams. Shea, an attorney, brought the Mets to New York and got the stadium built. The stadium is named for him.

Shayne tried to get dates for 1972 for the Coliseum. He argued that since the N.H.L. wasn't going to expand until 1974, why not let his team in until then? This put pressure on the Coliseum— and the N.H.L. The N.H.L. didn't want a rival league anyplace, but especially it didn't want one in New York. And the Coliseum didn't want to wait for hockey. It wanted to open with that sport as one of its attractions. Yet, it didn't want a league that hadn't proved itself. It stalled on talking to Shayne, while Shea held extensive conferences with Ranger management about getting an N.H.L. expansion team into the Coliseum for 1972.

Finally, the N.H.L. acted. In an about face, a week after the W.H.A. had announced it was in business and was going to have a New York franchise, the N.H.L. suddenly granted franchises to New York and Atlanta and was going to expand in 1972—two years earlier than it had planned to. In addition, it said it was going to expand again in 1974, and planned to have 24 teams in North America by the decade's end.

Cynical observers saw the league's move to Long Island, and further expansion plans, as a ploy to rid itself of the W.H.A. The Coliseum would gladly take the N.H.L. over a W.H.A. team. And by moving to Atlanta, the N.H.L. also got the inside track at the new Atlanta Coliseum, which the W.H.A. had hoped to invade. The N.H.L. for the first time was in the Deep South.

A host of repercussions followed the N.H.L.'s new expansion. Shayne immediately started a $33,000,000 lawsuit, charging the league with violating the United States's antitrust laws. His major contention was that the league had stated publicly it didn't intend to expand until 1974, and suddenly it was breaking its own time-table. In addition, the way it did was somewhat bizarre. The league decided that a unanimous vote wasn't necessary after all to expand in 1972. They had interpreted their rules wrong, they said. Twelve votes were needed of the 14 members. What was required unanimously was a vote to restructure the divisions. However, this was seen as a move to get past Charles O. Finley's expected negative vote for further expansion. Finley owned the Seals. His club was in difficulty. As it was, the good teams didn't visit Oakland that often. Further expansion meant that the top clubs would make even fewer visits.

A 16-club league meant lessening playoff excitement if the two divisions were retained. So the league contemplated creating four divisions of four teams each, while retaining the 78-game schedule. Which club went in what division was a sticky problem. In order to keep the 78-game schedule, there would be imbalance. Teams would face the other clubs in its division six times apiece. That's 18 games. That left 60 games to play against 12 clubs. The league decided to keep the two existing divisions and just to add teams.

The four-division alignment is bound to come. Some owners wanted the four strongest teams—the Rangers, Bruins, Canadiens, and Black Hawks—to play in the same division. This would give weaker clubs in each of the other divisions a chance to finish on top of their division, or at least be competitive. The stronger clubs, of course, balked at this idea. Other weak teams wanted the strength spread out, since that would mean a Montreal, say, in their division would make more visits than if they were in another division.

The four-division setup would work like this: The league will be split into two sections, with each having two divisions. At the end of the season, the first-place club in one division will play the second-place team of the other division in its section, and vice versa. The winners will then meet for the sectional championship. The sectional champions then meet for the Stanley Cup. Thus, it will still take three rounds to win the Stanley Cup, but on a percentage basis fewer teams will qualify for the playoffs, since only half—eight of the 16 teams—get in.

There are good advantages to this system. It creates more heated rivalries, since a four-team division makes for ready identification. It also cuts down on travel, since the divisions are, more or less, based on geographical proximity. But it also means that a nondivisional team visits a city only five times every two years.

For the first time since 1942, when the Brooklyn (née New York) Americans dropped out, the N.H.L. has two teams from the same area. The Long Island franchise wound up paying an indemnification fee of $4,000,000 to the Rangers. In addition, all the overlapping 50-mile radius of the new franchise belonged to the Rangers. Actually, the indemnification to the Rangers was more than $4,000,000. The new franchise did not expect to share in money received from the 1974 expansion.

Since the new Long Island and Atlanta franchises had to pay $6,000,000 apiece to join the league, the Long Island team wound up costing more than $10,000,000, with its indemnification (plus interest). The money was to be spread out over a considerable period of time—at least 10 years, perhaps as long as 20 years.

Was the N.H.L.'s new expansion designed to keep out opposition? Whatever the motives, it succeeded. Shayne didn't get his New York franchise because he had no place to play. Yet, there was an ironic footnote to the Long Island affair. When Shayne originally was given the New York area, he was also given New Jersey and Connecticut territorial rights. Although kept out of Long Island he still owned Manhattan and New Jersey. He had paid $20,000 for his territorial right. He sold the Jersey rights for $50,000. Thus, Shayne, who never even had a letterhead for his proposed team, had never hired a manager or coach, made a $30,000 profit.

As far as moving in on the W.H.A. was concerned, Campbell had a simple answer when asked if the league's move to Long Island could be construed as monopolistic. "We didn't have to announce our intentions," he said. "After all, does Macy's tell Gimbel's?"

The Draft

One of the most significant changes hockey underwent during its booming expansion years has been overlooked by the vast majority of fans. Yet, because of the dramatic change, there may never again be dynasties as typified by the Canadiens or Red Wings. The change was the universal draft, also known as the amateur draft. Essentially, this system means that every amateur hockey player in North America, when he reaches the age of 20, can be drafted by anyone. He belongs to no one.

In the old days (before 1967) the system perpetuated the old dynasties, and locked out the consistent losers. It worked like this: Every club had the rights to youngsters in its 50-mile territorial limits. In addition, it had the right to deny any other N.H.L. team from placing a minor-league or amateur team in its territory. What did it mean? It meant that the Rangers, for example, had the rights to Hoboken. But the Canadiens and Maple Leafs had the rights to a million potential hockey-playing youngsters. Since most of the good hockey was being played in Montreal and Toronto, the chances were that the Rangers, or Bruins, or Black Hawks, or Red Wings couldn't move in and get local youngsters. But the Canadiens and Leafs had amateur teams all over the place.

During those years, players agreed to perform for an N.H.L. club by signing a "C" form. Even if the youngster were 13 or 14 that meant that, in effect, he became the parent club's property. The big club then assigned him to one of its junior affiliates.

Years later, after the system was ended, Campbell admitted that if a boy who turned 21 had wanted to fight the system, he could have. The youngster, after all, had signed for a team at a time he was really too young to be legally bound. "But no one ever fought it," said Campbell.

This system of N.H.L. teams sponsoring junior clubs was the

bulwark of the dynasties. At one time, the Canadiens had six clubs vying for the prestigious Memorial Cup, an amateur competition for players under the age of 20. The secret for other N.H.L. teams was to develop top amateur teams in other centers of Canada. It took money, but eventually the Black Hawks got a productive Junior A squad in St. Catharines, not far from Niagara Falls. The Rangers and Bruins weren't so lucky, or at least so perceptive in finding young talent that hadn't already been locked up by the Canadian clubs. Such stars as Boom Boom Geoffrion, Henri Richard, and Dickie Moore came up through the Canadiens' farm system.

The Bruins got lucky. They reached Bobby Orr when he was a 13-year-old and signed him as soon as they could convince his parents that he should join the Bruins. For the next five years all that Boston fans heard about was this teen-ager up in Ontario who was going to make the Bruins a contender some day. The fans were asked to be patient. They were, and Orr didn't disappoint them.

But an Orr doesn't come along even once a decade, and many of the other franchises couldn't be saved unless some drastic changes were made. In addition, there was governmental pressure to get the N.H.L. out of amateur hockey.

There was another consideration: expansion. If the system had continued, how could any of the new clubs hope to compete? They had no farm clubs, they had to shell out millions to join the N.H.L., they had no amateur affiliates. If the established clubs were allowed to keep their junior players, the new teams couldn't possibly get even for at least 10 years.

Thus, the whole system was wiped out, and a new one put in. All N.H.L. clubs were to rid themselves of amateur ownership. They would have no more tie-ins. All amateur clubs were then turned over to local control, under the general leadership of the Canadian Amateur Hockey Association. But first, the league didn't want its members who had paid to develop these teams to be out entirely. So on January 1, 1966, all player lists were frozen. That is, every player on the list remained the property of the parent club. Then, in 1967, all the amateur teams were turned over to local sponsorship. The league and the C.A.H.A share the cost of this venture. The N.H.L. contributes about $1.2 million a year to the cost of the program. The C.A.H.A. in turn gives $5,000 subsidies to each of the Junior A and Junior B teams in Canada.

Another change was made. All the amateurs in Canada (except those on the frozen player lists) were then eligible for drafting by the N.H.L.—provided they are at least 20 years old by December 31. There had been enormous pressure in Canada to keep boys in school. Under the former system, many youngsters turned professional when they were 15, 16, or 17. They never even finished high school. Under the new ruling, no player may become a pro until he's 20, when his junior eligibility ends.

For the first three years of expansion, the West Division teams were allowed to select first in the amateur draft, in ascending order —the club with the worst record went first, next worst second, and so on. Then the system was changed to an overall draft. Any club, whether it be expansion or established, went in order of its record. Of course, concessions were made to the brand-new teams. In 1970, the expansionist Sabres and Canucks were allowed the top two draft choices. In 1972, the new Long Island and Atlanta teams each was given the right to make one pick before the other teams chose.

There is no limit on the number of amateurs to be taken. In 1971, for example, the 14 clubs drafted 115 players. That gave each team the right to negotiate with the player. Once a team chooses an amateur, it must reimburse the C.A.H.A. $3,000. Then it attempts to sign the youngster. Just a few years ago most boys signed a bonus of from $3,000 to $6,000. Now it takes about $15,000 to get a boy to agree to play with a club.

To make sure that many of the mistakes of the past aren't repeated, the league doesn't permit new expansion teams to trade away its top draft choice. The 1967 crop of expansion teams unwisely did just that, and some of them never recovered, unable to build a young club. They took established players in return for giving up draft choices. Then the players aged, and the teams had nothing.

Over the long run, teams should become more nearly equal with the amateur draft. If a club is bad for several years, it will get some high draft choices. If it picks wisely, it will have a couple of superstars. In today's hockey, where so many players are mediocre, the team with a pair of stars can become a contender.

There are no more ready reserves of players in the amateur ranks for one team. Thus, a club has to draft extremely wisely, and then build up a minor professional backlog of players. Or, it has to trade for players. In either event, astuteness counts. You only get one chance at your No. 1 draft choice. Under the former system, there were dozens of amateurs available. Out of all those numbers there was a good chance that a few would turn out well. The problem today is that there is enormous pressure on getting good players on the ice. There are more expansion teams than established ones, and most of them post losing records. So they'll usually play their top draft choices immediately. It takes time for a rookie to adjust, and in other times a first-year man would be sent down to the high minors for seasoning. Not today. Yet, because of the watered-down play, it's easier for a good rookie to make it. When Buffalo and Vancouver chose 1, 2 in 1970, they came up with a couple of good ones—the Sabres got Gil Perreault and the Canucks got Dale Tallon. Each became an instant star. In the teams' second season, they again had high choices. The Canucks took Jocelyn Guevremont and the Sabres got Richard Martin. The unusual part of the 1971 draft was that each of the five top choices got to make the big club, and four of them established themselves quickly as big-leaguers—Guevremont, Martin, Lafleur, and Dionne. Interestingly, those four are French-Canadian. The Canadiens would have had two of them under the former system that allowed them to choose the top two French players. They wound up with Lafleur, but only because they had gotten the Seals' draft choice. It would have been frightening for the rest of the league if that system hadn't changed. In 1970, the Canadiens could have acquired Perreault.

The other significant draft is the expansion draft. This is where the new clubs acquire the bulk of their players. The basic draft works like this: the new clubs have to be stocked with players, 18 or 19 or 20. They get them from the established clubs. But the established teams don't want to lose their best players, of course. So they protect themselves by making out a "protected list." It can be 12 or 14 or 15 players who the new teams can't touch. Now the new teams choose, their order usually selected by a flip of the coin or, perhaps dramatically, a spin of the wheel of fortune. A team wins the flip and is ready to choose. It has the choice of all the players—except for the protected ones and first-year pros—who are under contract to the other N.H.L. teams. Say the team picks a Montreal player. Montreal then "fills," or protects, another player. In other words, once a team loses a player, it can then protect another player. So if, for argument's sake, teams are allowed to protect their top 15 players, and will lose three players, they don't lose their 16th, 17th, and 18th top men. They will lose their 16th man, true. But then they fill in with whom they consider their next best man. So on the next round they will lose their 18th top man. Then they protect again. On the final selection, they'll lose their 20th top man. In reality, then, an expansion team will wind up with players whom the established squads consider the 16th, 18th or 20th top players in the organization. Put another way, for practical purposes the established teams figure that these players have no chance to make their own teams.

Goalies naturally are included in the expansion drafts. Generally, the established clubs are permitted to protect their two goalies, and can lose a maximum of one goaltender from their organization.

One thing can be said for the expansion draft: it provides bodies. However, it certainly doesn't provide quality, as a rule. There are several reasons. One major factor is that often new general managers for expansion teams may not have been wise enough, or experienced enough, to spot potential in an unprotected player. Often, they went for the name, an established player. But perhaps as important a factor was the behind-the-scenes maneuvering that preceded each of the drafts. Certainly, it seems bizarre that no one took the Canadiens' Claude Provost when he was left unprotected. Or Boom Boom Geoffrion, when New York left him off. Or Rod Seiling. The bylaws call for an open draft. If a player is left unprotected, you're supposed to be able to get him. But what happens in reality is that deals are made: You leave my man alone, I'll do a favor for you sometime. Or, if you do take a certain player, you can have him for a year and then return him for another deal.

But the major statement about expansion, after the maneuvering, or the poor selections, is that the players generally are of lesser quality, or over the hill. When the expansion of 1967 took place, 120 players were drafted. Each of the six new teams took 20 players apiece. Yet, in 1970, when the second expansion took place, only 28 of the original 120 draftees were still with their clubs. The North Stars, three years later, had only two players still around. The club with the highest number was Los Angeles, with seven. Los Angeles finished last the season before. Of the 28 players, six were goalies, which meant that half of the original 12 goalies drafted were still with their teams.

Much talk was made in expansion that it would give good players, who before never had a chance to make it, a shot at the big league. If this was the case, how come only 28 of 120 players were respected enough to be retained?

7 | Strictly Personal

The French Connection

Hockey is the only sport not bothered by confrontations between blacks and whites. There are probably less than 10,000 Negroes in Canada. If hockey is polarized at all—and it really isn't—it would occur between the so-called Anglos and the French.

Much garbage has been said about the French players in hockey, and perhaps the only true generalization to make is that it's virtually impossible to make generalizations.

However, the French like to think of themselves in certain stereotyped ways. Most of them believe, for example, that they are better skaters, that they possess a Gallic freedom in their movement. A long-time official of the Canadiens, who is French, says, "We seem to have a certain ebullience on the ice."

Anyone watching the Canadiens skate must agree. They are the only predominantly French team in hockey, and have been since they were a charter member of the N.H.L. in 1917. Indeed, they were created to give Montreal's French-speaking community a representative of its own. There is absolutely no city in the world of sport (not even Green Bay) that is so inseparable from its team as Montreal is to its Canadiens. There are mixtures of sociology,

politics, and emotion involved here that are impossible to separate.

For much of this century barriers were imposed on the French-
speaking population of Canada. This wasn't official discrimina-
tion. But in order to get most jobs, civil service or private, a
person had to speak English. But most French-Canadians were
brought up in households and schools where French was the only
language spoken. By the time they were ready for the outside
world, they found they had difficulty communicating in the language of big business—English. Thus, the French for the most
part were blue-collar workers. But they had the Canadiens. Here
was an outlet for them. The Canadiens were the symbol to many
of how far a Frenchman could go. He could reach the top. The
love affair between city and team has continued. The league even
recognized the necessity for the Canadiens to have a flow of
French youngsters, and allowed the team to have the option of selecting the top two players of French extraction. However, if they
took the option, they'd lose the draft choice they'd otherwise have
for any player. This didn't bother the Canadiens in the least.
There was always a goodly supply of French youngsters.

In time, every city's hockey team comes to represent the life-
style of their fans. There are certain generalizations to be made
about the styles of play of certain teams, which reflect the city
they play in. Montreal was fast and exciting. Toronto, British-ori-
ented, was traditional and, perhaps, a bit dull. Chicago was big
and burly. The Bruins were boisterous, almost barroom in their
style.

No place else, however, was the analogy carried through more
than in Montreal. The fans, 85 percent French-Canadian, made
godlike creatures of their heroes. Hockey was on the minds of the
people constantly. A loss in Cup play was a shattering experience,
sending the city into virtual mourning.

But the French players on other teams were in the minority.
Often, in fact, Toronto didn't have one Frenchman on the squad.
Over the years, several things were said about the French: They
stick together, they get moody, they shy away from fights. Perhaps

that's true. Perhaps it's all true, or just some of it, or none of it. The thing is that the other players believe it.

In recent years, the belters on the Canadiens weren't named Tremblay or Beliveau or Lemaire. They were named Ferguson, Harper, Harris.

When Ferguson joined the team, he knew what he had to do. "I accepted it," he says. "I know the French guys are more concerned with playing hockey than fighting. That was my job on the team." Ferguson doesn't say it in disparaging fashion. Rather, he simply accepts the fact that that's the way things are in Montreal. Or used to be, at any rate. Marc Tardif and Guy Lapointe, two young Canadien stars, are willing fighters. Yet, it doesn't take much to bring the French-English rivalry to the surface.

When Vic Stasiuk was the coach of the Flyers in 1971, he got annoyed because several of the French players spoke French to one another during the practices. He forbids the language to be spoken when the clubs are on the ice. His reason? "I can't be worried that one of my English players won't understand what his teammate is saying. It might cost us a goal." Stasiuk, however, even forbid French spoken in the dressing room.

When Scotty Bowman took over the Canadiens in 1971 he spoke English to the team in group meetings. But the bilingual Bowman spoke French to the players when addressing them privately.

"It's traditional that you speak to the whole club in English," said Bowman. "The chances are the English players have more difficulty with French than the French do with English." Bowman wisely used the more familiar language when talking with Guy Lafleur, his prize rookie, who was having a difficult adjustment period because of the publicity he had arrived with.

One coach insists that French players need more constant encouragement than the English, that they "are up more and down more, like Yo-Yos. You never know how they'll react to a game."

English players who've appeared with Montreal claim they feel a certain antagonism from the players and the fans—especially if they're not stars. "The fans don't even want to know you," says

Red Berenson. Dave Balon has spoken of feeling like an outsider on his own team.

Because there is such a common bond among the players on the Canadiens, and because they feel they are representing an ethnic segment of Canada, they probably have had more reason to be successful than other teams. It must be more than management that has enabled them to win more Cups than anyone else, or finish first more times than anyone else. For the most part, they've won under different owners, different general managers, different coaches, different stars. There is a Canadiens' mystique. As Derek Sanderson of the Bruins said, after bowing to them in the playoffs: "We tried to upset a dynasty. And when you try to do that, you have to have luck. For some reason, the Canadiens always seem to have the luck. So it must be more than luck, huh?"

The Clutch

Losers talk about luck. They say the puck isn't bouncing right, or that they hit the post, or that the goalie slipped. Sure, there's luck for a play, even a game, even a few games. But luck has little to do with finishing first, or winning Stanley Cups. Listen to a team that's just lost a clutch game and they'll say, "Geez, we hit three posts. Those shots go in, we win." That's just the point. The shots didn't go in. And when a team is composed of professionals who've taken thousands of shots of practice, who've scored 20 or 30 or 40 goals in a season, and the shots just miss, then the point is not that they've come close—but that they've missed. This is what choking is all about. When you get tight, you miss the shot that you'd easily put in on other occasions. So you hit a post. You hesitate a split second too long before shooting, or perhaps you rush the shot that split second, or perhaps you trip just when you're going in for a breakaway. Look at a team that's slumping and gets an injury. You can bet that there's going to be another injury pretty quickly. It's on the players' minds.

Although their overall record isn't as imposing as the Canadiens, in some ways the Toronto Maple Leafs may be hockey's great clutch team. The Maple Leafs are the only team to win the Cup more times than they've finished first. In other words, they didn't necessarily have the best team, or the team that could be the best over the long haul. They were just good enough to win what they had to win. In the Leafs' first 50 years, they captured 13 Cups, the same number as the Canadiens. But the Leafs made the playoffs only 38 times over that span, compared to 43 for Montreal. Thus the Leafs won one-third of all their Cup competitions, while the Canadiens won one-fourth.

The Leafs showed only seven first-place finishes during the first 50 years, while the Canadiens finished first 17 times. The Detroit Red Wings, who finished first 13 times, could win only seven Cups.

On the other hand, consider the record of the Rangers. In 1950 they got past the first round of play, but dropped the Stanley Cup final. Over the next 20 years they managed to make the playoffs eight times—not once did they win a series. If this had happened over a short span of time, one could say that it was only one team's inability or that the opposition was consistently stronger. But over such a span of time it is more. Their fans called it a jinx. In a sense, it was. Everyone on the team knew they couldn't win. Something would always stymie them, and it would seem like a good excuse at the time. Indeed, at the time, the excuse was logical. But put them all together, and you've got a history of choking. It seemed that as soon as the uniform was put on, an apple would be given with it. How else can one explain the fact that in six straight playoff appearances, stretching 14 years, no Ranger club won a road game during Cup play? A team has to work mighty hard at producing a record like that. The excuses? They were legion. Once, goalie Gump Worsley stopped a shot. It was under his head. No one could get at it. So what did he do? He picked his head up and Red Kelly poked it in. Later, Worsley claimed he thought the whistle had blown. Since he believed play was halted, he lifted his head.

A few years before, the Rangers went into the sixth game of the final round leading the Red Wings by three games to two. The

Rangers blew a two-goal lead, and lost. In the seventh game, they blew a two-goal lead and lost in overtime. There was perhaps a valid reason in the 1950's for the Rangers' dismal record. They had to play their "home" games on the road since the circus usurped Madison Square Garden. The home games were played on neutral sites, but certainly didn't have any of the benefits home ice would afford.

Following a four-year lull, the Rangers made the playoffs in 1967, in what was to be the first year of the Emile Francis dynasty. The New Yorkers got in by finishing fourth, after spending more than half the season around second place. This gave their tired fans more food for thought—the Rangers fade in the second half. But this time, at least, they got into the playoffs. Their opponents were the Montreal Canadiens. Boom Boom Geoffrion scored for the Rangers against his former teammates and the Rangers were off and running. With the final period almost half over, they led by 4-1. The lead should have been insurmountable, especially in Cup play, when everything is so tight. Then some funny things happened. The Canadiens began to move. A goal made it 4-2, and another one quickly made it 4-3. Suddenly the complexion of the game changed. The Canadiens were pressing and the poor Rangers, diffused and uncertain, couldn't even halt play to stop the Frenchmen's tempo. What happened after that can be chalked up to either (a) the Montreal mystique or (b) the Rangers' failure in the clutch. The Canadiens won, 6-4. Later Francis was to say that the loss of Phil Goyette, his most heady player, had hurt the club. Goyette was the type who knew how to take command, slow things down to his tempo. The Rangers were swept out of the playoffs in four straight games, blaming the opening contest as the reason for their swift exit.

The next year the Rangers finished second and faced the fourth-place Hawks, a club that had given more goals than it had scored during the regular season.

The Rangers won the first game smartly at the Garden, and anticipated the second meeting. But between games, the Reverend Martin Luther King, Jr., was assassinated. Sports called a moratorium. The game was delayed a day, and immediately everyone speculated what the delay would do. The Rangers were high. They had gone into the playoffs with momentum and had captured the opening game. They didn't want an extra day off now. And there was something else to consider: two Hawks' players had been injured and weren't expected back for a few days. The delay would allow them to return.

The Rangers won the second game, but didn't look as convincing. Still, they had a two games to zero lead in a best-of-seven series. The Hawks, however, won the next two at Chicago, to even the series. The clubs came back to New York. Another thing happened then, another "jinx" effect that Rangers fans had come to expect. It was a close game. But on one shift one of the Hawks wanted to get off the ice, so he took a 90-foot shot at the Rangers' end of the rink, merely trying to dump the puck in. Jim Neilson, the defenseman, was standing about 20 feet in front of Giacomin. He deflected the puck—and it sailed past his own goalie. The Hawks won the game, and the next one, and ousted the Rangers. The New Yorkers pointed to the delay because of King's death, and the fluke goal, as the reasons for their downfall. And they were, weren't they?

There was another excuse the following year. The opponent was the Canadiens. There was a tight game going on. The Rangers' Larry Jeffrey was killing a penalty, and one of his teammates had successfully iced the puck. But Jeffrey, for some reason (jinx? Canadiens' mystique?), forgot that even when you're killing a penalty, if you touch a two-line pass it's an offsides. Jeffrey touched the puck. The play was called back to the Rangers' end. There was a face-off. The Canadiens scored, for the winning goal. The Rangers lost four straight.

The Bruins were the opponents in 1970. The Rangers lost the first two games—on the road, of course. That gave them 10 straight defeats in playoff competition. They came back to win the two games in New York, and went into the fifth game tied at two victories apiece. Then another strange thing happened. The Rangers turned an advantage into a disaster. They were leading, 2-1, midway through the second period, and had the game well under control. Then Phil Esposito accidentally cut Jean Ratelle. It was an automatic five-minute penalty. No matter how many goals the Rangers would score over that span, Esposito had to remain in the penalty box. Ratelle, however, was the Rangers' prime mover. His injury was so severe he couldn't participate in the power play. The New Yorkers suddenly looked bad, and with each thrust that the Bruins broke up, the Boston fans began to back their heroes. Soon, the crowd was cheering madly for Boston. The Rangers didn't score. They didn't even get the benefit of the full five minutes. One of their players committed a penalty with almost two minutes remaining in Esposito's penalty, and the clubs were again equal. The Bruins came back to win the game in the final period, and then took the next game in New York. The reason this time was the injury to Ratelle.

The jinx ended, sort of, in 1971, when the Rangers finally got past the first round and finally won on the road. They defeated the Toronto Maple Leafs. But they lost the second-round series in seven games to the Chicago Black Hawks. Again, bad luck. Bobby Hull got only two goals in the series. Each won a game, though, and each came on a shot following a face-off the Rangers lost in their end.

In successive years from 1968 to 1971, the Bruins finished third, second, second, first. They won the Cup only once. The three times they were ousted from Cup play, their tormentors were the Montreal Canadiens. The only time the Canadiens didn't make the playoffs was when the Bruins won.

Is that more coincidence? Or do all these things taken together tell you something about clutch play and choking? There is a cliché in hockey, but it's true: Losers, they say, talk about luck.

The Stanley Cup

The playoffs are a whole new season, say the players—and they're right. The Stanley Cup is part of the fabric of Canadiana, making the United States's World Series and Super Bowl mere diversions by comparison. Except, perhaps, for the World Cup in soccer, which takes place every four years, nowhere does a country's pride rest with a sports symbol with such intensity.

Ironically, the Cup was never meant to symbolize professional hockey supremacy. When the Governor-General, Frederick Arthur, Lord Stanley of Preston donated the Cup in 1893 (for its now famous purchase price of $48.67), he intended it to go simply to Canada's top hockey club. There were no acknowledged professionals in Canada then. Until the early 1900's the Cup indeed was captured by the simon-pure. But then the pros began to take over and fielded the best squads. They began to compete for the Cup. With the expansion of the N.H.L. in 1926, the Cup became the league's exclusive property. Before, it had gone to any team from any league that had challenged for it. But from that date on, only the N.H.L. could compete for the Cup. Lord Stanley never saw a Stanley Cup game.

The Cup itself is beautifully simple. It is supported now on a three-foot-high sterling silver base. It costs more money just to engrave the names of the players on a winning team—$150—than it did to buy the Cup. Indeed, more than $8,000 has been spent on engraving the names of the players. You get your name on the Cup only if you've actually appeared in Stanley Cup play that season. If you were a star of the team, but got injured and missed the playoffs, then your name may not appear.

The Cup sits in the Hockey Hall of Fame, just outside downtown Toronto. It is removed from the hall only for repairs, engraving, or presentation. Theoretically, the Cup is under the command of two trustees, the venerable Cooper Smeaton and Red Dutton, who were born before the turn of the century. The trusteeship is a throwback to the days when Lord Stanley donated the Cup and stipulated it be managed by trustees. They were in charge of making sure the challenge for the cup was legitimate, and often decided which clubs could challenge for it. The trustees today make sure that ineligible players don't get their names on the Cup.

Since the Cup stands for worldwide hockey supremacy (the world's best teams, after all, are competing for it, even though they're confined to North America) it is easy to see why so much nationalistic pride is involved. A World Series, a Super Bowl, or a basketball championship ultimately is the victory of one city, not a nation. But when Montreal or Toronto—or someday, Vancouver —win the Cup, it is as though the Cup has returned to its rightful owner. Is the Cup truly symbolic of the world's best? Without a doubt it is. The World Series, the Super Bowl, and basketball's champions are called world champions—but that's academic. Few countries compete in these sports on any sort of scale. Yet, hockey is a big-time sport in dozens of countries. There's no question that the Stanley Cup winners would beat the top teams of other countries. But in the other sports—who would there be to play?

The Cup's broad silver base is indicative of the minimum time the N.H.L. intends to keep it around. It is big enough to accommodate the names of players until the year 1999.

Just what does Cup competition do to the players? Some get fired up, performing better than they should be expected to. Others, even the great ones, go into a sort of panic state. Unquestionably, the greatest playoff performer on offense, over the long haul, was Rocket Richard. The Rocket was one of the great ones in the regular season, of course. With an average goals per game of .556 he compiled the finest average of any modern player until Hull and Esposito came along. But in the playoffs, Richard was even better, in a class by himself. He averaged .616 goals a game. No one in Cup play comes close. His record of 82 goals in 133 playoff games is nine goals better than Beliveau's—and Beliveau played in 29 more games. Although the Rocket played in 19 fewer games than Gordie Howe, he scored 15 more playoff goals. Richard also was the only Stanley Cup performer to amass five goals in a game. His career record of six overtime goals is twice as much as any player ever had. He had seven games in which he scored at least three goals. No player ever had more than three hat tricks in Cup play.

On the other hand, there was Frank Mahovlich's playoff performances, which had been extremely erratic. Until 1971, Mahovlich had been one of the prime disappointments in Cup play. In 49 previous playoff games he had eight goals—one every six games.

Yet, during the regular season he had averaged just about one goal for every two. Perhaps the change of scenery helped Mahovlich. He set records for most goals and points in one playoff year with the 1971 Canadiens.

The idea that a change helps was never more evident than with Phil Esposito. In 29 playoff games with the Black Hawks, he had four goals. But in his next 35 with the Bruins, he accounted for 24 scores.

The playoffs seem to exaggerate statistics—positively and negatively. Players simply aren't the same. When the Canadiens' Ferguson retired in 1971, he had compiled the highest penalty-minute average per season in history—152 minutes a year. The playoffs, as we know, are a tight time. Clubs try to avoid penalties. Yet, Ferguson was even more protective of his teammates during the playoffs. He had 260 penalty minutes in only 85 playoff games, a seasonal average of about 240 minutes.

There are just as dramatic differences in playoff performances by the goalies. Perhaps the most unusual case is the Rangers' Giacomin. The goalie with the salt-and-pepper hair had this record over a four-year regular season stretch: First-team all-star once, second-team all-star three times; 30 shutouts (leading the league twice); goals-against averages of 2.61, 2.44, 2.55, 2.36. Yet, in the playoffs, he appeared in 18 games, with his club winning only three. He turned in no shutouts. His goals-against average in Cup play was 3.41, 3.00, 3.33, 4.13. While his regular-season average was 2.62, his playoff average was 3.45. Over those four years, he never appeared in fewer than 66 games. In fact, he appeared in more games over that span, and turned in more shutouts, than any other goalie in the National Hockey League. So what happened? Why should a goalie who averaged one shutout for every nine games played during the regular season, when the scores are higher, not even turn in one in 18 appearances in the playoffs, when traditionally the scores are lower? And how could his average zoom so spectacularly? And how could a goalie who made the all-star team four straight seasons, whose team during the regular season won 148 games and dropped 99, post three victories and 15 losses in playoffs over the same span?

It is easy to make the mistake of blaming it on Giacomin alone. The club generally performed poorly those playoffs, and didn't give him much scoring help. But that only increased the pressure. Ultimately, everyone came to believe that the long seasons took their toll. Each year he played more games than any other goalie. The minutes added up, and finally broke him in the playoffs. Yet, Giacomin insisted he wasn't tired. If he wasn't, then was he choking? Perhaps he didn't feel tired. But he looked tired, or tight at any rate. Shots that he would have batted aside with ease went past him. It was apparent to many that Giacomin was simply continuing the so-called Ranger jinx. His coach, Francis, insisted that Giacomin wasn't tired. Giacomin insisted he wasn't tired. But in the 1970–71 season, Giacomin was rested. He played only 45 games during the regular season. Result? In the playoffs his goals-against average was a sparkling 2.21. He appeared in 12 games and his team won seven.

Glenn Hall was another outstanding netminder whose playoff average was considerably poorer than his regular-season mark. In 16 full seasons, he never yielded an average of three goals a game. He retired with a career average of 2.51. Yet, in 15 playoff appearances he gave three or more goals seven times. During the regular seasons he averaged one shutout for every 11 games. In the playoffs, he got one for every 20 games he appeared in.

Except for one brief stretch early in his career, even Terry Sawchuk—who many say was the finest ever—did not match his regular-season work in the playoffs. His career average during regular play was 2.52 goals a game, compared to 2.64 in the playoffs. Sawchuk, however, did have a higher shutout average in playoff competition, turning in one for every 8½ games, compared to one for every 9½ in regular-season play.

But Plante is far and away the superior playoff goalie, perhaps the best ever. In 15 playoff years his average was a superb 2.09. It was better than his regular-season mark of 2.34. His 14 shutouts were a record as he averaged one blanking for every eight Cup games, compared to a regular-season mark of one for every 10 games. During one stretch he posted the best playoff average for five straight years, and he led the playoff goalies six times. His average in Cup play was under 2 in eight different years, over a span of 17 years.

Defensemen are more difficult to rate because their scoring figures don't tell the story. But Tim Horton was around long enough to make an evaluation based on his statistics. During 20 seasons, he averaged .291 assists for every game. In the playoffs, it rose to .319. Since he was around for such a long time, the figures should be nearly equal. Yet, they're rather far apart, showing that his productivity rose during Cup play. Although he never even came close to a point-a-game average during the regular campaign, he once amassed 16 points in 12 playoff games, including a record 13 assists.

A measure of the importance of the Cup to the league might be illustrated with this vignette. It was 1966, and the Canadiens and Red Wings were battling in the final. The Canadiens were taking a train to Detroit for what might be the last game. Whenever a team has won three games in the final round, the Cup automatically is sent along, so it can be wheeled out in case the championship is decided in the final game. Excitement was so high that two armed guards, each carrying shotguns, were assigned to accompany the Cup to the train. As it was loaded aboard they stood on either side of the steps, looking like bank guards protecting a million-dollar gold shipment.

The moment of triumph is electric. At first, there is a lull, as though the victory hasn't set in yet. Then suddenly the players leap and hug one another. As though programed, the winners come from the bench, or the various parts of the ice, and form a receiving line. The losers skate by and each player of the losing squad shakes the hand of the winner. Then the red carpet is rolled out. Campbell walks behind the wheeled table that supports the Cup. He presents it to the winner's captain, who then holds it aloft. The captain takes a victory lap around the rink, waving the Cup high to the fans. Afterward, of course, is the champagne.

Index

Abel, Sid, 47, 82, 141
American League, 96, 97, 116-117
Andrews, Ron, 155-158
Arbour, Al, 83
Ashley, John, 105
Atlanta, Georgia, 196, 198, 201

Backstrom, Ralph, 95
Balon, Dave, 13, 60, 85, 208
Barkley, Doug, 79-80, 82, 83, 139
Beliveau, Jean, 75, 76, 80, 162, 180, 207, 214
Berenson, Red, 38, 39, 183, 208
Berry, Bob, 60
Blair, Wren, 74-75
Blake, Toe, 19, 86, 108, 138
Boston Bruins, 15-16, 27, 28, 31-32, 34, 37, 41, 48, 50, 52, 57, 59, 60, 65, 66, 79, 81, 85, 90, 94, 105, 107, 109, 121, 130, 137, 141, 149, 150, 168-169, 174, 176, 184, 189, 192, 194, 197, 199, 200, 206, 208, 211-212, 215

Bowman, Scotty, 27, 28, 34, 76-77, 80, 82, 89-90, 207
Brown, Arnie, 61, 62-63, 166
Bucyk, John, 174, 192
Buffalo Sabres, 34, 39, 66, 102, 157, 168, 175, 181, 187, 191, 193, 201, 202
Buffey, Vern, 16, 106-107
Byers, Mike, 60

Calder, Frank, 164
Calder Trophy, 180
California Golden Seals, 15, 24, 29, 34, 70, 81, 82, 94, 95, 102, 137, 175, 187, 189, 194, 197
Campbell, Clarence, 37, 38, 94, 107, 108, 112, 114, 115, 116, 119, 120, 152, 169, 170, 184, 185, 186, 188, 191, 194, 198, 199, 217
Canada, 9-11, 18, 26, 73-74, 100, 102, 128, 148, 159-160, 162, 187, 188, 190, 194, 200-201, 205-208, 212-217

Canadian Amateur Hockey Association, 74, 200, 201
Carr, Gene, 94
Cashman, Wayne, 59
Central League, 94, 106, 134
Chabot, Lorne, 30
Cheevers, Gerry, 27, 31, 34, 71, 109, 130
Chester, Hawley, 161
Chicago Black Hawks, 10, 23, 25, 29, 33, 34, 35, 40, 43, 45, 47, 48, 50, 63, 64, 81, 82, 85, 86, 113, 128, 139, 141, 149, 165, 166, 171, 174, 177, 180, 181, 184, 185, 186-187, 191, 193, 197, 199, 200, 206, 210-211, 212, 215
Clancy, King, 90
Clarke, Bobby, 181
Cleveland Barons, 117
Coaches, 72-90
Connell, Alex, 31, 117
Cournoyer, Yvan, 56-57, 60, 80
Crozier, Roger, 34, 45

Daley, Joe, 34
Day, Hap, 87
Defensemen, 61-71, 134, 181, 217
DeJordy, Denis, 27
Delvecchio, Alex, 58, 59, 139
Denneny, Cy, 157
Desjardins, Gerry, 29
Detroit Red Wings, 14, 15, 16, 42, 45-46, 47, 57, 64, 67, 79-80, 82, 83, 86, 87, 102, 116, 117, 128, 132, 139, 162, 165, 166, 183, 184, 199, 209, 217
Dionne, Marcel, 79-80, 102, 202
Draft, 199-204
Drillon, Gordie, 87
Drouin, Jude, 181
Dupont, Andre (Moose), 66, 134
Dutton, Red, 213
Dwyer, Big Bill, 117
Dye, Babe, 157, 164

Eagleson, Alan, 165, 166
Ecclestone, Tim, 38

Ellis, Ron, 38
Esposito, Phil, 48, 57, 59, 85, 168-169, 176, 192, 212, 215
Esposito, Tony, 29, 33, 180, 181

Fairbairn, Billy, 180, 181
Favell, Doug, 27
Ferguson, John, 11, 48, 207, 215
Finley, Charles O., 197
Fisher, Red, 152
Fleming, Reggie, 9, 49-50, 77, 142
Foley, Rick, 63
Fontinato, Louie, 63, 64
Forwards, 35-61
Francis, Emile, 12, 28, 39, 76, 81, 86-87, 93, 94, 95, 116, 141, 153, 169-170, 180, 181, 210, 216

Gadsby, Bill, 82
Gardiner, Charlie, 35
General managers, 90-97
Geoffrion, Boom Boom, 12, 25, 35, 37-38, 57, 132, 133, 162, 200, 204, 210
Giacomin, Ed, 12, 23, 26, 28-29, 32, 177, 178, 211, 215-216
Gilbert, Rod, 57, 58-59, 87, 141, 166, 170, 189
Glover, Fred, 29, 82
Goal judges, 12, 14, 17-35
Goaltenders, 12, 14, 17-35
Gordon, Jackie, 101
Gottselig, Johnny, 35
Goyette, Phil, 60, 67, 210
Grant, Danny, 180
Green, Ted, 50, 66-67, 70
Guevremont, Jocelyn, 181, 202

Hadfield, Vic, 39, 50-51, 58-59, 93, 169, 170
Hall, Glenn, 17-18, 19, 27, 33, 34-35, 165, 216
Hamilton, Allan, 102
Hamilton, Canada, 164
Harkness, Ned, 83, 140, 141
Harper, (Terry), 207
Harris, (Ted), 207

Hart Trophy, 177, 182
Harvey, Doug, 182
Henderson, Paul, 38
Henry, Camille, 56-57, 60
Hillman, Larry, 66
Hillman, Wayne, 66
Hockey Hall of Fame, 213
Hockey News, The, 153-154
Hodge, Ken, 59
Hood, Bruce, 109
Horton, Tim, 166, 167, 173, 182, 217
Houle, Rejean, 49
Howe, Gordie, 16, 48, 58, 75, 103, 107, 139, 162, 163, 167, 192, 214
Howell, Harry, 94, 182
Hull, Bobby, 10, 17, 25, 40, 45-49, 146, 163, 167, 173, 174, 179, 180, 189, 190, 191, 192, 212

Imlach, Punch, 39, 82-83, 87, 94, 133, 139, 165
Ingarfield, Earl, 166
Ion, Mickey, 108

Jeffrey, Larry, 53-54, 211
Jennings, William, 67, 116, 186
Jewison, Norm, 155
Johnson, Tom, 79
Johnston, Ed, 27, 34

Kannegiesser, Sheldon, 134
Kelly, Red, 67, 141, 209
Keon, Dave, 38, 39, 52, 177, 182
Knox Brothers, 187
Krulicki, Jim, 14
Kurtenbach, Orland, 50, 97, 135, 136, 166

Labossiere, Gordon, 95
Lady Byng Trophy, 45, 67, 179-180
Lafleur, Guy, 80, 95, 101, 102, 135, 168, 202, 207
Lapointe, Guy, 207
Laprade, Edgar, 135

Laycoe, Hal, 37, 81-82, 181
Layton, Eddie, 66
Lemaire, (Jacques), 207
Lindsay, Ted, 165
Linesmen, 111-114
Lorentz, Jim, 94
Los Angeles Kings, 27, 29, 60, 82, 95, 96, 131, 175, 186, 187, 188, 189, 194, 204

MacNeil, Al, 166
Magnuson, Keith, 50, 63, 64
Mahovlich, Frank, 57-58, 80, 83, 140-141, 152, 165-166, 173, 214-215
Maki, Wayne, 67
Maniago, Cesare, 12, 26-27, 177, 178
Maple League, 52
Marshall, Don, 60
Martin, Pit, 166
Martin, Richard, 202
McCormick, Hughie, 31
McKenzie, Johnny, 15
McLellan, John, 88
Media, hockey and the, 146-162
Mepham, Eddie, 118
Metz, Don, 87
Metz, Nick, 87
Mikita, Stan, 23, 25, 43, 122, 179-180, 191
Milford, Jake, 74
Minnesota North Stars, 26, 74, 95, 100-101, 171, 175, 176, 177, 181, 186, 187, 188, 194, 204
Molson, David, 186
Montreal Canadiens, 10, 11, 18, 19, 25, 33-34, 38, 42, 45-47, 48, 49, 51, 53-54, 63, 70, 74, 75-76, 79, 80, 82, 85, 86, 92, 95, 100, 101, 108, 113, 121, 122, 126, 135, 137-138, 159, 162, 173, 174, 175, 184, 186, 187, 189, 193, 197, 199, 200, 202-212, 214, 215, 217
Montreal Maroons, 30-31
Moore, Dickie, 200
Morenz, Howie, 86

Morrison, Scotty, 103, 105, 106, 109, 110, 112, 114
Mulcahy, Charles, 94
Musial, Stan, 94
Myre, Phil, 33, 34

National Hockey Association, 18, 163-164
National Hockey League Services, Inc., 158
Neilson, Jim, 64, 211
Nevin, Bob, 60, 100
New York Americans, 117, 198
New York Rangers, 11, 12, 13, 14, 16, 19, 20, 23, 27-28, 30-31, 32, 34, 39, 49, 50, 52, 53-54, 56, 58, 59, 60, 62-63, 64, 66-67, 76, 79, 85, 86, 93, 94, 97, 100, 101, 102, 105, 107, 116, 132, 135, 141, 153, 157, 163, 166, 169-170, 176, 177, 178, 180, 181, 182, 184, 186, 194, 196, 197, 198, 199, 200, 209-212, 215-216
Nicholas, James A., 13
Norris, Bruce, 82
Norris, Jack, 27, 28
Norris, James, 82, 181, 187
Norris Trophy, 181-182

Officials, 103-127
O'Neill, Brian, 120
Orr, Bobby, 48, 61-62, 63, 64, 65, 69, 70, 71, 98, 100, 102, 167, 168, 177, 180, 182, 189, 192, 200
Ottawa, 31, 163

Paiement, Rosaire, 193
Parent, Bernie, 27, 88
Park, Brad, 16, 49, 64, 71, 93, 149, 157, 169, 170
Patrick, Joseph, 18
Patrick, Lester, 18, 30-31, 97
Perreault, Gil, 39, 157, 168, 180, 181, 193, 202
Philadelphia Flyers, 27, 61, 74, 75, 82, 88, 96, 100, 166, 171, 175, 181, 186, 187, 188, 207

Pilote, Pierre, 182
Pittsburgh Penguins, 14, 26, 34, 96, 166, 167, 173, 175, 186, 187, 188, 189
Plante, Jacques, 18-20, 26, 27, 28, 32, 33, 34, 88, 177, 178, 216-217
Players' Association, 131, 165-166, 173, 183
Players' Emergency Fund, 123
Poile, Bud, 96-97
Pollock, Sam, 92, 95
Popein, Larry, 67
Pratt, Bob, 97
Professional Hockey Writers' Association, 173
Provost, Claude, 45, 46, 48, 204

Ratelle, Jean, 39, 58-59, 93, 169, 170, 212
Reay, Billy, 63, 81, 139-140, 180
Referees, 103-111
Regan, Larry, 29, 82, 96
Reibel, Earl, 67
Reichert, Arthur, 116
Richard, Henri, 76, 135, 162, 200
Richard, Maurice (Rocket), 12, 36, 37-38, 40, 86, 162, 214
Riley, Jack, 96
Rolfe, Dale, 64
Ross, Art, 37, 121, 163-164, 176
Ross Trophy, 37, 121, 176, 182
Rousseau, Bobby, 100-101
Routine, 137-146
Ruck, Don, 158-161
Ruel, Claude, 48, 75, 76, 85

St. Louis Blues, 19-20, 27, 33, 34, 38, 67, 76-77, 82, 83, 89, 94-95, 128, 158, 171, 175, 176, 183, 186-187, 188, 190
Salaries, 162-183
Salk, Jonas, 94
Salomons, 187
Sanderson, Derek, 12, 14, 28, 32, 41, 52, 54-55, 59-60, 168, 180, 208
Sather, Glen, 85

Sawchuk, Terry, 20-21, 22, 30, 34, 147, 165, 216
Schmidt, Milt, 65
Scorers, 114, 119-121
Scouts, 98-102
Seiling, Rod, 13, 59, 63, 64, 69, 204
Shayne, Neil, 195, 196, 198
Shea, William A., 196
Shepart, Alan, 94
Shero, Fred, 61, 74, 75, 82, 100, 135
Shore, Eddie, 116-117
Sinden, Harry, 27, 85, 90
Skov, Art, 105
Smeaton, Cooper, 213
Smith, Al, 26
Smith, Dallas, 64, 71
Smith, Gary, 24, 29
Smythe, Conn, 90, 164, 182
Smythe Trophy, 182
Snider, Ed, 75
Springfield Indians, 96, 116
Stanley Cup, 212-217
Stapleton, Pat, 64, 68-69, 166, 177, 178
Stasiuk, Vic, 70-71, 82, 207
Statisticians, 114, 123-125
Stewart, Nels, 30
Stewart, Ron, 44, 48-49
Storey, Red, 107, 108
Sullivan, Red, 163

Tallon, Dale, 181, 202
Tardif, Marc, 207
Timekeepers: game, 114, 125-127; penalty, 114, 121-122
Tkaczuk, Walt, 60, 93, 169, 170
Toronto Maple Leafs, 10, 19, 20, 32, 38, 44, 58, 82, 83, 87, 88, 90, 118, 129, 133, 152, 159, 164, 165, 166, 167, 175, 177, 178, 182, 184, 185, 187, 199, 206, 208-209, 212, 214
Torrey, Bill, 94
Trainers, 142-145
Tremblay, J. C., 63, 70, 138, 207

Udvari, Frank, 103
Ullman, Norm, 38, 166, 167

Vachon, Rogatien, 33-34
Vadnais, Carol, 94, 101
Van Impe, Ed, 166
Vancouver Canucks, 10, 15, 34, 81, 96, 97, 159, 175, 181, 186, 187, 191, 193, 201, 202, 214
Vezina, Georges, 33, 86
Vezina Trophy, 32-35, 90, 178, 181
Villemure, Gilles, 28, 181
Voss, Carl, 107

Wakely, Ernie, 33
Walton, Mike, 185
Warren, Earl, 94
Watson, Bryan, 47, 48
Westfall, Ed, 52, 55, 60
Wharram, Ken, 166
White, Bill, 63, 64
Widing, Juha, 60, 135-136
World Hockey Association, 194-195, 196, 198
Worsley, Gump, 153, 209

Young, Scott, 152